The Hollywood Parents Guide

To Toria & Cat

Advance Praise for The Hollywood Parents Guide:

"If you have a child who is interested in getting into 'the business' THE HOLLYWOOD PARENTS GUIDE is an absolute MUST READ. Bonnie writes from the heart and the result is not only warm and funny, but full of useful information. Real stories from real parents of real kids working in the industry - tips and advice from casting directors, agents and other industry professionals. It's like arming yourself with a mini toolbox full of all the tools that you'll need to help guide you as you venture along this journey with your child. I should make it required reading for the parents of all of my clients! "

Pamela Fisher
Vice President Abrams Artists Agency
Head of Youth and Young Adult

"From A to Z *The Hollywood Parents Guide* answers every question I have received as a Casting Director and more. If your child wants to be a professional actor, the first thing you need to realize is that acting is a business and as in any business, there are rules to help guide you. Bonnie Wallace has given parents a How to Guide that is a must read."

Suzanne Goddard-Smythe
Casting Director
Nominated for two Artios Awards for Outstanding Achievement in Casting

"First let me say that *The Hollywood Parents Guide* is a fantastic book! Finally there is a guide to help parents steer their kids performing career. Thousands of parents have asked me for just such a book. There are a couple on the market already but they are written by agents or acting coaches. What parents have needed is a book written by one of them! And Bonnie has done a superb job writing it. The information is not only current but from the heart. If you have a little tyke that is driving you crazy to be on TV pick this one up!"

Chambers Stevens
Author of the Hollywood 101 Series
5-time winner of the Backstage Readers Choice Award

"An absolute play by play of how to best help your young, budding artist become a healthy, fully-functioning Hollywood success. Not only is my mother an incredible writing talent, but she also possesses a true depth of experience in parenting a Hollywood hopeful. User-friendly and guided by an open, generous voice with first hand knowledge of the industry, this book is one I can truly call 'masterful'.

Dove Cameron
Actor and singer
Star of *Liv and Maddie, Disney Descendants,* and *Barely Lethal*

"What a delightful rarity, an actual book written from the point of view of somebody who truly has experienced and is currently experiencing everything that they are talking about. I feel so lucky to have played a small part in Bonnie and Dove's Hollywood journey. It is truly through the remarkable, grounding force that Bonnie has, as a parent, enabled her remarkably talented daughter, Dove, to achieve such profound success at such a young age and in such a short period of time. In reading Bonnie's book, I found myself repeatedly saying, "Yes! Yes! Yes!" and now know, when asked by people in the future interested in a 'how to' for Hollywood, that Bonnie's book will be my first recommendation. To top it all off, Bonnie has remained as kind, loving and gifted a person as one could ever hope for in dealing with the madness that is Hollywood. Stop reading my longwinded spiel and start reading Bonnie's eloquent and informative book."

Andy Fickman
Award-winning Executive Producer/Director of *Liv and Maddie,*
Director *Parental Guidance, Paul Blart: Mall Cop 2, Race To Witch Mountain, You Again, Game Plan* and *She's the Man*

The Hollywood Parents Guide

YOUR ROADMAP TO PURSUING YOUR CHILD'S DREAM

Bonnie J. Wallace

Published in the United States by Hollywood Parents Press.

ISBN 0986351105
ISBN 9780986351105
1. Performing Arts. 2. Acting and Auditioning.

Library of Congress Control Number: 2015909637
Hollywood Parents Press: Los Angeles, California

www.HollywoodParentsGuide.com

For my daughters,

Claire and Dove

You make my life the loveliest adventure.

Gratitude

This book would not exist without the incredible generosity of a number of people. Pamela Fisher, Dove's agent at Abrams, first suggested that I consider writing a guide for parents and then agreed to be interviewed. Bonnie Zane agreed to be interviewed and bring the perspective of a Hollywood casting director to the book.

One of my favorite aspects of this book is the voices of the young stars' parents, each of whom I am grateful and honored to call a friend. Knowing them and their kids is one of the best parts of this adventure. Their immense generosity in sharing their candid stories helps make this guide come to life and shows that there are many different ways to approach this adventure. Heartfelt thanks to the following parents who agreed to be interviewed for this book:

Amy Anderson	(Aubrey Anderson-Emmons)
Kenda Benward	(Luke Benward)
Victor Boyce	(Cameron Boyce)
Pat Fisher	(Jordan Fisher)
Kim Holt	(Olivia Holt)
Pam McCartan	(Ryan McCartan)
Clark Trainor	(Tenzing Norgay Trainor)
Allison Zuehlsdorff	(Cozi Zuehlsdorff)

Special thanks also to Domina Holbeck, Dannielle Thomas, Katie Rhodes, Patti Felker, Molly Kaye, Corey Barash, Chambers Stevens, Betsy Sullenger, Andy Fickman, Suzanne Goddard-Smythe, John Beck, Ron Hart, Gigi Michaels, Roberta Raye, Kate Carruthers, Ann Wilkinson, Cheryl Schneiderhan, Dana Wells Boyd, Catherine Kennedy, Debra Gilmore, Mark Power, Steven Fogell, and Dinah Manhoff.

Eternal appreciation to my parents—Bob Wallace, June Wallace, and Kristin Wolfram— for their constant love, for encouraging me by example to look for where I can make a contribution, and for always believing in my ability to write.

Greatest and deepest love and thanks to Claire and Dove, who are my greatest teachers and my true inspiration. I am so honored to be your mother.

Note on Pronouns

The English language makes it difficult to write in gender-neutral terms, and I don't really like the standard use of the masculine as the standard pronoun. I also find it distracting when writers attempt to balance this issue by switching between *he* and *she*, either by sentence or by paragraph. My solution is to use the colloquial, though technically incorrect, *they* when talking about a kid or a person if the gender is neutral. This seems to be adopted more and more in conversation, and it feels like a decent compromise.

Note on Use of the Word "Hollywood"

Hollywood is a place, an industry, and an idea. It is specifically a geographic area of Los Angeles. When I use the word, I am generally using it to refer to the film and television industry, or "the business." The idea of Hollywood has always been bigger than its geographic borders, and the dream of it will always be bigger than even the industry itself. The city of Los Angeles may be the actual center of film and television production in the United States, but when they talk about the business, most people will still say "Hollywood."

Contents

Introduction

Five years ago, if someone had told me that my teenage daughter—who had little more than community theater on her resume—would soon be the star of her own Disney Channel show, star in four movies in three years, and have multiple songs on iTunes—I would have told them they were dreaming.

Today I can tell you: amazing adventures begin with dreams.

This is the book I wish someone had given me five years ago, when I was standing on the edge of deciding whether to leave everyone and everything I knew to support that dream. My daughter Dove had spent every day of the previous year lobbying me to move to Los Angeles, and her mentors—from her acting coach to her voice teacher and even the local LA-affiliated casting director—were all telling me that my child needed to be in Hollywood to fulfill her potential.

Fast forward: today, Dove is a happy, grounded, and successful young woman with a thriving acting and singing career. She has numerous credits at this point, but she is best known for starring as both Liv and Maddie in Disney Channel's *Liv and Maddie,* Mal in *Disney Descendants*, Liz in *Barely Lethal*, Beth in *Monsterville: The Cabinet of Souls,* and Charlotte Anne Jane in *The Mentalist.* She also has a growing number of songs on iTunes. I mention this because I refer to my daughter Dove Cameron a lot in this book, and I am aware that not everyone who reads the book may know of her.

Dove's accomplishments—and the incredible learning curve we traveled to get here—have put me in a position to be able to truly help others who are considering this journey. I speak from experience. I know what it's like for a parent to start from scratch and get their kid up and running with a successful career in Hollywood.

This was not a predictable outcome for us: I come from a small island in the Pacific Northwest. I'm not an LA person and certainly not "Hollywood." My sole experience with Los Angeles had been going to the convention center downtown twice a year for twenty years, and I didn't like it. The idea of moving there filled me with dread.

But I watched my kid come alive every time she acted and sang, and I watched people's reactions to her when she performed. And while I knew she was determined enough not to be stopped even if I made her wait until she was eighteen and came down on her own, I also knew that her chances of actually making it were significantly better if she had a head start.

So I looked at my finances, listened to my heart, and said yes. What I didn't know about what I was doing would fill a bigger book than this one. But what I have learned is worth sharing, especially if it can make the journey easier for other dreamers. And if our story—and the many other stories here from the parents of other young stars, and from industry insiders—can help and inspire you, then I'll feel truly successful.

What you'll find here is accurate, experience-tested information on every step needed to give your child the best possible opportunity to make it in Hollywood, as well as inspiration and resources to help you on your own journey, and even help you decide if this dream is right for you and your family to pursue at all. After all, there are infinite dreams to chase, and this is just one of them. It is, however, a pretty amazing one.

PS—I have discovered that I love Los Angeles and its hardworking, creative people. One more stereotype bites the dust.

Hollywood Kids 101: Basics

CHAPTER 1

Questions to Ask before You Start

When I ask other parents of young actors if they had a background themselves in performing, it doesn't come as a surprise that the answer is frequently yes. This makes a lot of sense: if we are made up of a combination of both nature and nurture, many of these kids got their passion from both sides of that equation. In our case, Dove grew up watching me perform in community theater, helping me memorize lines and hanging out backstage. The upside to being a performer yourself is that you often have a better sense of whether your child might really have what it takes to make it professionally. The downside is that you risk the very real danger of projecting unfinished dreams onto your kids.

This isn't an issue that belongs solely to acting, or solely to parents. The world is full of people who pursued one profession or another because they felt it would make their parents happy. Kids often unconsciously pick up cues from their parents—especially the one they most identify with—and decide to follow in their footsteps or complete a journey that was never finished. Pay close attention to why your kid wants to be an actor. Is it to please you? Make sure your kids know that you will love them regardless of what they do for a living or how successful they become.

A bigger problem, in my eyes, is the relentless glamorization of fame in our culture. The number of kids I've talked to who say they want to be an actor but have never once taken an acting lesson, been in a play, done extras work, or had a single audition astounds me. They have no idea what it takes, if they even like it, or if they might be good enough to be hired. All they see is the fame and its accessories: red carpets, magazine covers, imagined riches. What they don't see are the often hundreds of auditions, years of acting lessons, and disappointments before something finally happens, if it does. And they definitely don't see the many thousands of hopefuls who flock to Los Angeles and New York every year in hopes of making it—and the thousands more who finally give up the dream each year.

You also want to consider the needs of the rest of your family. In my case, I was recently divorced, and my older daughter, Claire, was off to college, so our situation was relatively simpler than what many people face.

This is not meant to discourage you, or your child, from what might be the adventure of a lifetime. It is, however, meant to be a reality check. Professional acting is not for the faint of heart. If your child wants to be an actor more than anything else but has no experience or training, help them get some of both before you take the leap and try the big markets. You may both discover that they are more in love with the idea of being an actor than with the work itself.

Maybe your child can get a taste of the business from where you are—or near to where you are—right now. **Every state, and most major cities, has government-run film commissions, and if you check with them, you can get information about what projects are filming and who might be casting local roles or hiring extras.** This may also be a good way to get some film or TV work on your child's résumé. If your child is cast and the experience is a positive one, you can be a little surer that the expense of even a trial trip out to Los Angeles may be worth it.

Visit http://hollywoodparentsguide.com/bonus/ to get your free contact list of state film commissions. And don't discount local theater. Many directors consider theater training to be the best for an actor. In any case, please help your child have a fighting chance and arm them with some kind of experience before you come to LA—they will be competing with kids who may have impressive résumés.

If after some lessons and experience, your child is more passionate than ever—and you see evidence of a consistent work ethic and commitment to lessons and rehearsals over other pursuits—you can consider a move, or an exploratory trip, to Los Angeles.

Why do I say Los Angeles? You can make a living as an actor in other cities, but LA is the capital of film and television. While New York certainly is second in that market (and first in live theater, though that's not the subject of this book), many if not most of the principal roles for shows and films shot there are actually cast in Los Angeles. This is even the case for Atlanta, which is a growing market. Extras and smaller roles will always be cast from the local pool of actors, and this can be a nice way for your child to cut their teeth on the basics. But no one I know dreams of being an extra! So if you want to get your child in front of the people who could cast them in a role that could lead to a career, the place you need to be is LA.

Tips and Takeaways:

- Why does your child want to be an actor? Make sure it's because they love to act, and it's not about pleasing you, or about the idea of fame.
- What are the competing needs of the rest of your family? Is this doable?
- Look for opportunities to get your child experience before coming to LA. State Film commissions are a great place to find local film and TV projects. **Visit http://hollywoodparentsguide.com/bonus/ to get your free contact list of state film commissions.**

- Look for opportunities for your child to participate in local theatre, which provides great training.
- You can be an actor anywhere—and make a living as an actor in many places—but the city where nearly all the major roles in film and TV projects are cast is Los Angeles.

CHAPTER 2

Stories: How Do You Know?

Hollywood Parents Share Stories of How They Knew Their Kid was Meant to Be an Actor

Kenda Benward

Mother of Luke Benward, best known for *Ravenswood, Cloud 9, Good Luck Charlie, Minutemen, Dear John, How to Eat Fried Worms,* and *Because of Winn-Dixie.*

You know, I think if parents are really honest with themselves...you can look at each of your children as individual people. And their giftings and their talents—they're pretty evident, if you're honest about it.

I have three different children, and they're not all actors. They're not all dancers; they're not all softball players. Each of them has their own unique thing.

I began to see that in Luke from a young age. He would go outside and play basketball or play football with his friends. But most of the time, he was wearing a Spiderman costume with a Batman cape, holding a sword with an Ice Wolf Ninja mask in the tree. He was in make-believe world all the time.

He was in a make-believe setting in his mind all the time. And I thought, "OK, there's something to this."

He really had a lot of natural instincts I didn't have to teach. So that's kind of how I knew...maybe there's something here for him.

Victor Boyce

Father of Cameron Boyce, best known for *Jessie, Gamer's Guide to Pretty Much Everything, Disney Descendants, Grown Ups, Mirrors,* and *Jake and the Never Land Pirates.*

I used to ask Cameron—you know, early on, when he first started booking commercials—I was like, "Do you still want to do this? Do you want to do this? Are you sure? Because I need to know." Because at this time I was still taking off work, and it was scary for me.

"Yes!" He would say yes, but he was only like eight, nine, ten. How do I trust this little kid?

I just recently stopped asking him that because now you know he's fifteen. He's deep into it, and I see him doing things on his own. I know he is committed. When we were on hiatus, he said, "Dad, Dad, when do we go back to set?" So I don't have to ask him—he is telling me.

"When do we go back? I'm so bored. I want to go back!"

"Go relax. Go play basketball. Go swimming."

"Argh! I want to go back to set."

So I'm finally completely at ease. He in fact loves this; this is what he wants to do. Because some people are like, "You're pushing him." No. I didn't even want to do this. Honestly, I did not want anything to do with this. I'm glad now, totally. Totally happy now. But before—no. Even after he did a couple of commercials...I don't know...I was so skeptical, such a cynic about everything. But now he's on his way. It's great. I love it, and I wouldn't turn back. I have no regrets.

Clark Trainor

Father of Tenzing Norgay Trainor, best known for playing Parker on *Liv and Maddie.*

In theater camp, depending on the size of the camp, you could end up getting lost. And I think that there was a lot of talent at the theater camp that didn't get recognized because there's only one play that they're working on. There are only so many roles. But Tenzing did luck out. In that first summer, the first week they go through the audition process so they can settle the camp and figure out who's going to get which roles. He landed one of the larger roles, and he had never acted, so that's when we kind of opened our eyes: "OK. That was surprising. Didn't see that coming."

We didn't put him in theater camp to pursue acting. I actually wanted him in theater camp because I wanted him up on stage. I wanted him to be able to present himself, whether as an actor or as the manager of a company talking to employees or the CEO of a company talking to shareholders—whatever. Or an attorney, which is what I am. Presenting yourself. That's what these organizations—Toastmasters or whatever else—are about. Your ability to communicate with others is critical.

That's why we put him in it. But then when he came home and he had landed one of the [major] roles, we were very surprised. It just went from there.

Pam McCartan

Mother of Ryan McCartan, best known for *Liv and Maddie, Summer Forever,*
Royal Pains, Monsterville: The Cabinet of Souls, and *Heathers the Musical.*

It has been consistently said since Ryan was seven years old that he has natural instincts. And interestingly enough, when Ryan was cast at seven years old, he was double cast. It was a big show. It was very demanding—it was three and half months long over the holidays. They cast two boys. One actually was ten and the same height as Ryan, and Ryan was seven, but they cast both boys. And the other boy had a little more experience at the age of ten. He was sort of their A-team boy, and Ryan was the B-team boy...until Ryan had a chance on Halloween during a rehearsal when the ten-year-old decided to do something and go to a party for Halloween, and Ryan was it. And they were like, "Wait a minute—we have the wrong A-team boy." And the director came back and said, "I have not given your son enough credit. This young man has incredible instincts. He has instincts beyond most adults that I've directed, and I think this business is for him."

And that was at age seven. And then we continued to hear it, but now that he's an adult and isn't around us as much, we don't hear it as much as he does. But he continues to hear it. So it was more about instincts. He was kind of a natural.

Kim Holt

Mother of Olivia Holt, best known for *I Didn't Do It, Kickin' It, Same Kind of Different as Me,* and *Girl Vs. Monster.*

[Olivia] did a few of our local plays, and our theaters were pretty... they're pretty big productions. She did Annie *and* Through the Looking Glass, *and I could just tell she really, really had a love for it. She went*

to a voice coach, and she started with that. He is the one that said, "I would really like to take Olivia to LA to meet some of the agents and stuff out there."

She was actually a competitive gymnast before that. She was out on the top national team. I thought she would at least be going to Alabama when she graduated and be a college gymnast. We spent a lot of time in the gym. We would spend at least thirty hours a week in the gym—five or six hours a day of practice.

Allison Zuehlsdorff

Mother of Cozi Zuehlsdorff, best known for *Dolphin Tale, Dolphin Tale 2, Sofia the First, Mighty Med,* and *Liv and Maddie.*

Our family has always been interested and into the arts, so when Cozi's dad and I saw her giftedness starting at around age three, we always made it possible for her to delve in where she felt interested. Piano lessons were our idea, but she's been playing for about nine years now, and the effort has been well worth it, from getting several music-related commercials to writing and producing her own music. As a family, we've always been of the mind that talent plus working hard on your craft is the ultimate winning combination.

Pat Fisher

Mother of Jordan Fisher, best known for *Teen Beach Movie and Teen Beach Movie 2, Liv and Maddie,* and *The Secret Life of the American Teenager.*

Well, you know, I kind of "let nature take its course" because [Jordan] was a very active gymnast. He was in the men's regionals and won several gold medals, and we thought we were on the path to the Olympics.

And when he was in fifth grade, he was kind of discovered by his drama teacher and his music teacher at school. They sent him outside of school to do an audition at a community theater. He booked the role, of course, and he got a lead role and a solo in the show. And there were members from Red Mountain Theater Company in the audience, board members, and they recruited him right there on the spot, his first performance outside of school or church.

So he was still doing gymnastics at that time, and gymnastics is a very rigorous schedule, and it finally got to a point that he had to choose. And I just said, "Jordan, you are going to have to make a choice." You know, my line to him always was, "I've learned how to be at two places at one time, but I can't figure out how to be in three." And so he finally seriously had to make a choice, and he chose acting. By the time he had to make a choice, he was well into it for a year or so. So he found his passion, and I supported him. The whole family did.

CHAPTER 3

First Things First:

Headshots, Resumes, Coogans, and Work Permits

Before your child gets even the most basic audition, you need a few things in place:

- a headshot
- a résumé
- a Coogan account if you are in California, New York, Louisiana or New Mexico
- A work permit for your child if you are in California (as well as some other states, link to state websites listed in the resources section of this book)

Headshots

Headshots can be expensive, but they are important. In LA, a session with a good photographer should run in the ballpark of $150 to $300. If it's much more than that, you are being sold some kind of unnecessary package. Photographers frequently charge more outside of LA since there is less competition to keep prices down.

It's important to work with someone who actually specializes in industry headshots—not a portrait photographer, for example. A good headshot feels natural and gives a sense of how your child really looks. Ideally it captures a sense of their inner spirit. For girls, it's important to keep makeup at a true minimum, if any is worn. Kids are cast to look like kids! Headshots are not glamour shots. Hair color and length should be as close to their current status as possible. Clothing should be a solid color (especially avoiding black, white, or busy patterns). You'll likely be aiming for two different looks: one commercial and one dramatic. Your agent can help you decide on the final choices.

Because kids change so quickly, headshots really need to be updated once a year or so, which is why it's important to find an affordable photographer and not order more prints than you are likely to need. A good photographer will give you a contact sheet (digitally these days) for you to choose your favorite shot or two. Many will include a slight retouch on one or two of the images you've chosen. Then you should be given the finished images on a disc (or in an electronic file) to give to the printer of your choice. Fashions change and opinions vary, but the basic result these days should be an eight-by-ten color photo of your kid with their name printed on the border. The printer can do the simple setup of the border and name for a small one-time fee. The finished headshot will end up stapled to the back of the résumé.

A word of caution: please only use a photographer with a good reputation or references. There are unfortunately some awful stories out there. Make sure the photographer would never use your child's photos inappropriately or ask them to pose in a way that makes them (or you) feel uncomfortable. If that happens, walk out. We were fortunate: before we moved to LA, we used the services of a friend who is a professional photographer; when we landed here and Dove signed on with an agent, we went to one on the agency's list of recommended photographers. My experience is that most good talent agencies will be happy to share their list of recommended photographers, even if you are not yet a client. Finally, beware if there appears to be some kind of financial arrangement between your agent or manager and the photographer they want (or, worse, require) you to use. Clearly they are placing their own agenda above your child's. This is not uncommon in smaller markets, but it is actually illegal in Los Angeles.

Some people believe that the résumé should be printed on the back of the headshot because it is "nicer," but very few people actually do this because it's just not practical. The minute anything changes on the résumé (a new role, a new coach, different contact information), you are wasting expensive photos instead of inexpensive paper.

Résumés

A résumé can be a little tricky for a kid just starting out, as you may have little to put on it. Two standard format examples are included in this chapter, as well as in the resources at the back of this book. One ironclad rule: never invent or embellish to have your child appear more impressive or experienced than they actually are. Los Angeles is a town where everyone pretty much does know everyone. Casting directors will often ask kids about something on their résumés just to make a little small talk—to get a feel for them as people and to break the ice a little. You don't want to put your child in the position of having to lie or—just as bad—answer honestly that they don't know what or whom the director is talking about!

Similarly, don't exaggerate skills. If your kid can ride a horse or swim at a certain level, that's great—put it down under Skills. But if they can't and they end up getting cast in a role that requires that skill, you could be actually endangering them, as well as setting them up for massive stress, embarrassment, and a possible loss of the job, not to mention their reputation.

When we came out to LA from Bainbridge Island, Dove had mostly community theater on her résumé. She'd been in two locally produced films (a featured extras role in an independent feature and a supporting lead in a short film) and recorded two things (vocals on a demo and backup vocals on a few songs for an album). She'd worked with an acting coach and a vocal coach, both of whom we could list under Training, and had a small role in a locally shot commercial: nothing that would specifically suggest she'd make an excellent bet for an agent or casting director, but enough to suggest that she had some experience both performing and taking direction. Anyone can (and probably *should*) be able to have a résumé that suggests this by the time they arrive in LA. There are so many kids competing for roles that you should arm yours with some sort of track record before coming here. But if all they have to show is small and local stuff, no worries. That's all most kids have before coming to Los Angeles.

Some cautions for résumés: these things end up everywhere, and you must be very thoughtful about what personal information is on them. For example, limit contact information exclusively to that of your manager or agent, if you have one. If that person is you for the time being, include your own cell phone number and e-mail address only—no physical address and no details that could help someone with less than honorable intentions track down your child or sound like a family friend. This means no school names, team names, and so on. Give the minimum details necessary for professional communication, and nothing more.

The basics for all résumés include the following: Keep the fonts simple and the size at ten to twelve point. Use standard white paper, nothing fancy. When listing categories of experience, film and TV are listed separately, and the list is in this order: film, TV, theater, commercials, and training. Skip any categories that aren't relevant. List your child's experience—where they have any—in the three columns: (1) the name of the project, (2) for TV, the type of role (series regular, recurring, guest star, or costar); for film, the type of role (lead, supporting, principal, or featured); for theatre, the actual name of your child's role, and (3) for film and TV, the name of the production company; for theater, the director.

Finally, never list extras or background work on a résumé, except perhaps under Training. It is not considered relevant by casting directors or agents.

A small but important note for young actors who are over eighteen but play younger: do not put your actual age or date of birth on your résumé. Just type "legal eighteen." No one needs to know you are actually twenty-four if you look fifteen! And since an audition is technically a job interview, it is illegal for casting directors to ask. So let them think you are younger if it helps you get the role.

Meanwhile, if your child is under eighteen (and not a "legal eighteen"), do put their age on the résumé. It is required for casting to know exactly how old they are in order to know how many hours they are allowed by law to work.

Below are two examples of résumés: one for a child with little professional experience and no agent, and another for a child with more experience as well as an agent. Copies of these can also be found for easy reference in the back of the book, in the section on Résumé Format Examples.

Sample résumé format for young actor with no agent, little professional experience:

CATE RUIZ

(555)111-1234, catesmom@ymail.com

Hair: Dark Brown	Weight: 95
Height: 4′10″	Eyes: Brown
Age: 11	

THEATER

ANNIE	Orphan#4	Dir. Deirdre Cory
THE WIZARD OF OZ	Munchkin	Dir. Theresa Smith

COMMERCIALS

Kingston Toyota	Principal	Sunrise Productions

TRAINING

ACTING—Improv Class	Arthur Sackler
LITTLE STARS SUMMER CAMP	Denise Smithson

SPECIAL SKILLS

Singing, swimming, tennis, horseback riding, gymnastics, dance, basic guitar. Can wiggle ears and do "the wave" with eyebrows.

Sample résumé format for young actor with an agent, some professional experience:

SUPER FINE TALENT AGENCY

8888 Sunset Blvd, suite 100, Los Angeles, CA 90069
(555)111-1234, talent@superfinetalent.com

CATE RUIZ

SAG-AFTRA

Hair: Dark Brown
Height: 5′1″
Age: 11

Weight: 110
Eyes: Brown

TELEVISION

THE PERFECTIONIST	Guest Star	CBS
MAGIC COAST (PILOT)	Series Regular	Disney Channel
GUILTY AS CHARGED	Featured	Warner Bros.
LOST AGAIN	Costar	ABC

FILM

NOW OR NEVER	Lead	Disney Channel
ALMOST KILLERS	Supporting	SKY Pictures
GIVE ME A SIGN	Featured	Traverso-Raye Prod.

THEATER

ANNIE	Annie	Dir. Deirdre Cory
ONCE UPON A MATTRESS	Nightingale of Samarkand	Dir. Daniel Fox
THE WIZARD OF OZ	Dorothy	Dir. Theresa Smith
LES MISERABLES	Little Cozette	Dir. Steven McAfee

RECORDING

YOU AND ME	Prod. Sam Jones	Wildwood Records

COMMERCIALS List available on request

TRAINING

VOICE	Mary Reynolds
ACTING—Scene Study	Arthur Sackler
ACTING—For the Camera	Samantha Scrivener

SPECIAL SKILLS

Singing, swimming, tennis, horseback riding, gymnastics, dance, basic guitar. Can wiggle ears and do "the wave" with eyebrows.

Coogan Account

The Coogan account was named in honor of Jackie Coogan, one of the first truly huge child stars and one of the first whose fortune came in part from heavy merchandising. His earnings amounted to between $48 and $65 million in today's dollars, but when he came of age and asked his parents for his money, Coogan discovered that they had squandered nearly all of it on extravagant living. This profound injustice led to the so-called Coogan law, which requires that 15 percent of all earnings by a minor in the state of California be set aside in a blocked trust until the child is eighteen.

As of the time of this writing, the states of New York, Louisiana and New Mexico have similar laws. Check your state's website for specific labor laws. If you live in Texas and your child is shooting a movie in Texas, you may not need to set an account like this up. But if you live in California and your child is shooting a movie in Texas, the Coogan law will apply. A good source of direct links to state laws regarding minor blocked trust accounts is the SAG-AFTRA State Statutes page, which can be found at http://www.sagaftra.org/content/state-statutes.

Note: On January 1, 2014, the California law was modified. It now reads, in part, "It is required that 15 percent of the minor's gross earnings be set aside by the minor's employer, except an employer of a minor for services as an extra, background performer, or in a similar capacity." In other words, if your child is working as a background player or extra and making something like one hundred dollars a day, the requirement to deposit 15 percent of that small check has now been waived. This makes sense and reduces an unnecessary paperwork burden for everyone.

Still, if you and your child aspire to have them performing in featured or speaking roles, you need to set up a Coogan account. It is easy to set one of these accounts up, though not all banks offer them. A partial list of California banks that do is provided at the back of this book in the Resources and References section.

An important aside: another aspect of the Coogan law makes clear that 100 percent of the minor's earnings in fact belong to the minor. There seems to be a lot of confusion about this. The balance of your child's earnings—after the 15 percent is secured in the Coogan account—does *not* belong to the parents or family. This can be a difficult truth for parents. It can be challenging to make ends meet if you are living on only one income because one parent is providing full-time support for the child's career. If you are a single parent, it can be incredibly difficult. Some families deal with this by cutting a parent in as a "manager" for 5 percent, 10 percent, or even 15 percent, though this is still not enough to support a family. Whatever your family decides to do, make sure there is clear communication about it with your child so there are no bitter feelings on either side later.

Work Permits

Work permits are another new issue for most parents. And while they can be a slight hassle, they are important and are in place to protect your child. Below are the basics.

The State of California requires any child under the age of eighteen (with a few exceptions) to have a valid and current work permit before they are allowed to work in the entertainment industry. The first thing to notice about this is that if your child lands a job where they begin shooting the next day or so (which is not unusual), you will have a serious problem unless their work permit is already secured. So take care of this before they begin auditioning. This applies not only to acting jobs, but also to commercials, modeling, and vocal recording. The permits are valid for six months and renewable every six months while the child is under the age of eighteen.

There are services that will take care of this process for you for a fee, but using them is really unnecessary. The six-month permits are free of charge, and the first time you apply, you will need to supply a birth certificate or other legally acceptable proof of birth date. Both the first application and all renewal applications for the permit must include approval from the child's school. Specifically, an authorized school administrator must verify that your child's attendance and grades are satisfactory. Note that this is an excellent incentive for your child to keep up their grades and attendance. The school's approval is a necessary part of getting the work permit. If your kid's grades are not up to par, it can cost them months of opportunity until they can get them back up and demonstrate that with a new report card.

If you are applying for the first time (or renewing) when school is not is session, you can supply your child's most recent report card and a letter from the school principal stating that your minor is satisfactory in all academic subjects, attendance, and health.

If your child is homeschooled, as so many young performers are, you will need to complete the application and attach it to an affidavit from whichever private school or local school your child's studies fall under. Again, the requirements of satisfactory attendance, academic progress, and health are the same.

State laws vary in terms of their requirements for minor work permits. A great list of links to information regarding laws on the employment of minors is here: http://www.sagaftra.org/content/state-statutes.

NEW

As of January 1, 2012, there is a ten-day temporary entertainment work permit available for online application. It has a different list of requirements, as well as a fee. To apply for the temporary permit, your minor child must be between the ages of fifteen days and sixteen years, have never applied for a six-month Entertainment Work Permit, and have not previously applied for a ten-day Temporary Entertainment Work Permit. This appears to be designed for first-time, emergency use, as it has a fee and is only good for ten days, versus the standard permit, which is free and good for six months.

Contact information for the California Entertainment Work Permit for a minor is provided in the back of this book in the Resources and References section. Permits can be applied for online, by mail, or in person at the Van Nuys, California office.

Full disclosure: I learned about work permits and Coogan accounts the hard way. In August of 2011, Dove had been auditioning for a full eight months—without being cast in a single role—when suddenly she booked her first gig: a recurring guest star on a critically acclaimed cable show. She needed both a Coogan account and a work permit in about thirty-six hours. I panicked and spent about a hundred dollars to have a service take care of the work permit for me, as I needed to know without question that we would have it in time. I then dropped everything else, did some fast research, and set her up with a Coogan account. Please save yourself the stress, and do this up front! Done without rush, this is all free.

Tips and Takeaways:

- Get a great headshot for your kid.
- Make a professional resume, even if your child has little experience yet.
- Open a Coogan Account when you land in LA, and if your child is working outside of California, check to see what the laws are in your state regarding minors, labor laws, and blocked trust accounts. A good resource is: http://www.sagaftra.org/content/state-statutes.

- Secure a work permit for your child before they start auditioning for paid projects. The permit is free, and required by law. A link to the different laws regarding work permits and minors by states can be found here: http://www.sagaftra.org/content/state-statutes.

CHAPTER 4

Audition Basics

When you come to LA, whether for a short-term or longer-term stay, the objective is to get work. But not all work is created equal. There are different levels of auditions available: the ones anyone can get, the ones only someone with an agent can get, the ones only someone with a top agent can get, and the ones that are only offered to established stars.

Auditions for Anyone: No Agent Required

The most basic audition opportunities can be found posted on job boards for actors, like CastingNetworks.com, ActorsAccess.com, and Backstage.com. For a low monthly fee, you can post your child's headshot, résumé, and special skills. Auditions that match their basic information, like gender and age range, will come into your e-mail inbox, and you can decide whether to pursue them. Some are fun, and some will not be appropriate. These auditions are never going to be for big projects or lead roles. But they are useful to help your child get comfortable with the audition process, and if some lead to actual work, they can help fill out a résumé so a potential agent might take your child seriously.

Working background can be a great way for your child to learn some of the special language and protocols of a set. It's decidedly unglamorous but another good way to test the seriousness of their commitment. Are they willing to go through the tedium of a long day of mostly waiting and then likely repeatedly performing a simple action, like crossing behind the star through a hallway on the call of "ACTION"?

What extras work will *not* give is the fantasy that I suspect many young actors dream of: that they will be noticed, or "discovered," in the course of working as an extra. While technically anything is possible, I know of no one that this has happened to, and in every set with extras that I have been on—television or film—the extras are largely segregated from the stars and director.

Since Dove did not work as an extra, I can't speak much for what to expect if you do pursue background work, though there are some basics for anyone on a set that are covered in Chapter 28, in the section on set etiquette. In general, know that you are likely to need to manage and provide your child's own wardrobe, hair, and makeup and that they will be kept in a holding area with the other extras while waiting to perform. Of course you should stay with them the entire time. Assistant directors can't be responsible for your child—only you can!

The fact that background actors are treated differently from the main cast has everything to do with sheer logistics. There are sometimes dozens, if not hundreds, of background players on a shoot, and organizing the services for that many people is a major undertaking. An example of this in action is the fact that background actors eat lunch after the cast and crew. Principal actors need to eat first, as they will have to go back to hair and makeup, and may well have a wardrobe change, before returning to the set. The leads will often be ushered to the front of the lunch line for this reason. The crew works very long hours and will also likely have to return to the set while the extras are still eating. In general, there are good reasons for everything you see done on a set, even if those reasons are not always obvious.

Student films are another entry-level opportunity that can provide real experience and add some material to a résumé. However, since they are by their nature nonunion and typically run by young people, be especially careful around questions of safety. My older daughter, Claire, acted in a student film when she was eighteen, and the director—another eighteen-year-old—wanted her to jump off a rooftop in an action scene! He had placed a mattress on the ground for her to land on. When I asked her about this later, she admitted it hadn't occurred to her that she could say no. Luckily she walked away with only muscle soreness and a good lesson. Unions are great for many reasons, not the least of which is safety regulations. Be alert wherever your child is working, but especially if the project is amateur or nonunion.

Auditions Requiring an Agent

Most auditions can only be accessed through an agent, and this goes for just about all roles in recognizable TV or film projects. The breakdowns (detailed descriptions of a project, including director, producers, casting director, story line, and roles available for casting) are only listed on Breakdown Services, to which only licensed agents have access. You can only get an audition if your agent submits you. Clearly, if your child is going to be able to do the kind of work that they actually hope to do—and, let's be honest, no one goes to LA in hopes of working as an extra or in student films—then they will need an agent. Getting an agent is one of the toughest parts of the process for many people. Dove was no exception. I'll cover finding an agent in Chapter 13. For now, just note that nearly all work with the possibility of an entry on IMDb (the Internet Movie Database—an online who's who of all film and TV) can only be accessed with an agent.

The Audition Itself

At its most basic, an audition consists of getting an appointment with a casting director looking to fill a role. Unlike auditioning for a play, where you have to come in with a prepared monologue of your own choosing (and maybe a song!), when you audition for film and TV, you prepare a scene or scenes from the material you received when you got the audition appointment. These scenes are called "sides." It is strongly preferred that your child come in with the sides memorized if possible, as this will help them be more natural—not sound like they are reading—and be able to make eye contact with their scene partner (usually the casting director's assistant). Sometimes, given the short notice given for an audition and the possibly excessive length of the material, memorizing the sides entirely is impossible. If that's the case, just help your child be as familiar as they can be before going in so they are as comfortable as possible with the material. The sides will be attached to an e-mail confirming your child's appointment. You'll want to print them out and possibly highlight your child's lines. In general, the younger the child, the shorter the sides will be.

Even if your child knows their lines cold, they should still enter the room with a copy of the sides. This is because the casting director may ask them to change something about their read ("This time, try it as if you are feeling angry" or "OK, pick it up from the middle of page two, but more urgent this time"), and that can sometimes throw actors off if they don't have their material available.

But before your kid gets in that room, you have to get to the casting office! Los Angeles is a big place, and its traffic is legendary for a reason. Auditioning is stressful enough without wondering if you will be able to find the location or if you will be late. For that reason, always build a large cushion into your drive time. It's a cliché because it is true: fifteen minutes early is on time; on time is late. Being late is just unacceptable. There are too many other people out there who can fill a given job for casting directors to take a risk on an actor who can't show up on time. If you are ever late on set, you can cause hundreds of people to wait, and cost the studio many thousands of dollars. Not OK! I used Google Maps to get a visual and time estimate before I set out to get Dove to an audition and a GPS in my car to get us there reliably. The best GPS devices allow you to change your route if severe traffic is detected, which can be a godsend in Los Angeles. Phone apps with map functions are a cheap and easy solution, too.

This may sound excessive, but another thing LA is known for is its confusing, restrictive parking signage. Most casting offices have only street parking, and it is really easy to get towed if you don't pay close attention to all of the signs. Be armed with lots of quarters (not all meters take credit cards yet), and allow extra time for finding a safe place to leave your car.

Once you walk into the casting office, look for the sign-in sheet. Typically it will ask for your child's name, the role they're auditioning for (sometimes the project, if the agents are casting more than one project that day), and the time they arrived, as well as the appointment time. It may also ask for their representation or agent. If you don't have one yet, just say "self" and list your own phone number. Never list your child's phone number (if they have one).

In the waiting room, you're likely to see other kids who are clearly there to audition for the same role as your child. This can be both funny and a little disconcerting, especially if they all look very similar. Once we walked into a room where literally every young woman in it looked like a clone of the next. In our case, they were petite, blond, and dressed as cheerleaders! Hilarious and weird.

Waiting rooms outside casting offices can be stressful places. Do what you can to help your child feel relaxed. Find out where the bathroom is so they can use it before going in to the audition. If you're there fifteen minutes early, there will be time for this. Bring water. Nerves can make for a remarkably dry throat. Little snacks for the car can be good, but they're probably better not brought into the office. If your kid needs to run lines, it's better to do this where you won't disturb the other people waiting.

People I've talked to are divided about whether it's better to talk to others in the waiting room or not. I'd let intuition be your guide. I've seen some parents and kids deliberately try to psych other kids out in various ways, which is as astonishing as it is horrible. I've also seen kids make long-term friends in a casting room—a process that can be aided by the fact that after a certain point, you are likely to see the same people over and over again in different rooms across town. Generally you can't go wrong being quiet and polite and keeping it at that.

Finally, your child's name will be called! At this point, they should take their headshot and résumé and follow the casting director's assistant back into the casting office. You will not be following. This may seem wrong to you, but it is absolutely standard and very important. Kids often behave quite differently when their parents are right there, and it is critical that the casting director gets a feel for how a child acts in a professional situation when their parent is not directly influencing them. Some kids are more relaxed when their parents are out of sight, and some are much shyer. But when it comes down to it and your kid is in front of a camera with the director calling the shots, they need to be reliably comfortable and professional, and this is the first opportunity a casting director has to test that.

You will be nearby, waiting in the casting room along with the other parents and kids. It should go without saying to never make phone calls in the waiting room. Auditions go surprisingly quickly, given how much time it takes to prepare for them and drive to and from them! Your kid will be out before you know it.

When they do come out, make sure to thank the casting assistant as you leave. Casting assistants work very hard and have stressful jobs.

Leaving the audition, it's the most natural thing in the world to ask your child how the audition went. But asking this is unfair because it creates a sense of pressure. And honestly, they have no idea how it went. The casting director could have been purposefully poker-faced (and many are) to not get your child's hopes up. So your child may feel that they did horribly. Or they might have been extremely encouraging (which in fact can unnecessarily get your child's hopes up). Not only do they not know how it went, but also how they FEEL it went may be completely off the mark. A number of times, Dove felt like she really nailed an audition, only to never hear back for a callback. More often, however, she felt she did terribly and then *did* get a callback! Your kid may in fact have turned in a fabulous audition, but one of many, many things out of your (and their) control will mean that they won't be cast. More about those elements later.

So what *can* you say when they come out from the audition room and you've left the waiting room together? My personal instinct is to let them lead the conversation—most likely they will want to share their experience. You might ask how they *feel* about how the audition went, which is something they do know about, and which matters very much. If they feel triumphant, you can celebrate with them.

If they feel less than happy about how it went, ask if there is something that they might do differently next time. If they felt unprepared, maybe more time spent learning their lines or considering how to interpret them is in order going forward. Or maybe something happened in the room that threw them. Oftentimes the casting director will ask them to read the sides in a different way—in other words, give them direction! It's not unusual for a casting director to test an actor—even a young one—to see if they are capable of following direction. Being able to follow direction is one of the most valuable assets an actor has. But if your child has *over-rehearsed* their lines (yes, this can happen), they might have a difficult time veering from the deep groove they have developed and speaking the lines differently. Maybe working with an acting coach on the next important audition would be a good idea. Finally, it's possible that your child didn't feel good about the audition simply because they were just so very nervous. The best remedy for this is to simply go to more auditions, until they get a chance to really see clearly that there is always another audition around the corner. The fate of the world does not rest on getting a particular role. Keeping a sense of perspective on this will go a long way in helping your child do the same.

Tips and Takeaways:

- Basic audition opportunities that your child can get without an agent can be found on job boards like Actors Access, Casting Networks, and Backstage.

- Working background may be good for education, but it will not give experience that will be taken seriously by agents or casting directors.
- Most auditions for decent-sized roles can only be accessed through an agent.
- Fifteen minutes early is on time!
- You will typically not be allowed to watch your child audition.
- Every audition your child does gets them closer to booking their first role.

CHAPTER 5

Basic Players

A section on the basics in a book like this would be incomplete without a list of the basic players in this landscape. Some are necessary and will be part of the picture from the beginning; some will come later, as your child becomes more successful; and some may never enter into your child's world. But it's important to understand the people in the world you are entering into, as they are all a part of the system you need to navigate for your child's success. Listed below in alphabetical order are the basic players.

Agent

An agent, also known as a theatrical agent, represents your child and is primarily focused on obtaining work and negotiating contracts on their behalf. Agents should be licensed by the state they work in.

The number of clients they represent can vary from just a few to many (something to consider when looking for a good match), and they typically are limited to charging 10 percent commission. I would *only* sign on with one that is SAG-AFTRA franchised. You can check with SAG-AFTRA at http://www.sagaftra.org/professional-representatives/aftra-franchised-agents for a list of their franchised agents, organized by major market.

Ideally, you would sign on with one who is also a member of the ATA, or Association of Talent Agents, the nonprofit trade association of professional talent agents. You can go to their website (http://www.agentassociation.com) to see whether the agents you are considering are listed. Just because an agent hasn't joined the ATA doesn't mean they aren't reputable. But if the agent is a member, it means they are accountable to an additional supervising body of peers.

Important: In the major markets, such as LA and New York, there are youth divisions and agents who specialize entirely in representing young people. These are the agents you want to find. They generally are in that line of work because they love young people and are familiar with the special rules, regulations, and issues of employing and working with minors. They are also the ones casting agencies contact for roles that call for young people. In my opinion, youth agents are a very special breed.

Commercial agents are a little different, as they are engaged in finding not acting jobs for your child, but commercial jobs (i.e., TV or radio commercials or modeling for print ads). Many agencies have both kinds of agents, and some kids pursue both types of work and therefore have two different agents. We did not go that route, and I suspect that is another book entirely.

It is really important to understand that just because your child has an agent, this does not guarantee that they will go out on many, if any, auditions. Yes, agents only make money if your child works, so it would follow that they would want to send as many of their actors out as possible all the time. But the truth is that until your child has a legitimate TV or film role under their belt (something that would get them a legitimate entry on IMDb, as opposed to a vanity entry), their odds of actually being cast are slim, and so they are less likely to be sent out. Yes, it's a catch-22.

Assistants

Assistants are the intelligent, hardworking people who manage the gritty details of every aspect of this business. Your agent, manager, casting director, lawyer, and business manager all have assistants, and they are the secret glue of this industry. From the moment you walk into a waiting room to the moment you leave, you make an impression on these guys, and it is important to understand that how you treat them and what they observe are part of the process. It's just common sense that people who are difficult when they don't believe they are talking to someone "important" will be difficult on set, which is another way to say that you are auditioning, too, and generally for the assistants, who report back. So be smart, and be kind. Many of these people will be running their own agencies and firms someday.

Business Manager

A business manager is generally not needed until your child is making fairly serious money on a regular basis. But at that point a manager can be crucial, as the fine points of taxation for actors can get quite complicated when multiple commissions, residuals, and even multiple state (or country!) taxes get involved. For example, in her first year shooting *Liv and Maddie*, Dove did projects in California, Utah, and Georgia within one calendar year. The next year she was shooting in Canada. If your child is fortunate enough to reach that tipping point where they are making around $200,000 a year (not many kids do this, but if you are a regular in a series, it can happen), then a business manager can help you through the incorporation process. It's critical that this person have an impeccable reputation, as your child's earnings will be in their hands. Make sure you get recommendations and do real research before signing on with one, if you ever get to that point.

Casting Director

The terms *casting director* and *casting agent* are often used interchangeably, but the correct one to use is casting director. These are the folks who decide who gets the role or at least whittle the choices down to a very few before the director and producers weigh in. Typically when your child auditions, they step into the room with the casting director and their assistant, and the audition is filmed for later review. Casting directors may work on multiple projects at once, both film and television. After your child has been auditioning for a while, you will begin to notice that they are going in front of some of the same people repeatedly, for different projects. This can be good for a number of reasons: your kid is likely to become more comfortable and turn in a better audition if they are familiar with the casting office, and frankly if a casting director is familiar with your child, they may even request that your child come in to audition for a certain role. This is one of many reasons that it's important to go out on as many auditions as possible—not only is your child getting better and more practiced with every audition, but they are becoming familiar to the people who may keep them in mind for future projects.

Lawyer

A good rule as to when it's time to find a lawyer is when a project or contract comes up that involves a serious time commitment or serious money (or both). If your kid is working as an extra or getting guest star roles for one or just a few episodes or cast in a small role in a movie, your agent should be able to take care of making sure the contract is appropriate. But if your child has been offered a series-regular role (lead or not) or a larger role in a film, I would engage an entertainment attorney to review the contract and represent you in negotiations. There are so many aspects to a contract that even an intelligent, educated parent cannot manage. A good contract is fair to everyone and will not leave a bitter taste in your mouth over time. A bad one can be a nightmare. And frequently, a good lawyer can negotiate small things that make a big difference to your kid's happiness in addition to a better financial deal.

It's also a very good idea to have a lawyer review a contract you are considering signing with an agent or a manager. In my opinion, lawyers are worth every penny of the 5 percent they typically charge when you engage one on retainer. And if your kid is fortunate enough to be moving into the levels where a lawyer is a good addition to the team, having one available for advice is another blessing. It probably should go without saying, but what you want is an entertainment lawyer, not a general practitioner.

I asked Patti Felker, Dove's attorney, about how she would advise parents to find a great attorney for their young actor. Her advice was to go to IMDb Pro, look up the actors whose careers you admire, and see who represents them legally. In the listing of actors' representatives, agents, and managers, their legal representation is often listed as well. She also recommended searching *Variety* and *The Hollywood Reporter* for references to attorneys of successful actors you admire and seeing if their names show up in interviews. Ultimately, this business is all about relationships, and the conversations and social capital that make or break an actor's career are often greatly shaped by their legal representatives. So find a great entertainment lawyer, and treasure them.

Manager

Does your kid need a manager? It depends. Some people have an agent but no manger; others have a manager but no agent. Many have both. Managers generally have fewer clients than agents, so your kid is likely to get more of their attention. However—and this is important—unlike agents, managers are not licensed by the state or franchised by unions. In other words, pretty much anyone can call himself or herself a manager. Of course, great managers are like gold.

In New York and California, managers are not permitted to secure work for their clients without the assistance of an agent. Why have a manager when an agent can (and must) do this for you? Because while the main role of agents is to get their clients work, the main role of managers is to look after the big picture: to shape and look after their clients' careers. Strategy, choices, and long-term thinking are the domain of a manager. An agent is generally focused on the day-to-day, which is necessary for securing auditions and managing contracts. Think of it this way: the manager watches the forest while the agent watches the trees. For this service, most charge between 10 percent and 15 percent commission. More on this in Chapter 11, Agents versus Managers.

Public Relations Team

Another group of people who are central to the workings of the industry—but not necessary (or even appropriate) until your child reaches a certain level in their career—are PR, or public relations. Publicists are the folks who can secure your kid a meeting with the editor of a leading fashion or entertainment magazine, hook them up with designers or stylists to borrow fabulous clothes for red-carpet appearances, or book them a spot on a news or talk show. They are typically the liaison for interview requests. Clearly this will only be necessary (and possible) if your child's work warrants that level of interest. And this is just as well—the services of a good PR team are not cheap! Unlike everyone else on the team (agent, manager, lawyer, business manager), they do not work on a commission basis, but on a fixed monthly fee. And that fee can be staggering. So if your kid is lucky enough to need a PR team, hopefully they are also lucky enough to be able to afford one! That said, if you can sign on with a great team, they can be invaluable to building your child's public image and thereby their perceived value and career opportunities.

CHAPTER 6

Stories: How Did They Get Started?

Hollywood Parents Share Stories of How their Kids Started in the Industry

Kenda Benward

Luke got started in the acting business by association. I'm an actress, and he wasn't acting at all when he actually booked his first film. My agent knew I had a five-year-old son. And so she called me the day the Mel Gibson film [We Were Soldiers] came through Nashville. And she said, "Listen, they're looking for a five-year-old kid to play Mel Gibson's son. Do you think you could bring your child?"

And I paused because, number one, he can't read. He's too young to read. And he doesn't know the lines; he doesn't even have time to learn them. He's never auditioned for anything this major before. Maybe a commercial here and there, something little. But she goes, "Well, just bring him."

So I brought him to the audition. And there were about a hundred kids there. They were all practicing their lines. They were all dressed in khakis and white starched shirts. And he was not in khakis and a white starched shirt. He was in football sweats. His hair was all messy because he had been at kindergarten all day. And he looked to me with this face like, "I don't know what I'm doing here. Why am I here?"

And I said, "Listen, don't worry about the lines. Just go in and do the Pledge of Allegiance. You know that. You've memorized that."

Five years old, he walked in and auditioned with the Pledge of Allegiance and his citizenship pledge. And about two days later, after Randall Wallace saw the audition tape, casting called and hired him—booked him. Five years old.

They were doing a national search, and there were five kids they were looking for. In fact, Taylor Momsen from Gossip Girl*—she played Cindy Lou Who in* How the Grinch Stole Christmas*—she played his older sister. A lot of great kids. Devon Werkheiser, who was on Nickelodeon—he was on* Ned's Declassified*—he was in the cast.*

And it's just amazing to see. You see these kids working together as kids. And now they're adults. And you've been able to watch their journey over the years—how their friendships have grown and how they've gone on to do different things.

It's a pretty amazing process. But, yeah, a national search for five roles. They came through Nashville; they were shooting in Fort Benning, Georgia. And before they went to Georgia, they stopped and looked at some kids in Tennessee.

We had never even been to LA at this point. It wasn't even on the radar at all. I was acting, and I was doing the occasional national commercial that would come through Nashville. The occasional feature film, local music videos, local commercials—just whatever I could get workwise, I was doing. I lived in Nashville, and I was raising a family. I had no desire to go to LA at that point. It really just came out of the sky. It was out of the blue.

Allison Zuehlsdorff

Cozi got started on a whim one day when I asked her if she might want to be in a local production of Annie. *She commented that she would rather go see it than be in it but went to the audition just to see what would happen. She was cast that day as Annie and has been interested in musical theater, film, and TV since then.*

Amy Anderson

Mother of Aubrey Anderson-Emmons, best known for playing Lily on *Modern Family.*

When Aubrey booked Modern Family, *she had just turned four—like had been four for a month—so she was a newly minted four.*

The honest truth is that I had not intended at all to get her into this business. I had been in the business for years, and people would always ask me after I had her, "Do you want her to be a comedian like you, or do you want her to be an actress?"

I always would say, "No. I want her to have a normal life. I don't want her to struggle. I want her to have paid vacations and health insurance and all that stuff." I just never really thought about it. When she was a baby, I took her on a couple of commercial auditions with me where they were looking for moms with real babies because my agent had submitted me. Never booked anything. I took her on one print ad and didn't book it, and I just hated it, having to get her all dressed and queued, waking her up from her nap, driving across town, and all that. I just told my agent, "I don't really want to do that anymore with her. Can you just focus on me because it's too much work?"

She had been to a couple of auditions with me where I had to bring her because I had no one to watch her, so she knew what auditions were, but what happened was they decided to recast the role of Lily, and my agent saw it in the breakdowns. She just called me one day and said, "Hey, they're recasting this role. You should really submit your daughter because she's the exact age they're looking for, and she looks a lot like those other girls."

I was like, "No, I don't want to set her up for a failure. She's going to be going up against kids with experience; some of these kids are going to be professionals. The odds of her booking it are just nil. Why would I put her through that?" I talked to her a little bit about it—my agent was pushing for it—and I said, "Let me talk to her. It has to be her decision, even though she can't fully understand the magnitude of what I'm asking her." But she really wanted to try.

Yeah, she was just four at that point; she knew what an audition was. I said, "Do you want to go into an audition for you to try out for a part on a TV show?"

She said, "Ooh, yeah. I want to be on TV."

I was like, "Well...but you don't totally understand. Look, this is just a try to see if you like it, because you're probably not going to get it. They're going to see a lot of little girls, and they're only going to pick one, but this might be a chance for you to see if you like acting. But if you do get it, you also have to understand that it's a lot of work. It's grown-ups telling you what to do all day, you have to follow a lot of rules, it's long days, you'll be tired, and you still have to do your schoolwork. So I really want you to think about this."

She goes, "But I really want to be on TV." I was trying to explain to her what that even meant.

I said, "It would be a show where each week you would be on the show a little bit. Shows have things called episodes. You know how when we turn on SpongeBob*, it's on every day, and you see different episodes? Or we turn on* The Fresh Beat Band*, and we see them?"*

And she goes, "Oh, yeah. I totally want to do that because it will be all about me."

She said that—literally, I quote. And I'm like, "Oh my God! She was born to do this." Ten days later, I was signing her network contract, and it's been this wild roller coaster ever since. Yeah, she went on two commercial auditions and one print when she was an infant, and that was it.

I'm very honest about this, but I still question whether I made the right choice, because obviously it's changed our lives tremendously. It's not like she's just a kid who is going and trying out for pilots and commercials and sometimes books something and has a job here and there. She's on a major network show, and she's famous now. It's been a lot for us to deal with. Of course, there are pros and cons, but I question all the time whether we did the right thing. I feel confident that she's a really happy kid, and I think I would know if she were unhappy. She would tell me if she didn't want to do it anymore.

It's been tricky, but I also tell people it's just like anything that any kid does. Some kids are really good at soccer, some kids are on the math team, some kids play chess, some kids are good at art. My kid just really happens to like to act, and she also sings. I always tell her that's her choice. If she ever wants to stop doing it, she can. I always tell her, "When Modern Family *goes off the air..." I recently had to tell her that the show isn't going to be on forever, because it dawned on me at one point that she didn't realize that. I think she thought she was going to do it for the rest of her life.*

Because it's been like a lot of what she remembers of her childhood so far. I said, "You know, in a few years, this show isn't going to exist anymore, and you, at that point, can decide if you want to keep acting or not. You just do whatever you want then; you don't have to decide now."

And right now she says, "Oh, well, I like acting for now, but I think I want to be a YouTuber."

I'm like, "Oh, God." Although some of those YouTubers are making a lot of money.

Kim Holt

[Olivia's] sister was actually really into theater, her older sister. They started out doing summer camps and theater camps when they were, like, three. She did theater probably up until she was ten. Then she started professionally acting at ten years old.

Clark Trainor

Tenzing got into acting when he was eight by doing a summer theater camp, which I still to this day think is the best introduction to even television and film. Because on stage there is no cut, reset, back to one, start over. If you want your kid to learn total immersion into a character, there's no other place to do it than on stage. Because when that play is going, if a special effect doesn't happen, if a sound cue doesn't happen, the play has to continue on. If the other actor drops a line, you have to be able to improvise and cover right on the spot.

He started in summer theater at age eight, didn't do anything in the fall or the winter, and then did the same summer theater again the following summer. And then we moved to Los Angeles [from Florida], and that's when the business side started.

Victor Boyce

I didn't want to do this. This was not my thing. The reason it happened is because Cameron was dancing. He was doing dance lessons and going to dance school, and two or three of the other kids—including Booboo Stewart—were already doing this. We met Booboo in dance, years before we started. Booboo was, I want to say, nine or ten.

I remember Booboo was on a lot of ads for Mattel for Hot Wheels. As a kid I was always big on the Hot Wheels, so I thought, "Wow, that's really cool," but I never thought about Cameron doing it. But the kids kept saying, "You should try, you should try, you should try." So I think his uncle, Libby's brother, sent some pictures of Cameron to different agencies, and that's how we got with our agency. So we started going on auditions, and again I was not expecting anything. I was still hesitant. I was very cynical and skeptical about the whole thing. Like I said, we kept going on these auditions, and he never booked anything. I was just getting frustrated, taking time off of work and whatnot, until we booked that first job. And from that day on, he has never, ever stopped booking.

Yeah, it's been a really, really interesting thing because, like I said, I wasn't chasing this—I didn't want anything. All I could think about was all the kids that had been...I won't name names, but you know all the horror stories, especially child actors, and I've met a couple. But long before we got into this, I knew a guy [who had been a child actor] and I was like, "Oh my God! I don't want anything to do with this." But as you get in and you meet people, you realize those are the sensationalized stories. For every bad story, there are a thousand good stories, I think, and it turned out really well.

Dance was the door opener for all of this. Dance was the precursor because if it wasn't for dance, we wouldn't have met the other kids who were already doing the auditions. It was just a fluke.

It just happened to be that. Like I said, Booboo was the main one. He was working the most. Other kids were going out. I don't know if they were booking anything, but Booboo was the one who was actually out there and working. Another kid, Turner White, who is part of Cameron's X-MOB crew, he was on not-Barney. It was like Barney, but it was Hip Hop Harry. *Imagine Barney as a bear who does hip-hop—there was a show like that. It was just like* Barney *and called* Hip Hop Harry. *So he was doing that, and he was also dancing with us. So between those two, that's what sparked it.*

Pam McCartan

Ryan was seven when he did his first stage performance. However, both my kids were three and a half when they started dancing. That's performing, too, I guess. Dance classes, recitals, and competitive dance. Not in the same classes, but at the same institutions.

Ryan was diagnosed with juvenile diabetes at the age of six, and prior to that, we had had him in all those typical boys' sports, like T-ball, basketball, and soccer. And by the time he was diagnosed with juvenile diabetes, we were noticing that his interest level was diminishing because he wasn't feeling so great. You know—because sugar levels continue to need to be monitored, and obviously he was insulin dependent. He would get exhausted so easily and look at us like, "Please don't make me continue this. I just can't do this." And so, whether it was his athletic ability or his diabetes, in any case, he really wasn't interested in sports. He did some tennis and some golf, which were more individual sports he could do on his own and not have to compete with someone and keep up. That seemed to work out a little bit better for him.

But he really fell into the acting thing primarily because of his sister and his sister's voice teacher. When Alison was ten and taking voice lessons, Ryan would come along because I was one parent with one car and had two kids, and he would be basically dragged along. John [Alison's voice teacher] had asked the question, "Does this boy sing?" He had been contacted by the history theater in Minneapolis—they were looking for a seven-year-old boy—and, sure enough, if Ryan was seven and could sing, he was worth looking at for the audition. And so we went, and he landed his first role. At seven. Because he could sing, really.

CHAPTER 7

Training

Most actors and directors would agree that training is an essential part of being a great actor. But after that one point of agreement, there can be a lot of divergent opinions. How much training? What kind? And what even constitutes training?

For many people, the definition of a properly trained actor is one who has a BFA or even an MFA in acting. But that's out of reach for the child actor or those who want to be professional before their early twenties. What does that leave parents who want to help their kid be successful?

My first suggestion is one that is frequently overlooked: encourage your child to read aloud. A lot. Strong reading skills—especially reading that does not sound like reading—are important for actors of all ages. Similarly, encourage practice memorizing short monologues. Reading and memorization are both skills that improve with practice, and will help your child stand out in auditions.

Just about any town of a decent size has acting classes for children. Often run through the local community theater, they can be a good introduction to the basics and are available to anyone who signs up, regardless of experience or talent level. This is an easy place to start, though the quality of instruction can be unpredictable. It's also a good way to see if your kid likes the idea of acting more than the process itself.

Many regional or professional theaters have special training classes for young actors. These are more likely to require auditions and have a higher caliber of both teacher and student. And some towns are fortunate enough to have dedicated acting studios with a range of instruction: Acting Technique, Comedy/Improv, Voice and Movement, Acting for the Camera, even private coaching. Los Angeles, of course, is groaning with acting schools and private coaches. A Google search on Los Angeles acting schools for kids turns up pages of dizzying choices.

Perhaps most important of all, encourage your child to audition for *everything.* It turns out that the majority of "work" for actors of any age is just auditioning! And the more you do it, the better you get. Not only that, but there are some overlooked opportunities for young actors in fantastic places—including professional Equity theaters, which may produce plays that include roles for children.

Have you noticed that I've mentioned a lot of *theater* training? This is because many directors believe it is the best foundation for actor training. Luckily, outside of Hollywood it is also easier to find plays to audition for than movies and television.

What should you do? I think the answer is different for everyone, and in the stories and interviews that follow, you'll see that fact illustrated over and over in the incredibly different paths of each of these successful young actors. Every kid is unique and shows up with their own strengths and gifts. And every one of these kids had access to different opportunities. Very few came from Los Angeles originally, but most arrived with enough training or raw talent that they attracted an agent or manager and began to get work.

If you decide to look for an acting coach or school, do your research. Look online to see who has been nominated or voted best acting coach or school in your area. If you live near LA, I recommend the annual Backstage Readers' Choice Awards, which you can find online. Yelp is often helpful, too, and successful actors will sometimes mention their coaches in interviews. Word of mouth can be a good source, but consider who is giving the recommendation: are they getting work, or are they another hopeful with no track record? This may go without saying, but you want to take the advice of people who are actually successful, not just someone you know who likes the person they are taking classes with. Certainly, if you have an agent, ask them for recommendations.

When you find someone you think might be a good fit—either a coach or a class or school, see if you can try one or two classes before any major financial commitment is made. Chemistry is important. You don't want to pay for a dozen classes just to discover that your child and the teacher aren't a good match. You may end up trying out a number of different coaches or classes before settling on one. That's OK. The right acting coach is an incredibly important partner for many people and can mean the difference between booking and not booking—or knocking it out of the park after you do book. One famous young actor had a coach on set for the entire time she filmed a movie—and that performance got her an Academy Award nomination. The nomination changed her life more than the movie probably did, as it opened up an entire career of top-notch roles.

Dove is the kind of kid who learns best by doing. She had very little formal acting training. Instead she learned by auditioning and getting roles and learning with each successive role, starting with community theater at the age of eight. She did sign up for classes with a well-known acting school for kids when we arrived in LA, but she dropped out after about three classes when the schedule conflicted with her high school show choir rehearsals. That being said, she did spend three full years on vocal training before we came to Los Angeles, and she still works with a vocal coach when she can.

Tips and Takeaways:

- Make sure your child has SOME training before they come to Hollywood.

- Training can be classes, coaching, or learning by doing (i.e. auditioning for and acting in plays, etc.).
- Practice auditioning is as important as acting practice, as they are different skill sets.

CHAPTER 8

Stories: Training

Hollywood Parents Share Stories about their Young Actors and Training

Kenda Benward

When we lived in Nashville, [Luke] never took acting classes. I taught him right at the house. I would teach him based on my own training. And mainly, his experience in acting was when we were making tapes. That was really when I was coaching him.

I think auditioning is one of the best learning tools there is. Not only the act of doing it on tape and reading with somebody, but then looking at it and watching yourself and what you did. And going, "Oh, wow. I didn't even realize I was doing that with my hand." And then you can redo it, or—if it's great—you can send it off and see what feedback you get from casting.

But for Luke, he was very natural. I didn't have to teach him a lot. I had to help bring things out of him sometimes, like emotions. I had to help him when he was doing a scene where he was very sad about something. I had to help this young seven-year-old child get into that moment and stay in that moment and make it honest and real.

Pat Fisher

When [Jordan] actually started in the business, he was thirteen, but he started acting in school plays, church plays, and so forth when he was about two. From kindergarten on, he got the lead role in everything he ever did.

He was with the Red Mountain Theater Company in Birmingham, Alabama, which is the only professional theater company in the Southeast, and he was a year-round member with them for seven years.

Yeah, he really just learned by doing. He had never really had any acting classes or voice classes or anything like that. Being in professional theater taught him the ropes of the business and of course enhanced his skills as well. But he maybe had three or four vocal classes ever, still to this day.

Victor Boyce

Cameron has never taken one acting lesson. And the reason why—when he was eight, we got an audition for a movie, and the movie was Mirrors*. Again, the biggest thing he had done was, "Mmm, pancakes" [in a commercial]. He had never had a speaking role, never done any acting like that. So we go to this audition, and, first of all, they needed a kid who was biracial because it was Paula Patton [as the mom] and Kiefer Sutherland as the dad, and even though Paula is very, very fair, she is obviously...she is mixed—she is biracial. So Cameron fit perfectly for that, but he didn't have much acting experience. But when the director, who was Alex Aja, saw him in casting, he told me, "Don't ever give him acting lessons."*

I'm like, "Why is that?"

"Because he is so natural that you would ruin it."

I took his advice, and I have never, ever given him acting lessons. I know, I know. But I only did it because Alex Aja, who knew a whole hell of a lot more than me, Mr. Green Guy—I took his advice. Now that doesn't mean I have never gotten him coached. We do big auditions; I'll get him coached. That's different. But acting lessons...He said for a kid—Cameron was eight—"He is very, very natural, and I love how he's delivering what I'm telling him to do."

And I said, "OK. What do I know?"

He's learned on the job, and it's been the best thing ever. A lot of people won't have those same opportunities, so I'm not saying acting lessons are bad or couldn't help you. But in our case it was beneficial not to do it because he did get that early opportunity to work with Alex Aja and be in a big movie, and he worked with Kiefer Sutherland and Paula Patton, Amy Smart. Now since the years have gone, he's done all these things and TV shows, and now we are checking out different directors and styles in every aspect of it, not just acting. So he is learning as he goes. As you know, he worked with Keanu Eagan, which was amazing, to work with him. The guy is genius, and when you are around someone like that, you soak it up, and you combine that with your previous experience and your own talent and creative ideas, and then you develop as an all-around actor or director or writer—whatever it is you want to do. When it all comes together like that, it's really fortunate and really great.

Pam McCartan

(Author's note: Ryan eventually went on to win the National High School Musical Theater Award—the Jimmy Award—for Best Actor).

Ryan had applied for Young Arts, which is a scholarship program for artists today between the ages of fifteen and eighteen. At that time, it wasn't as young as fifteen. He applied, was chosen as a finalist, spent a week in Miami, and actually won. He was a silver-award winner, and as a result of being a silver-award winner, he actually was called back to New York. He won ten thousand dollars or something. You know—a full scholarship.

They're amazing, and I would like to really plug that because if people have great artists in their families, they should really look into Young Arts. It's an amazing scholarship program, but bigger than that, it's life changing. Ryan would describe it as life changing. To spend a week in Miami with artists in several different disciplines, not just acting. I'm not going to recite all nine disciplines, but everything from poetry to videography to dance...opera vocal, theater, and musical theater. Anyway, it's amazing.

It was life changing. Truth be told, Ryan was going to be an English teacher. He had applied for one college, the University of Minnesota. Education was his path. He had had so much success, and yet he wanted to be an English teacher. We have education in the family, and that seemed logical. Both his dad and I chuckled to ourselves, wondering if that goal would really be met, but that's OK. We never stood in his way; that's what he wanted to do. Who would we be to say, "Why?"

Young Arts, though. It was Young Arts that said, "OK, so you're planning on going to the University of Minnesota. Have you thought about auditioning for their BFA program, which is sponsored by the Guthrie, because, you know..."

And that's when he said, "Well, maybe I should."

Validation. There was a representative from the Guthrie there in the audience who approached him and said, "You haven't missed the deadline for auditions. We'd really like to have you audition." And this was not a game changer, even at that point, because if he was accepted, which he was, he still could have changed his mind come

September. But to circle back, so then he went to New York for this in-the-studio, out-of-the-studio big Young Arts presentation. He had also applied to be a Presidential Scholar.

The only way to get in as a Presidential Scholar in the arts is though Young Arts. It is the only path, so as a result of being in Young Arts as a finalist, he was able to apply. And they only take one male and one female in that discipline, and Ryan was granted that. That was amazing.

And so he went to Washington, DC, for a week, and we were able to attend, and we watched him perform just the most amazing numbers with some spectacular people at the Kennedy Center. It was incredible. And then we get back, and he's contacted by Young Arts again because he's been chosen by Patti LuPone to do an HBO special. And he does that. I believe they won an Emmy. Not for that particular one, but this was in an Emmy-winning program. Then he was contacted again to go to Germany with Bobby McFerrin. Now this was all because of Young Arts. And he's seventeen.

Clark Trainor

Tenzing's not in acting classes right now only because we are so adamant about him having things away from acting when he's not here [at the Liv and Maddie *set]. And when you are shooting the show, to leave after rehearsing all day and having a run-through just to go to an acting class is just not something we want to do.*

While he's working, we're not so big on having him in classes. On a hiatus, it's great if he's in class.

Amy Anderson

She [Aubrey] hasn't. I get asked that a lot because people think that she must have had classes or something before. She didn't, and she hasn't. She's at the point now where I feel like she really could benefit from some because I don't want her...because she learned how to act on the set of Modern Family.

She literally learned by just watching the other cast members, because even the kids had been on the show for two years already. So even though this was their first huge show, they really knew what they were doing at that point. The adults obviously are very seasoned. She's an observer, so she would just sit and watch them, what they would do. She would watch them reset their props, she would watch them do their little things that they would do to prepare, and then she would just imitate them. Those things are good, and she's learned in the best classroom ever. But she's only had to play one note at this point, and I don't want her to be stuck there and to forever be pigeonholed as Lily because she can only do dry sarcastic.

She's good at Lily, but she, I think, has a great range in her. I thing she has the potential to do so much more. We're getting more and more inquiries now for future stuff—for animation voices, stuff like that—and I want her to really be ready for it. It's a tricky age, too. I think a lot of parents don't really think about this. Because she can read, but she reads at a seven-year-old level. It's hard for her to go in and do certain auditions, or to do animation. They really want kids to be able to read. She has some challenges ahead of her if she wants to continue. I think that during this next hiatus, I might get her into an acting class just to stretch her. And she's also been doing some local theater, which has been really good. Her dream is to do Broadway.

Yeah, so just kind of taking those steps to do what she needs to do to prepare for that.

Kim Holt

[Olivia] never really had any acting training, except for the theater that she did, and nobody really trained her. She picked up choreography

really well because of gymnastics. They do a lot of ballet in gymnastics as well. All of that kind of stuff came pretty natural to her. She just loved to perform, and even in gymnastics, she loved to perform when they had their floor routine or beam routine. The performance was always her thing.

Her music coach is the one that took her out to LA. We didn't take it seriously still. We did go out to LA—we thought it would be a fun family vacation. [Olivia's voice coach] actually knew somebody that did one of those things that's like International Presentation of Performers, IPOP.

I think the majority of people that go there are through one of those [acting/modeling] schools. We never did that, but he knew somebody that ran that. He took Olivia there, and she had maybe forty callbacks from different agencies.

At that time, I personally was like, "What? Is her picture just the top of the list?" You know what I mean? Because she had never done any [professional] acting. She had never done anything like that.

She was ten, but she was at a really good age, and that's something that people don't really understand, especially if you're a little bit older. She was at an age where she was tiny. So she could play even tinier roles. She was only like four four, I think, when she started.

Allison Zuehlsdorff

Cozi is learning by doing. Being in the movies, her very first line on camera was in Dolphin Tale. *She had been in several commercials before, but none of them had any lines for her to say. And then I think for her it's a matter of being observant in life and being just very perceptive and instinctive.*

We do go in for coaching. We have an awesome coach. We go in especially when there is a new project she's auditioning for, especially if it's some character she has never played before and she needs help figuring out how she wants to play it. Learning your craft—working hard to flesh out an audition piece—is essential, really. Cozi is always a better actor after a big audition than she was before she started working on it, becoming one with the material.

From what I've seen, a child who is especially observant and has good instincts is the one I often see being able to get inside at character in a very real way.

CHAPTER 9

Scams

Before launching into this section, I want to emphasize that there are *many* legitimate acting coaches, acting schools, photographers, and so on out there. And these professionals are a critical part of the industry. Training is important, and photographs are part of the calling card for an actor of any age. The best ones are identified by their reputations, which can be easily researched online and through word of mouth. There are enough excellent and authentic acting coaches, schools, and photographers that there is just no reason to get tangled up with the questionable ones.

Scams are one of the sad facts of this business. I cannot tell you how many times I've heard of parents approached in a mall by someone who says they can get their kid into the business or even make them a star. The person may claim to be a talent scout or an agent or manager. Suddenly you are being pressured into signing your child up for a slew of expensive classes, and usually a package of linked services—you are required to use that person's photographer for headshots, for example.

This kind of scam is particularly cruel because it plays on both the secret hope of most parents (my child is so special that even a stranger can see it!) and most kids (I'm going to be a star!). Our need to be and feel special is so strong that it can easily blind us to what common sense might tell us are warning signs, and keep us from doing the bit of research that might show us that these people are not in fact able to deliver what they are promising.

Some operations are more technically rip-offs than outright scams. They cost serious money, offer fairly generic training, and frequently wrap up representation in the package—in other words, you are paying the person who is supposedly acting as your child's agent, which is actually illegal in some states, including California. Interestingly, these sorts of operations are more often found outside of Hollywood, where the parents are less likely to know better.

Representation mixed with classes, workshops, or fees is perhaps the biggest red flag: a legitimate professional agent *never* asks for or requires payment. Agents *only* make money on commission when your child is paid for performing, and then they get 10 percent. If I can save even one parent hard-earned money with this paragraph, I will feel very happy. To restate: *legitimate agents and managers do not ask for fees.* If you are talking to someone who promises to represent your kid for an up-front fee, run the other way.

An important distinction: schools and training programs will generally take anyone with money. They are selling services. Real agents and managers do not sell services of any kind. Agents and managers make money if and when your young actor does. There is nothing wrong with companies that are selling services, as long as you understand that this is their business and that a company that is selling a service is not also a legitimate source of representation.

Additional red flags to be aware of include long-term contracts that require up-front payment, anyone who claims to be a "talent scout" (these are actually not used anywhere in the legitimate structure of the industry), and traveling groups who set up in hotels for "casting calls," "open calls," and the like but are actually selling services.

Yes, there are legitimate casting calls and open calls. But no legitimate casting directors *ever* charge fees for an audition. This is one way for you to know if you are looking at a legitimate casting call.

Legitimate casting directors also may hold workshops, for which they may charge. This is completely reasonable. However, you should be clear that a workshop is not an audition.

Don't lay out significant money or make a commitment to anyone or any business on behalf of your child before going home and doing some research online. Look up the people or businesses that are asking you to sign up, and see if they have been reported to the Better Business Bureau or have many entries in Google with the word *scam* or *rip-off* attached to their name. Of course, any business can have a couple of upset customers, and these days malicious trolls can do damage to even the best ones. But if you see many complaints or any sort of negative pattern, stay away. For that matter, if a company seems to change its name or location regularly, that is likely another red flag.

Don't just research the name of the business; research the names of any people running the business or working for it, too. Often the borderline scammers will move from business to business to stay ahead of their reputations. Interestingly, many of these individuals do not see themselves as con artists—just people who are trying to help young artists. But if they are mixing training packages with representation, they are only helping themselves—to your wallet.

Use social media as well as Google. See if you can find accounts on Twitter, Facebook, MySpace, and so on, for the people and businesses you are investigating. Is what they are posting consistent with what they are saying?

IMDb is a fantastic source for information, but the most relevant entries can only be accessed if you have a Pro account. These currently cost $19.99 per month or a discounted $149.99 per year. This may seem steep, but the details available through a Pro account can be truly valuable. For example, you can look up agents, managers, producers, directors, and actors, and see their connections and contact information.

In the case of researching agents or managers, you can see who they are representing and where those clients fall in the pecking order known as the Star Meter, a ranking that changes weekly and is based on algorithms that measure popularity or interest on their site. The lower the number, the higher the ranking. In other words, a ranking of five thousand is much better than a ranking of fifty thousand. Currently there are about 5.7 million people listed on the site.

I'll talk more about IMDb in other chapters.

Finally is the issue of modeling schools, pageants, and talent contests. We did not go that route, and so I can't speak from experience on this one. Many of these charge a small fortune and turn out a lot of hopefuls each year, some of whom do make it. As long as you recognize that the primary result of most of these schools and contests is to boost your child's confidence and poise, and you feel their fees are worth that, go ahead. Confidence and poise are useful in whatever your child ends up doing in life. But the odds of such a program leading directly to a professional acting career are probably slim.

The BizParentz Foundation (http://www.BizParentz.org) has an excellent section on spotting and avoiding scams, and I highly recommend reading it.

Every Hollywood parent has at least one story about scams. Here is one in Victor Boyce's words:

Victor Boyce
People get trapped by these scam artists in the malls who say, "Your kid is so cute. Come and give us twenty-five hundred dollars, and we

are going to give you a notebook full of stuff, and you will get jobs." It's such BS, and they are just scammed. My own little nephew got scammed like that. They gave him a bunch of tongue twisters, and he never landed an audition. Which is to say they took his money and gave him a bunch of BS, and that was it.

It makes me sick, and people need to be aware. Because everybody thinks their own kid is cute, so when somebody comes to them in the mall and says, "Hey, your kid is so cute. They should be in the business," you go, "Aw!"

"You just give us twenty-five hundred dollars."

"Oh yeah, yeah."

My number-one rule when people ask me is don't pay anybody anything—zero dollars, nothing. The only person who you pay is your photographer to shoot your headshots. That is it.

No, if they are on their job and your kid has some luck and some skill, you are going to get paid. And then *people get paid, but not beforehand. There is nothing to pay, and all these scam artists... I shouldn't say "all" because some are legit, but these scam acting schools and all, it's a bunch of nonsense. Some are legit, but I have had some really bad experiences. Not personally, because I stayed away from that from the beginning. But people I know have just been sucked in, and then they wonder what happened. And it's like, "Oh, man!"*

Tips and Takeaways:

- Legitimate agents and managers NEVER ask for or require payment or fees. They ONLY make money if and when your child does.
- Schools and training programs will generally take anyone with money. They are selling services, not representation.

- Beware any organization that says it is offering "casting calls" or "open calls" BUT which is actually selling services.
- Legitimate casting directors never charge for auditions. They may charge for workshops. But workshops are not auditions.
- Research an organization online before spending any serious money.
- Beware anyone who promises that they can make your child a star. No one can promise this with any truthfulness.
- Look up agents and managers using IMDb Pro to see what caliber of talent they represent.

CHAPTER 10

Before You Try to Get an Agent

Before you even begin to try to get your kid in front of an agent, you need to set a few things up. At the bare minimum, your child should have *some* kind of training or experience. While there are probably many agents out there who are willing to represent a kid with no experience or training whatsoever, please understand that these are not the kind of agents with much leverage in the industry.

When you actually consider the meaning of the word *representation*, the issue of what exactly is at stake with an agent becomes a little clearer. Agents' primary currency is their own reputation. They represent your child, but your child represents them, too. "Representing" works both ways. So in literally every audition your kid goes out on, they are representing the faith that their agent has in them. Agents who consistently send out actors who are prepared, easy to direct, easy to work with, and excellent at their craft have a secure reputation, and when they pitch a client for a project, they are likely to get a good response. The reverse is also true.

So now you can understand a little better why good agents are so careful about the clients they choose to represent. In addition to this basic issue is the issue of balancing out their portfolio. Having a bunch of kids who all fall into the same category in terms of looks or age or type does no one any favors. Agents need to have a good mix so that all of their clients get a fair chance at projects and they have someone for everybody. This sometimes means that some agents will pass on representing your child just because they already have your child's type covered. This can be disappointing, but it is ultimately in everyone's best interest.

It's a good idea to get set up with some basic casting services before you approach an agent as well. The two most widely used are Actor's Access and Casting Networks. It's a pretty easy process to register, upload a couple of headshots and your child's résumé, and fill out a form listing special skills. This shows the agent that your child has a presence in the industry, and it gives you the opportunity to learn about lower-level auditions and get your kid out for some auditioning experience—and maybe even some work experience!

Of course, you already have a headshot and résumé for your child, right? Don't even think about approaching an agent without these. Understand, however, that it is likely that once you succeed in getting an agent, they will probably request that your child get new headshots! And they will help you reformat your résumé to be consistent with the style their agency uses, all of which is part of the process.

Your child should have a couple of monologues memorized—one drama and one comedy. It is a weird truth that in the world of television and film, this is the only time your kid will need to come with their own material, but it does make sense. After all, going forward, they will be auditioning for a specific role, and that role will have sides. Finding great monologues can be challenging, so this is good news.

Where can you find good monologues? There are a few collections out there, but not as many as there should be. The majority of monologue books are for adults, and many of the few that are for kids are so tired! That being said, I like *Magnificent Monologues for Kids* and *Magnificent Monologues for Teens* by Chambers Stevens. Sometimes an effective place to look is simply on the Internet. Google key words like *monologues* and *children*, and see what pops up. The monologue can come from a play, film, or TV script. It doesn't matter. Some of the most interesting ones can come from fiction. Just make sure there is no description to interrupt the monologue's flow. And do try to make the monologues age appropriate.

Confession: Dove auditioned for Pamela Fisher with Meryl Streep's "Stuff" monologue from *The Devil Wears Prada. Not* recommended! Looking back, I can't imagine how crazy it must have looked to Pamela to see a fourteen-year-old girl performing a role written for a middle-aged woman! Luckily, she was able to see the talent through the very odd choice.

If your child can sing, it's a good idea to have them prepare a song as well. Kids who can do more than just act—particularly the classic "triple threats" who can act, sing, and dance—are simply more marketable. Singing along to a karaoke track should be fine in most agents' offices, although a cappella is always OK. Things get a little trickier when you are auditioning for a particular role: in those cases you will be told what your child needs to prepare, and it often looks more like several bars of a song along with sheet music for an accompanist. Check the Resources and References section at the back of this book for links to inexpensive digital sheet music and karaoke tracks.

Do you need to set up a Coogan account or work permit before trying to get an agent? Absolutely not. But both are free to set up, and if you are helping your child get comfortable auditioning by going out on auditions listed through Actors Access, Casting Networks, or Backstage, you should have these things done. If your kid books a role, the producers will expect the paperwork to be in order.

CHAPTER 11

Agents versus Managers

As I mentioned earlier, some kids have an agent, some have a manger, and some have both. You really can't get anywhere serious without at least one of them, as the auditions for better roles are only available through agents and managers. This may seem unfair until you consider the number of actors who would submit their headshot and résumé for every possible decent role if they were able to do so. It would overwhelm the office of every casting director daily. The system of submitting through agents and managers ensures, for the most part, that the choices casting directors have for auditions are relatively appropriate in terms of suitability for the role and capability. So the system works pretty well.

Technically you *do* need to have an agent in Los Angeles. In California, managers are not permitted to secure work for their clients without the assistance of an agent. So an agent relationship should be the first you develop.

I personally think that until your child is making a fair amount of money (obviously a subjective point) and or until they are getting decent-sized roles on a regular basis, there is just no real need for a manager. Again, if a manager's primary role is to manage the career of an actor, there has to be a career to manage! And frankly, after all of the other deductions from a kid's paycheck (15 percent to the Coogan,

10 percent to the agent, some percentage to taxes), why give away another 10 percent or 15 percent prematurely?

That being said, after a certain point of success, a manager can be invaluable. Remember that agents typically have many more clients than managers do. This means that no matter how hands-on and "managerial" your agent may be, they still are not likely to have the bandwidth to take care of daily issues and big-picture decisions the way a manager would.

When you decide it is time to interview managers, consider looking for firms that specialize in developing talent. The really big management companies only take established stars for the most part, and just like a youth agent, managers who specialize in developing young or emerging talent often have a true passion for doing so, which can serve your child well as they build their career.

What about the "momager" option? (Sorry, dads—my very unscientific poll shows that about 90 percent of the parents who primarily handle their kid's careers are women, not men). Opinions vary widely on this one. In my case, I never felt qualified to position myself as Dove's official manager. These people are professional for a reason. I may be intelligent and educated, but my knowledge of the industry comes largely from my experience and perspective as a parent, not from years spent managing the careers of multiple actors. Parents generally do not have the relationships and deep knowledge of the business that a seasoned professional manager does.

Many people in the industry consider it to be unprofessional when a kid has a parent as their manager, which can potentially harm your kid's chances at being taken seriously. If you are their manager by default—because their career hasn't reached the stage where a professional is warranted—it may be best to not officially list yourself as their manager. If your child has an agent, list the agent as contact on auditions, etc. If they have no representation yet, list yourself simply as their parent.

It seems to me that many parents who officially manage their kids are in risky territory for two reasons. First, they are likely shortchanging their kids' career since they are probably not as good as a true professional would be. And second, by being in an official business and financial relationship with their dependent child, they are further complicating an already complicated relationship.

The fact that your kid is more likely to have an agent at first than a manager—at least until they actually have much of a career to manage—can make many parents their kid's manager by default. If you are in this position, treat it as professionally as you would any other job. Track expenses, manage finances, and educate yourself as best you can about what is happening in the industry. Once your child starts to make money, you can set up an LLC and run their professional expenses through that account. Commissions, if you draw them, should probably be paid out the same way other commissions are (this might mean through your child's agent) for the sake of consistency. Later, if your child is making enough money to justify it, they can incorporate and write off even more expenses.

Even though Dove has a team of two amazing managers, was I effectively her *unofficial* manager? Of course. As her mom, I was basically mission control. Until she turned eighteen, I needed to be, legally. Now that she is technically an adult, I'm not required to play this role, but in reality she's both too young and too busy actually working to deal with all the communications and details that her career requires. We have been thoughtfully, organically transitioning these details over to her and her team over time.

It can be truly difficult to play both roles—parent and manager—whether they are official or not. Those roles have different agendas. Your kid needs you to primarily be their parent, and if you are not extremely conscious about this, it can be easy to slip into professional mode. When more of your conversations are about work than about life, you know you have a problem. And it can happen. It has even happened with me and Dove sometimes, despite constant awareness and our best efforts. And when it does, it feels awful for both of us.

I think the riskiest thing about a parent being the manager is that it removes an important protective layer between the child and the profession. If you have professional management, then you are free to simply advocate for your kid.

A producer friend pointed out another problem with parents as managers to me recently: as in all businesses, sometimes the need for a difficult conversation arises. If you are your child's manager, production may not feel comfortable having the conversation with you. A professional manager will be able to participate in that conversation objectively, represent your child in their best light, and convey information to you and your child free of emotion. If the parent is the one production must have a difficult conversation with, that conversation can become even more difficult: fraught with emotion, and issues around objectivity. This makes a good outcome for both your child and for production less likely.

Finally, sometimes the best interest of the child and the best interest of the child's career are directly at odds. In this case, parents need to step up and make sure that their kid's needs as a person are given priority. This is not always easy if the projects are big and the stakes feel high. But you are the only one who can do this. Managers need to be objective about the talent they represent, and parents, by nature, can't really be objective about their kids.

Tips and Takeaways:

- Your child needs an agent before a they need a manager. In California, only agents are legally allowed to secure work for clients.
- Managers are invaluable after your child has a career to manage—before that, they are probably unnecessary. Your child

will also be able to attract a better manager after their career has gotten off the ground.

- When your child is just starting out, you are essentially their manager by default. Officially managing your child after their star begins to rise can be risky for both your relationship and for their career.

CHAPTER 12

Spotlight Interview with Pamela Fisher

Vice President, Abrams Artists Agency—Head of Youth and Young Adult

Bonnie: *Pamela, you are an incredibly good agent, and I know this personally, not just from looking at the roster of truly amazing talent that you represent. Did you always know that you wanted to do this?*

Pamela: *No. Absolutely not. I grew up in New York, wanting to be Annie on Broadway. That's all I really wanted to do. I was a big musical-theater geek. I went to school for it. I went to camps for it. It's all I wanted, and I eventually owned a school that taught musical theater to kids and produced off-Broadway workshops with children in New York. Musicals.*

Through that, a lot of casting directors networked with me, and I was able to help make suggestions of what kids would be good and appropriate for their various projects. As I did that, I was told that I was really good at helping to select and eyeing the talent and that perhaps this would be an interesting path for me. That's what led me on this journey.

Bonnie: *That's amazing. So do you ever go out looking for new talent? Or does talent mostly come to you at this point?*

Pamela: *At this point, the talent is coming to me more, but it's hard to take the agent hat off. So I find myself looking, in a way that's probably inappropriate, at the grocery store or certainly any show that I go to see. I'm always scouting. It's hard to turn that off.*
But as far as actually attending things to scout at, I have wonderful assistants and associates who have taken on that role more and are always looking for us and bringing us talent, particularly at conventions out of town that they're attending. So they'll fly for us, go, attend these conventions, and bring back some of the top talent that they're finding.

Bonnie: *That's cool. And exciting, because that's one of the hardest things for people who are trying to break in—to get in front of a top-level agent. What do you look for when a kid comes in to audition for you?*

Pamela: *So the number-one thing that I'm looking for is always what's missing on my list. So when I see a hole and I see breakdowns are coming out and projects are coming out...They need a twelve-year-old Hispanic boy, and I don't have any of them on my list, and there's no one to submit or pitch. I know I desperately need that.*

So I'm always looking for what's missing because I know that person's going to come in and get out right away. However, I'm constantly looking for incredible talent. They walk in the room, and there's just something magical that happens. So...constantly just looking for incredible talent.

Bonnie: *What are some red flags that you see sometimes when someone comes in front of you and you think, "hmmm"?*

Pamela: *It's so unfortunate that we do have occasions where children come in to audition for us, and we ask them...We separate them immediately from the parents. So they come in alone. Although, we do make sure to always say hello to the parent before and after. But they come into the room alone so that we're able to sort of gauge what's really going on, and we always ask them, "So, you want to be an actor?"*

It's very, very sad that we do sometimes get the answer that they do not and that their moms have promised them a present if they do this. Or they don't want to do it, but their parents have asked them to do it. So the number-one red flag is always going to be...because they have to want this. It's so much work, as you know and as your child knows. It is such a lot of work. You have to just want it. I mean—you know that for Dove, there really wasn't another choice...

Bonnie: *No.*

Pamela:*...or anything else. She was born to do this, and those are the kids that we're really looking for. So the number-one red flag is going to be that, and then of course difficult parents, parents who just...you can just tell it's going to fall into the "life's too short" category.*

I definitely encourage parents to be advocates for their children and to ask questions and to be interested and take an interest, but there's a very fine line. Once you cross over that point where it's just going to be too much work, then that raises a big red flag as well.

Bonnie: *We've covered this a little bit, but what might lead you to say yes to representing someone, other than just, "Oh, gosh, finally here's somebody in the category that I've been looking for that I don't have, and they fit, and they're wonderful," or like, "Oh. This is magic." Are those the two main things?*

Pamela: *The magic factor is something that I can't really put into words. Something happens. I often call it a fire in the belly. I get a feeling and a sense. A kid just turns me on in a way that I feel like I have to represent them, and it's not always the best read in the room. Sometimes there's just something about...there's a star quality or something in them. I know they're not quite ready yet, but I have that urge to develop them.*

There's also something that happens after they leave the room. Sometimes I'll be on the fence, or they're really not ready, but I can't stop thinking about them. I go home, and that evening I'm thinking about projects that came by that I would pitch them for. That's when I know I'm excited. And I think that really we're successful when we're excited about the clients or the potential client.

It has to do with an excitement. So three very good agencies could all sign the same client, but it's really the one that has that excitement for them and that fire in the belly for them, because I think you work in a different way. You work harder, and you work smarter for them. So for me, it's just sort of an enthusiasm that you get for that person. There's something that we're trained to pick up on that just happens.

Bonnie: *It's almost like chemistry. When I think about that, I think that's perfect. Because as a client, you would want that more than anything. You would want your agent to feel a sense of excitement about representing you because if they're excited about you, they're going to do amazing things for you…*

Pamela: *No question.*

Bonnie:*…and see things that others might not see otherwise. Then similarly for you, too, you're going to end up doing better for the agency if you feel excited about somebody.*

Pamela: *Yeah. I mean, there's sort of a misconception that it's an easy job to get talent in the [casting] room, even at a larger-level agency. It's work. It's hard. Even if your child is six or seven, it's competitive. There is competition out there. So when we're making that call, you want us to be calling with a great amount of enthusiasm because we have to knock that door down and get them in there.*

Bonnie: *Yeah. Other than the couple of red flags that you mentioned, what are some other reasons that you might decline to represent somebody?*

Pamela: *Oh. I have had situations before where someone is so wonderful, and it breaks my heart to say no just because I have a commitment, and I've made a commitment that I take very seriously to the clients that we have on our roster. So sometimes if it's a thirteen-year-old blond, blue-eyed little girl and I know that I have three that are not working currently that I really have already promised and dedicated myself to, it wouldn't be fair to put another one in the mix. It wouldn't be fair to the new one coming in, and it wouldn't be fair to those that I've made a commitment to already.*

In the youth game, we like to think that it's a little gentler than in some of the other dog-eat-dog sides of this industry that you hear about. We do know each other, and we will call each other. Sometimes I will call another agency or the head of another young-talent division or developmental division and let them know that there is a talent that we just cannot take on but that they should really look out for. It hurts because I know they're going to book. I know it's going to happen. But quite often, when I say we have conflicts, I really mean it.

I really do have people who are conflicting, and it just wouldn't be fair. So quite often, that is the reason, and it pains us to say no. But then we'll be an agency that's just got fifty kids in every division, and I don't want to be that. I want to really dedicate myself to just having a couple of people, and we sort of operate in that small way. I want the clients to know and to feel that. So quite often we have to say no even though your daughter or your son has done a great job in the room. It's just not going to be the right match.

Bonnie: *That's got to be hard. Do you sometimes see kids who show potential, but they're just not ready yet?*

Pamela: *I do, but sometimes I'll take them on. The development of the client still excites me. That beginning moment when the dream is new and fresh and exciting is still a turn-on for me and gets me really high. So I will often take someone on even though I can tell they're not ready. There's something there that I feel like I want to be in on at the beginning, and to watch those succeed is extraordinary. It's wonderful—very, very exciting.*

Bonnie: *I'm thinking of how rough Dove was when she walked in front of you. Oh, man* (laughing).

Pamela: *She was, but that magic happened in the room. We just sort of felt that...that feeling, and wanted to be a part of it.*

Bonnie: *Have you ever told somebody that they just might want to reconsider trying to make it as a performer?*

Pamela: *Never.*

Bonnie: *Like, "You know, kid..."*

Pamela: *Never. I am not the be-all and end-all. I make so many mistakes. I cannot tell you the people who have walked out of my office and become famous. I just didn't see it. I didn't get it. That's what makes this business so interesting. I'm sure you see television shows and movies all the time where you think, "Why did she get that role? She's terrible. That's not what I would have seen at all."*

I think that it's a business that's full of that. That's why it's so hard to get anything cast around here. You have the studios and network executives, the casting people and producers. Everyone has a different favorite in the room. That's what makes horse racing. So for me, I would never tell anyone. Just because it may not be someone that I think is right at the time or that I think will book it, it doesn't mean that they won't.

So I would encourage anyone, even if they've gotten some negative feedback, to keep at it. If you want it, and this is all that you want and all that you can see yourself or your child doing, I wouldn't let an agent or anyone in the industry tell you not to.

Bonnie: *I love that. I love that because I think that the world is full of people who've been told, "You know what? This isn't for you, kid." If they let themselves, they can be stopped right then and there, and then you never know what might have happened.*

Pamela: *Never.*

Bonnie: *But for you to be able to say, "Who am I to say? I don't know," is beautiful, and I hope that people take that to heart.*

Pamela: *Absolutely.*

Bonnie: *They have to know in their hearts if it's right for them. And if it's right for them, they shouldn't be stopped.*

Pamela: *Yeah. I absolutely feel that way.*

Bonnie: *So what's the hardest part of what you do?*

Pamela: *The rejection doesn't bother me because I think everything is a learning experience, and I especially like working with young talent because the stakes are different in rejection. Whereas if a forty-year-old or a forty-five-year-old doesn't get a job, they may lose their health insurance. They can't put dinner on the table for their family.*

For young talent and for young adults, the stakes are different. They don't get the pilot, they're going to go back to school the next day or back to their lives. It's different. So I think they're a little more resilient because of that, but I do think that sometimes the rejection has no rhyme or reason.

We had a situation this year where we had a little girl who was eight book a pilot. The pilot was picked up to series. They picked her up along with the series. She shot eight episodes, and they decided to replace her—decided to go a different way with the character. There's just no rhyme or reason to have to tell that.

I mean, having to break that news is just horrible—really the darkest, lowest point of my job and what I do. So the rejection is tough for me to impart to kids when some of it just doesn't make sense. "Someone else was more right than you" is a little bit different, but this has happened a few times where we've had people replaced. Truly the injustices are really, really difficult.

Then it's hard when you are dealing with people who you know are depending on you. And families, because we don't just represent the talent. We really represent families, because [the actors are] young adults, or they're kids. For us, it's very difficult when things are difficult, when there's a problem on set, when they're overworked or overtired, or whenever there are issues. It's really hard for us because we do feel very much for them.

We're there as an advocate. Nobody gets into repping young talent unless they really are there in the protection game as well, different than pure adults. You're really there to protect them. There are certain laws that have to be upheld, especially when they're minors. So we're really there to protect them. And sometimes lines are crossed, and that's very difficult. We really have to advocate for them, and that's another one that's a toughie for us. Certainly the injustices are really, really, really horrid. No one wants to be the bearer of that news.

Bonnie: *On the other side, what are some of the best parts of what you do?*

Pamela: *We still get excited about calling someone and saying, "You booked a costar." I mean, even the little victories are so exciting for us. We find joy in it every single day. We just had a situation where I videotaped. A little boy booked a pilot. They're a family coming from the middle of Chicago, and it's been a struggle for them to try and come out here and give this a try. It's been a struggle family wise, financially. The family has to separate. Mom is here. Dad's home with the other kids. I mean, this is so difficult.*

This little boy's life is about to change forever, and he's going to be on a major children's network, on a show that's picked up to series, and he just happened to be up here doing a voice-over when we got the news. So we were able to bring him in, and I whipped out my phone without him seeing and videotaped the moment.

I play it for myself to remind myself why we do this. Such joy, and to know that you had a part in it. You know? You helped to find it. You helped to cultivate it and to watch it burgeon and maybe suggested the right acting class or the right coach and helped them with their feedback, and that in some way you were a part of it. It's wonderful.

Bonnie: *It's beautiful.*

Pamela: *A great high.*

Bonnie: *So when we moved down here, I didn't even know there was such a thing as a youth agent. We were that green. Where we came from, there were just agencies and agents. Of course, in this market, you've got to specialize. So what's the distinction? There's not a hard-and-fast rule like, "Oh, I only represent people under eighteen." You actually represent a number of people in their twenties who play younger. So how does that work? Where's that line?*

Pamela: *It depends on what agency you look at. For us, with some of the older clients, they're developmental still. So our adult division might not quite be ready to take them on because they haven't booked their big movie or big series yet. Some of them...I have a thirty-one-year-old client that just won't leave* (laughs). *They just feel they get a lot of special attention here. They feel close to us.*

I think once you're starting to play young mom or young dad, I really think the networks aren't coming. They're still coming to me for the twenty-six-year-old, twenty-seven-year-old, but CW still wants to come to me for, like, the hot young talent, especially somebody who might be new. So there's not that much of a distinction, especially at Abrams, because of the synergy between the departments.

We take all of our meetings together. We talk about all of the scripts together. So it's not as though I'm missing something for the twenty-six-year-old, because the adult division knows about them, especially those that have significant heat and are almost ready to transition over. So we're constantly talking about projects.

They'll bring me scripts—"This has a twenty-eight-year-old in it. You might want to look at it." We discuss our clients together when they go to visit networks and studios. So for me, it works very well. There's not a cutoff date. Some agencies are only youth agencies. But for us, in our division, we really don't have a date that cuts off, but maybe they do at other agencies.

Bonnie: *What do you think makes for an especially good youth agent, as opposed to just an agent, a talent agent?*

Pamela: *I think for young talent and development, you have to have the developmental eye. No one's getting rich on costars. So you have to really have the desire to do this. Part of it is getting them in the door [to casting directors].*

So for a while, it's an education. It has nothing to do with the booking in the early stages. It's about the process of getting in the room. What happens in the room? Do I look at the camera? Or do I look at the casting director? Do I slate? Or do I not?

So for those early auditions, we are not expecting clients to book. We're expecting to develop them, and that is part of that process—getting them out there. So to be developmentally minded, you really have to be able to provide not only those opportunities but also…

For instance, clients that we represent sometimes go in for a two-line under-five on something, some cable show. And then the next day, they go out for the lead in a movie. It depends. So they might find a mixed bag of things because we're broadly submitting in the early stages, trying to get them into lots of rooms.

Also, I think you need to get feedback. You have to know your casting director so that you can find out how that client is doing in the room—"Oh, OK. They need to work on volume and focus." And then you have to know the teachers, go to classes. We go to a lot of the acting classes. We speak to our coaches: "How did they do? What do they need to work on? They didn't book this. Why do you think?"

So there's a lot of work that goes on behind the scenes. So a truly good developmental agent and youth agent is able to do that. It's not just submitting, pitching, and getting them in the room. It's doing the work to help develop them so they can go to the next stage. Know when it's ready: "I think you're ready to go out for other things. I think it's time to leave the costars behind now."

(People are) going to think I have something against costars. I don't, but I just think there comes a point where you do have to start to narrow down what it is that you're looking at. But the early stage is very broad.

Bonnie: *So a passion for development.*

Pamela: *Passion for development, and obviously all of the things we discussed before about knowing the labor laws, minors, and all of the things that it takes to protect a minor, because that is part of our job.*

Bonnie: *That's huge. What are your thoughts on when is a good age for someone to start out in the industry? I mean, it seems like the earlier you start out, obviously, the more traction you've got. But the downside of that, in my eyes, is that the earlier you start, the less of a normal childhood you have.*

In our case, I deliberately dragged my feet. We didn't even come out here until Dove was fourteen. Yet she sort of barely got going in the nick of time, in some ways. I look at some of these younger people, or people who are her age who started much earlier, and their careers are...they've had a chance to get some traction. So it seems like there's an upside and a downside to either way you go. Right?

Pamela: *There is. It's so hard to make an actual recommendation on that. It depends on the child. We had one child when I was back at TalentWorks many years ago who had just a miserable childhood and became suicidal. In his school, he didn't fit in. He was teased. He didn't look like the other kids. He was made fun of, and just...I think someone saw him in a mall, and he took an acting class, and they said, "Hey, you're good. You're funny. You're silly."*

He ended up doing a slew of movies and television shows, moved out to LA, and has an amazing life. For him, I don't know what a "normal" childhood is. I don't know that that would have been the right path for him.

Bonnie: *Normal isn't always great.*

Pamela: *So yeah. I don't know. He was bullied and teased and was really an unhappy kid in the "normal" surroundings. So I think it really depends on the child. It really does. I think once you're eighteen, it's harder to become SAG. So if you really, really, as a kid want it, you might want to try and get in before that so that you can get into the union. It's a little easier to Taft-Hartley because the casting directors have to make their case as to why they can't find anyone within the union to cast.*

So it's easier to just cast someone who is already SAG. Whereas youth, they don't have to explain themselves quite as much because you're not born with a SAG card in your diaper. But truly I think that parents should just know there is a mommy-daddy radar, and I think you need to use it in all areas with your child, but certainly to know when that time's ready. I think for you, you probably knew, "I cannot hold this off anymore. I have to do this."

Bonnie: *Yes. There was no question.*

Pamela: *Not an easy choice for you—certainly not the easiest path for your own life. But you were kind of forced into it, and I think your child forces you in. You just know, "I have to do this."*

When that hits—when that little intuitive nudge from within pushes you, and you know it has to happen...it's something that an agent really can't define. So for the most part, we're going to depend on the parent to know, "This is time. This is ready."

Bonnie: *What advice would you give to someone whose kid is just starting out? They've got this dream, but they have not a lot of experience. What could they do to prepare, maybe even where they live now, if they're outside of a major market like New York or LA? What would you recommend that they do?*

Pamela: *Anything that you can get to do is great. It doesn't matter if it's school shows or your church show or the local regional musical or an acting class that you've heard of. Even if they're not going to get the best—they may not get a Stanislavski theory class. But I think any time that your child is performing and getting up in front of people, that it's a great learning experience.*

I would say go after anything locally that you can, anything at all. Then, from that point forward, it becomes difficult. You have to decide very carefully. I think I mentioned earlier that there are these conventions, and there's a lot of negative press that goes along with them because some of them—not all of them, but some of them—charge enormous amounts of money.

Your child really doesn't get any kind of real education, but it is a forum where they could potentially meet a casting director or an assistant or associate at an agency. If they are favored, and if they are someone that is singled out, they get the chance to come and meet with you. So there is that opportunity. You want to be really, really careful.

So maybe check it out online. Take a look, and see who might have come out of those schools. Check to see if that's real before you fork over five thousand, eight thousand dollars. I mean, it's really a lot of money for these families. It can break your heart. The other thing you can do is submit to agencies. Some of them end up in the garbage can. So you'll want to know that. We actually hand open every single picture that comes our way.

Bonnie: *Wow.*

Pamela: *We do. That's just us, but we do. I think there might be other agencies, too—particularly smaller agencies that are starting out—and there's nothing wrong with that.*

Bonnie: *As you know, one of the hardest things for us was getting in front of you, getting in front of a top agent. It was just so tough, coming in from nowhere and having no "in," because the top agents typically aren't going to take a meeting—can't take a meeting—with somebody that they don't have a referral for. So what advice do you have for how someone can get in front of a top-level agent for an audition?*

Pamela: *Yeah. A pretty blond Caucasian teenage girl was probably the last thing that I needed at that moment. So that was probably a picture that might have just gone right by. You know?*

Bonnie: *Yeah.* (laughing).

Pamela: *As opposed to something in a category that I might have desperately needed at that time. What you did was the perfect thing. You used every possible resource at your disposal—friends, family. Ask around. Find out. So I think that's what you have to do. You really have to look around.*

But definitely submit, because there are some agencies that will take the time to actually open up their mail and take a look. Make sure it's a good picture. I mean, we get people in, like, bikinis and all sorts of crazy submissions. You don't have to wear a ton of makeup and have your hair perfect.

So a nice picture and a very simple cover letter saying, "We live X, Y, Z. We've done some local theater, and we're really interested [in representation]." Then, if that doesn't work and there are no schools that have ins, continue to just try and build up that résumé. Because it means something if they did a show in school. It means something that they did a musical, and you never know who's there.

You really don't know who's in the audience or who might know somebody. So constantly networking and trying to find out who's doing it... If you come out to LA during pilot season or even episodic season, there are intensive classes that people give for pilots, where they invite agents to come and see. There are workshops that are given at various classes or schools, and we do go to some of them. So those are chances. Any time you can get yourself in front of someone from an agency is a great opportunity. I would take it.

Bonnie: *So similar advice, then, for someone who just would like to find a good, legitimate, trustworthy agent—even if they cannot get themselves in front of a top agent, just do the showcases. Do the workshops.*

Pamela: *Yeah. Top agent really doesn't matter. You know? I think I work for a wonderful company, and I'm very, very proud of it, but I think that a very ambitious agent at a small, boutique-y agency who is passionate about your child will do a better job than an agent at the largest agency, who may not be as passionate.*

So I would go with the person that you feel the most comfortable with. Remember that this is going to be a team member. You don't want to jump around from agency to agency. Hopefully this is a relationship that you're going to have for a long while, and they're going to be a team member, and they're going to be in partnership with you. This is a very important decision that you're making.

Whoever feels right. And you're going to get that good feeling that this just feels right and comfortable, and whoever shows the passion and really, really loves your child is going to do really well.

Bonnie: *I love hearing you say that because I think it's really true. It's about the connection. It's about the relationship, and it is about the passion. You really do work very, very closely together. So you better like and appreciate each other. There better be a sense of connection there.*

Pamela: *You want someone who you can get a hold of. With the biggest agency in the world, they have no idea who you are. You can't get them on the phone, and you can't reach them to talk to them. I mean, you and I had many issues that came up. Teenagers just do as they're growing up. Things that happen in their lives or time that they need to take off or whatever it's for.*

We have people who go off to do a semester away or whatever it is. They're in college for a while and want to take some time off. You want to be able to make a phone call, get your agent on the phone, know that they're going to support you through what it is that you are going through. And that they're going to be there when it's time to come back aboard.

Bonnie: *Well, that was huge for us. I mean, when Dove decided she wanted to take some time off and just be a normal high school student and do show choir for a little while, just as she was starting to get some traction in the industry, that must have been a hard phone call for you to hear. But you were one hundred percent supportive. That meant everything to us.*

Pamela: *Yeah. She was worthwhile to us. We knew, and we believed in her. So we supported that, of course. We want you to be a kid. We want you to be able to have those experiences. I also think I once had somebody come in here, a sixteen-year-old, and they said, "This is my whole life. This is all I've ever done. I've taken every acting class. I've taken it my whole life. From morning until night is just studying this. I've read every acting book. It's all I've done."*

I wanted to say, "Well, go do something else. Go horseback riding. Go take an airplane somewhere and travel. Go see something. Because you'll have absolutely nothing to bring to the work. I want you to be a well-rounded person. That will make you a better actor." Because kids, they'll say, "I'm playing soccer this season, and it's really important to me," or, "I'm in show choir," or whatever it is.

So we want to make sure that we're there to support, and you want to make sure that there's going to be someone that you're not terrified to call because you're afraid that you're not going to get the support that you need for your family and for your child.

Bonnie: *Which speaks again to the importance of the quality of the relationship. You mentioned something about bikini photos a few minutes ago. That's just scary to contemplate. So let's talk about pictures. Have you got some hot tips about headshots?*

Pamela: *Definitely. For us here in LA—because New York is a little bit different; obviously commercial is different. Commercial shots are always a little warmer, a little more smiley. For us here in LA, we like kind of a blank face. I don't know why, but it's almost as if the casting directors like to just see it as a blank slate.*

Then I wouldn't wear any jewelry or anything with logos on it. I love bright colors. If you're a teen, then look like a teen. If you're a college kid, look like a college kid. Don't wear a suit and a tie and age yourself up. T-shirts, bright-colored T-shirts, hoodies, and simple, simple, simple. Put on a T-shirt and jeans. Take off the makeup. Just a little light makeup, and that's it.

I mean, just enough so that you're not washed out in the pictures. I think young and fresh is what we're looking for. I think the tendency is to want to look very glammy, but I would try to work against that and look very fresh and very simple.

Bonnie: *What about résumés?*

Pamela: *I would say build your résumé. People think, "There's nothing to do. My child is six. What can I put on it?" But you'd be surprised. If they like playing with cars, put that on there—whatever it is that's interesting. Kids are so unique. They're all special. Every single person who's reading this book today has a child who's got something special about them. So find what it is, and put it on there. Because it may be interesting. We never know. You know?*

We never know that the child who likes to build something...we may need that someday. Certainly anything that they've done in school, don't discount. The church show, temple show, the choir, the local regional theater—anything that they've done. Put it on there. It does help. People feel it's not professional, but that's OK. We don't expect the six-year-old to have a professional résumé.

So I would say include whatever you can, whatever it is. Works well with pets—things that you may not think are important—or with animals. Loves planting, or something. We use things like that. It helps us.

Bonnie: *Well, when you're young, I mean, there's only so much you can put on a résumé. When we came down here, all Dove really had was a bunch of community theater on hers. A* lot *of community theater!*

Pamela: *Yeah.*

Bonnie: *But it was stage work.*

Pamela: *But it lets me see what she's doing. I can tell by looking at that résumé that she's a soprano because she's done this kind of role. It helps us to see those things. We know we're in development, and so we know we're not going to get people who have done...There are people have come to us who have series regulars, but we know that many of them aren't. We do both here.*

So for us, it's not always a heavy résumé that we're looking for. We're just looking to get to know who you are. Chances are, if your child has some talent, they're going to come in and do a pretty good job. But we're also going to meet with two hundred other kids who can read the lines with expression. So what your child brings to the table that's unique and different about them is really what we're looking for, because so many others are going to be able to read the lines well.

There are a lot of people who can act out there and have nice reading abilities. So what's going to set you apart? What's going to make you different? It's you. It's what you are. It's what that child—what that youth, what that client—is bringing in the room with them that's different. So that's really what we're kind of looking for.

Bonnie: *I love that. So any funny stories that you'd like to share?*

Pamela: *Yeah. I'm fine to mention this because she makes fun of herself, too. Jessica Garcia, who works with Dove* (Jessica plays Willow on *Liv and Maddie*), *did a fabulous monologue for me—really one of the best things I've seen ever in my office—and decided to sit on the floor during it.*

So I could barely see her. I had to peer over my desk and, like, climb onto the desk to look over the side to watch her. At the end of the day, we signed her because I thought she was so special, different, and gave such a great read. But I had to let her know that I could hardly see it and she'd made a terrible choice by sitting on the floor.

Bonnie: *That's hilarious.*

Pamela: *I've had people where they unfortunately wore a skirt that was too short, and they didn't realize they'd be sitting during their monologue. So maybe when you're sitting, take a look at what you look like in the mirror, because I could see everything. It was uncomfortable. I was averting my eyes. So, yeah, we have interesting things happen.*

Bonnie: *So is there anything else that you'd like to share for other parents out there who are considering trying to make some kind of effort to help their talented kids? It's funny. Part of what makes me feel like I'm on the right track with this book is something that happened when I was sending out requests for cover art. I've been working with a bunch of graphic designers who were sending in cover possibilities, and it's been a really fun process. One of the graphic designers wrote back and said, "I'm so glad you're writing this book. I live in New York. I have a very talented eight-year-old boy, and I just don't know what to do for him."*

That's the situation we're really all in at every level, including all of the other parents of young stars that I've interviewed. It's like, "We know we've got a kid with talent who loves to do this work. We just don't know where to start and what to do to help them."

Pamela: *Yeah. My parents were the same way. They didn't know what to do. They knew I wanted it. They had no clue where to start and how to sort of do it. It's difficult because the goal is out there in the distance, and there's just how to make that journey.*

So number one is what I said before, which is, absolutely, I encourage anyone. Don't let anyone discourage you. Be encouraged. That's not to say don't take any constructive criticism. We often say, "This person's not ready. There's something there. They're not ready. Please, go take some classes and come back." But don't let anyone tell you that it's not something that you can do.

But at the end of the day, I think really doing everything you can to be as educated as you can be. Because there are so many wonderful, wonderful people out there, but there are also a lot of people who are not wonderful. There are people who are looking to make a fast buck off of your desires, needs, and innocence. Desire to help your child. So please be cautious. Do your homework. Look things up. Ask around as much as you can. We're lucky that we have the Internet today. We can look things up and see what people are saying about whomever it is that's looking to perhaps...Definitely look at whatever anyone is asking you to sign. Don't sign anything without someone taking a really good, hard, long look at it.

Bonnie: *And have a lawyer look at a contract before you sign it.*

Pamela: *Have a lawyer always. Always. I mean it's different when you're looking at an agency that's franchised by one of the unions. So this agency or even any boutique agency or the big agencies, we're all going to have very similar paperwork that's from SAG. So it's different. But someone locally that you don't know or that we may not have heard of, you really want to be careful before you just hand over your child—your very precious child.*

You're entrusting somebody with them. So do your homework. I encourage you. Because it can be a wonderful journey, but it can be very scary as well. So please make sure that you've really, really looked into who it is that you're trusting with the future of your child's career.

Oh. I want to say something.

Be a great parent. Something about working with you and with Dove. It's been a delight, obviously, and continues to be. But you were such a wonderful parent to work with. It really makes that journey so much better if the parent is on board to get everything done.

We have so many things that we need. There's paperwork that needs to be signed. There are classes that need to be taken. You have to drive them and take them and show up at certain times and wherever. You were always on top of it. So being on it for your child is extraordinarily important. I'm not sure where that will fit into these questions. But in addition to the child being really talented and us doing our job, this is a partnership with the parents. So working with wonderful parents is extremely important to the success of the child.

CHAPTER 13

Finding and Signing with the Right Agent

Finding and signing with the right agent is honestly one of the most difficult parts of the process. It certainly was for us. While it feels like there is an agent on every corner in Los Angeles—and there might be—*an* agent is not what you want for your child! You want *the* agent.

Who is the right agent? It depends on you and your kid. In the abstract, it is the best agent your child is able to interest who is also a great fit for you both in terms of personal management and communication style. As in some other close relationships, getting it right on the first attempt is not guaranteed, and getting out can be tricky, so it's best to take your time and make sure you have a really great fit before signing a contract.

Some people have luck sending out their kid's résumé and headshot with a cover letter. If you go this route, your cover letter should include the actual name of the agent. You can verify this with a phone call to the agency. Don't just send the letter to the agency with a generic salutation ("Dear Sir or Madam"). This is a fast way to the recycling bin. Include a few lines about what your child has been doing lately ("Katie just played Annie in our community theater's production of *Annie*") and that you would like to speak to them regarding representation. Specify whether you are seeking commercial work, theatrical work, or both. Theatrical work is film or television; commercial work is print or commercials. Although many people want both, some do not, and you might meet with different agents depending on this distinction. Also let them know if your child has had any training.

Keep it to one page, keep it simple, and make sure to include contact information so they can get back to you. There is absolutely no need to send anything else with this letter—not a reel or a tape or permits or social security numbers. Don't bother sending an SASE—headshots are rarely returned.

Unfortunately, there is a direct correlation between the level of expertise or reputation of an agent and the difficulty involved in getting an audition—typically referred to in LA as a meeting—with them. Your odds of getting a meeting with a top agent during pilot season are next to impossible, as this is the busiest time of the year for agents, and they have their hands more than full taking care of their current clients. If you want even a chance at meeting with a top agent, aim for May through November, with the understanding that many will be on vacation in July or August.

When we arrived here, I went online and researched the best youth agents (after discovering that youth agents existed). A great place to start is the Talent Manager's Association's Heller Awards, which have, among other categories, one for Best Youth Agent. These are peer-nominated awards, so to me they carry more weight than others. A few names popped up on the nominations list repeatedly, and then I did some further research. Most of these folks keep a pretty low profile, so this is not always easy. The more people you meet, the more you can ask for word-of-mouth recommendations to add to your list of potential representation. Again, be thoughtful about who you are asking for referrals. Someone who loves their agent but has little on their résumé and isn't getting much, if any, quality work is probably not your best source.

After you create a list of potential agents, cross-reference with the list on the SAG-AFTRA website to make sure they are all franchised. Then go online again and research each agency: this includes the agency's website as well as whatever a Google search turns up. If this sounds like a lot of work, it is! But it's a critical piece to finding someone who could be in your lives for years.

Something I would do now, in addition to looking up winners and nominees of the Heller Awards for Best Youth Agent, is what I recommended earlier in the section on avoiding scams: use IMDb. It's an incredible resource. Again, the most relevant entries can only be accessed if you have a Pro account. For the purpose of finding an agent (or a manager, later) you can look up any agent on the site and see their connections and contact information. Obviously, very successful agents or managers will have some high-ranking actors in their client lists. If nearly all of an individual's client list is lower ranking, you may want to keep looking. One note: it isn't important that the agents or managers themselves have a high ranking—these people usually keep a pretty low profile.

While you're on IMDb, if you have a Pro account, drill down more deeply into the client list of prospective agents or managers. What kinds of projects have their clients been doing? Are there a lot of short films, un-credited roles (which translates into background or extras work), or old entries? Are there a lot of roles for films or TV projects that no one has heard of? This points to a client list that is not actually getting quality work. And you may want to keep moving.

Getting the right agent can be one of the most challenging parts of this journey, but IMDb Pro and a patient attitude can go a long way in helping you make a great list to pursue.

After doing my initial research, I decided on a strategy: I would aim for the top and only start moving down the list after every effort to get Dove in front of the top agents had been exhausted. What I did not understand at the time was that the top agents *rarely* just meet with unsolicited potential clients. They are simply too busy taking care of their current clients.

This is where understanding how things work in Hollywood can save you a lot of time. I wasted two months repeatedly sending my kid's headshot and résumé to agencies that were never going to respond to that approach.

There is also an important distinction here: top agent versus top agency. There are some great agents at midlevel agencies, and middling agents at great agencies. In my experience, and according to the wisdom of just about everyone I've ever spoken to about this, the key is the agent—not the agency. This makes sense when you stop to consider that this is an entirely human-run business. And agents can change agencies.

Even if you are able to get a meeting with an agent at one of the bigger agencies, this is not always the best way to go. Larger agencies mean more competition for your kid within the agency—and less attention paid to their career. Sometimes the little boutique agencies are a better fit, especially for a kid who is looking to break out. Certainly the agency should either specialize in youth or have a youth division.

So there I was, with my brilliant short list, contacting these three people (yes, I was that confident and naive) every ten days or so via phone, e-mail, and post, giving them Dove's headshot, résumé, and the best cover letter I could muster. And I got back nothing. This went on week after week, until we were approaching the two-month mark. No one returned my calls or e-mails or responded to the large manila envelopes with my kid's face smiling out from the top. I was starting to question my methods and whether I had been crazy to move us here without managing to find an agent first.

In desperation, I contacted one of Dove's mentors, who had directed her back on Bainbridge Island and been one of the people who most encouraged us to take the plunge and go to LA. She has a very successful lifelong career as a professional actor and director and many contacts in the business. "Help!" I said. "I'm doing everything I can think of to get Dove in front of a great agent—save actually sitting in front of their door—and can't even get a meeting! What should I do?"

She asked who we were trying to see and knew one of the names. This one was in fact my favorite. She told me she'd call another agent in town that was very influential, and from her word to him, he would call our hoped-for agent and we would get a meeting. And like magic, within fifteen minutes my phone rang, and we were invited to meet with Pamela Fisher. I will love her forever for seeing the potential in Dove and taking a chance on her and for everything else she has done for us over the years since. Sometimes the stars do align.

Were we lucky? Yes. Does it take some kind of professional referral to get in front of one of these prized top agents? Yes, generally. And of course, getting into a meeting with someone is just step one. Your child needs to be ready to be represented by someone at that level, and the agency needs to have a space in its roster of talent that your child might fit into. If your child's type is already covered by that agency, they will likely decline, even if they think your child is perfect otherwise. Or perhaps the agent will tell you to come back after your kid takes more classes or gets some more experience. But every meeting or audition your child takes—whether with a potential agent or casting director—is an educational experience that increases your child's chance of success. It's important to remember this, as it can help you both keep perspective along the journey. If a potential agent declines to represent your child, it's ultimately because a better fit is out there.

So, some advice from our experience: if you are aiming for the top agents, you must have someone refer you to have a shot at a meeting. Who do you know that could vouch for the readiness of your kid to meet with this agent? If you know no one, then you have a two options: (1) continue auditioning, as every single job your child lands is an opportunity to network and possibly create a relationship that could lead to a referral and (2) revise your list to include perhaps more realistic choices given your child's experience level.

If considerable time goes by and you are still not getting bites from your list, consider having someone in the industry that you trust give you some feedback on the headshot and résumé, as well as your cover letter. Maybe something could be tweaked that would make a difference. Of course it's not a bad idea to do this before you send these things out in the first place!

There is a third option for finding an agent. Some of the larger or better acting programs for kids in LA have occasional showcases to which they invite agents and managers who are looking for fresh talent. While it is rare for a top agent to attend these, it can happen that junior agents from good agencies will attend, as they may be looking to fill their book with new clients. Many kids find great representation this way. Most junior agents have trained as assistants to more established agents and can be very knowledgeable. A less experienced but talented actor can be a great match with a less experienced but talented agent! They can grow together in the business. This logic applies to many other relationships in the business as well: stylists, hair and makeup artists, and other partners you may need later.

If your child develops a good relationship with a casting director before getting an agent, that director may be able to make the coveted recommendation that gets you a meeting with a great agent as well. One more reason to go out on as many auditions as possible, without waiting for representation.

Conventions (such as International Presentation of Performers, or IPOP, and the International Model and Talent Association, or IMTA) can be a route to representation for some people. We never took that path, but conventions have their share of success stories. Just be sure that the money you invest in them is spent with the clear understanding that there is no guaranteed outcome.

So let's say it finally happened: your kid got a meeting with an agent you believe is a good one. Yay! Now what? It really is just like any other audition in many ways: show up fifteen minutes early, let the person at the desk know you're there, and have your child's headshot and résumé. Of course, in this case there are no sides: the material is your own. Ask what the agent would like your child to prepare. They may want one or two monologues or just ask your child to come in and do a cold read. And don't be put off when it is just your kid, and not the two of you, who is called in to the agent's office. You may well be called in afterward, as many agents like to interview the parent as well. After all, the parent is someone they will be working closely with if they sign the child.

After your child has auditioned, you will both likely be thanked and released. That's it. You will have no idea if the audition was a success or not. It can be nerve-racking, but generally it is several days before you have an answer. In our case, I think it was three days later that we had a phone call from Pamela Fisher offering Dove representation, and by the end of the week, we received a contract in the mail.

Here is where you are probably tempted to run for the nearest pen and just sign every page of that contract, but you need to take a deep breath and read the contract very carefully first. If you are signing with a top agency, it is likely to be a standard, legally sound document. But if your kid is just starting out in the business, odds are that you are signing with a somewhat less well-known agency, and in this more likely scenario, the contract could have some questionable aspects. Look particularly closely at the subjects of commission (should be 10 percent and not more) expenses (generally there should not be any charged to the client) and length of contract (generally twelve to eighteen months, renewable). Make sure you know what the rules are for getting out if you find you aren't happy with this agent later. Most contracts should allow for leaving the agent with no penalty if a certain amount of time has gone by and no work has been produced. It can be trickier to get out of a contract after that.

In general I would recommend that you have a lawyer—preferably an entertainment lawyer—review the contract before you sign it. Since you are signing on behalf of your minor child, it is essentially you on the line legally. I used to be inconsistent about this step, but all you have to do is have one bad experience before you learn the hard way just how important legal review can be. Save yourself—and your child—that pain, and just get the document reviewed before signing it!

There is one more aspect to consider before signing with an agent, and this one is difficult but important: how did your child feel about the agent when they met? Did the agent feel warm and friendly? Scary? Interested or distracted? Your kid needs to feel a sense of trust with the person who represents them, and you do, too. It can be difficult to get a very accurate read on someone if you barely meet them yourself and are going largely on your child's impressions, but those, along with your own gut instinct gathered from all of your other impressions—from the vibe you get in their office to anything else—count for a lot. If you have any questions at all about whether this person is really the right one to represent your kid, ask for a meeting before signing. This is reasonable under the circumstances, and, frankly, you'll be in meetings with the agent after signing before you know it anyway! Some agents may want this as well since the reality is that their relationship with the parent can be just as important as their relationship with their talent, and in some ways they are signing you both.

If after all that, you just don't feel quite right, trust your instincts and keep searching. The right one will materialize. If everything looks and feels right, however, congratulations! Your child has an agent!

Tips and Takeaways

- Take your time finding a good fit for your child—this is an important relationship!
- Top tier agents rarely take meetings without a referral, though it can happen.

- Use IMDb Pro to research agents of young actors whose careers you admire.
- The agent as a person, and their passionate belief in your kid, is more important than the relative prestige of their agency.
- Best ways to get a meeting with a great agent: industry referral and acting showcases.
- Conventions are a route that works for some people, but they are not guaranteed.
- Have an entertainment lawyer review any contract before you sign it.

CHAPTER 14

Stories: Finding an Agent

Hollywood Parents Share Stories on How Their Young Actor Found an Agent

Allison Zuehlsdorff

We live in Orange County, and there was an event called the Actor's Forum that Cozi participated in. It's an event that a place called the Performers' Academy holds. They also have classes, but we found that the thing we liked best was the Actor's Forum, which they do a couple of times a year. They bring down agents and casting directors, and each kid that signs up gets a chance to go before these people with their headshot and a little monologue or a little snippet of a commercial and just be seen.

We actually found the agent that we are still with through that program. Her associate came, but agents trust their associates. Every one of the agents called Cozi back, which meant she got to then sit with the agents in their offices. We just found that this was much more efficient than randomly sending in headshots, hoping to get somebody to open a package and call you in.

It's funny—during the Actor's Forum, your child only gets about one or two minutes with each agent, but they are so savvy, it takes them just a couple of seconds to know if they like what they see and hear. I remember thinking, "Well, gosh, they just saw Cozi for twenty or thirty seconds." But then the proof was in the pudding. They all called her back, so then we had these appointments. So suddenly we had, like, four agents to choose from.

Actually, we did two of those forums. We got our first agent—we've had two agents—who was primarily a commercial agent, although he did say that he was both. After a while we noticed that ninety-five percent of the auditions we got were commercial auditions. And when we would ask to go out for more TV and film, he'd scrounge something up. But then it would always fall back into commercial auditions only. So, yeah, I think that it's super hard to know how good your agent is.

Think about it—you can't really ask other agents who's good, so when you're starting out, you just have to choose the best you can at the time and see how much coverage you end up getting.

You may end up having one of the departments (like theatrical or commercial) sending your child out all the time, but the other departments don't seem to know your child is alive. We've found that a lot. Building your child's team definitely takes years. I hope that doesn't discourage anyone out there. It's just the truth.

Anyway, once we figured out that our first agent was just going to be giving us commercial auditions, we had a decision to make. And don't get me wrong—commercials are wonderful, too. But Cozi really had a passion for telling stories and being a character, and you can't really do that in a thirty-second commercial.

It was so hard because we felt like we were being disloyal by going to another agent. But in the end, it was a real, necessary part of the growth of her career. We had to realize that this is a business. They were treating us in a businesslike way, but we still felt like we had a relationship with them and were cheating on them or something.

My suggestion now is always to step back and take your emotions out of it. If you're not getting enough auditions and you feel like your agent is not listening to your goals and helping you toward those, it may not be the best fit. There are times when you may need to make a change.

Let's face it—especially with kids, you really don't have that extra year to get your nerve up to make a change. I'd say first try and have a discussion with your child's agent so they know you're not happy. Who knows—maybe talking about it will bring a change. If not, don't be afraid to make a change.

Kenda Benward

*During the movie [*We Were Soldiers*], like I said, we met Taylor Momsen, and she had an agent. She had been working for a while, I guess. She had an agent in LA by the name of Mitchell Gossett, with CESD. And I just kind of boldly asked her mom, who had become a friend of mine, if she would feel comfortable giving Luke a recommendation so that he could meet this agent. And I don't know if she was comfortable with it or not, but she said yes.*

You need a good agent. And I think what makes a good agent is an agent that believes in you and your gift and talent and what you bring to the industry. And, of course, you don't know that until you meet with them.

But I could look at [Taylor's] career so far and go, "Wow, she's on a really great path." So far she's done two major films. And she has things in the works. So I want to meet the guy that's representing her and her career. And [her mom] was nice enough to give us a recommendation. So that was in May, when he shot that film. In July, we said, "Let's go to Los Angeles for the summer."

It wasn't the whole summer; we actually went for a month. We stayed at the La Estancia apartments in Studio City, which is right off of Vineland. We rented a one-bedroom apartment for all five of us.

I have two other children: a daughter that's two years younger than Luke and then another daughter six years younger than Luke.

We had never been. We didn't know what LA had to offer. We just thought, "Well, whoever's working seems like they're coming out of LA. So let's go to LA."

And again, I was still acting at the time. So I thought, "We can kill two birds with one stone here. We'll get Luke an agent. I'll start working out there. Who knows?"

We met with people around town. And there were about three agencies that showed interest. And really, that was all based off referral. We had another agent in Nashville that gave us a referral to Cindy Osbrink. And then…I forget how we got into Buchwald Talent, but someone recommended us there. And then, of course, we got to CESD through Taylor Momsen.

Victor Boyce

When we sent the pictures in, we talked seriously to two agents. We kind of shotgunned pictures to a bunch. We talked seriously to two, we met with them, and we picked one.

My wife and her brother…he is a screenwriter, so he had a little bit of insight. He doesn't have kids in the business. He is not an actor. But he has some insight, so he found them some way.

We had done research; we heard about them. We looked them up, and they had one very famous child actor who was like their bread-and-butter client, and so we knew, at least, they knew what they were doing. Because she was doing very well at the time. So that helped. And they had beautiful offices, lots of staff. It wasn't like a little hole-in-the-wall, fly-by-night type of thing.

Amy Anderson

The way it fell into place for [Aubrey] was just kind of a fluke because I've been an actress for years. At this point, I think it's been around seventeen years I've been in the business. I started in Minneapolis, and I moved here in 2001 to continue pursuing my career, and then Aubrey was born in 2007. It was my agent who actually saw the breakdown and kind of pushed me to submit her. So, by default, she just became her agent as well, so she's both our agent.

In that sense, for us, it was very easy, but I know [finding an agent] is one of the biggest challenges for people who come here, and it's hard. I feel like anybody can get a commercial agent if they try hard enough, but a theatrical agent is very difficult, and there's always a reason why it's hard. It's like, "Oh, it's hard because of your race, it's hard because you're not this race, it's hard because of your gender or your age, or you're not this age, or you are this age." Everybody has a reason why they will or won't represent you. So at the end of the day, you just can't take it personally. You just have to keep trying, but it really helps to know people. That's pretty much what it comes down to.

Kim Holt

[Finding the right agent] was one of the hardest things, I think, when we first started, though. We went and saw probably the five top agencies that were in LA, after that [showcase] happened, and I had no idea what we were even doing because, honestly, it wasn't like, "Oh, we're going to go get an agent." We just seriously were like, "This would be a fun family vacation. This will be fun."

Good excuse to go out to LA. I don't even really know if we had any expectations of anything. We went around to these agencies. They have you come in, and they have you read, and we'd never done it before. They were like, "Oh my gosh. We love her. We would love to sign her."

I'm like, "You really do? You love her?" I know I would never say something like that now, but I was...They all wanted us to move out there. They wanted to sign, but they wanted us to move out here, and I thought, "We can't move out here. We have a house back home. I have two other kids. My husband has a business."

We had a life. So we didn't. We did not move, and two of the agencies kept sending us stuff anyway, and they told us, "Just put it on tape." Finally one of the agents said, "If you just come out here for a month and she doesn't book anything, go home. We won't call you again."

We did come out here during pilot season, and we said we were going to stay for about six weeks. She booked commercial after commercial, and we stayed for seven months. I finally said, "It's time to go home." She was at that perfect age to do a lot of these toy commercials or kid commercials. We did that, and it was a lot of fun, and she loved it.

We went back home. She went to school, continued her gymnastics and theater. She actually started a theater program at her school, and then we would just come out for three months in the summer, if that. Sometimes we would only stay six weeks, and we would just do our stuff on tape.

We did tell Olivia, "If you book something that's substantial, we will make the move." I don't really think we thought that would ever really happen, though. We wanted her to still do her thing, but we didn't want to make any huge kind of commitment or move for our family.

She loved school. She was the vice president of her class. She was on the chess team. She was a cheerleader. She thoroughly enjoyed school. She enjoyed acting as well, and gymnastics. When it came down to it, we had to make her make a choice between gymnastics and acting, though, because they were both so time-consuming.

We did it a different way than most people do. I don't want to recommend that, just because I think [conventions are] super pricey. I do think that they have showcases that aren't like that, but I don't know. That was just how we did it.

We went through somebody that we knew, that knew somebody. I think just to sign up for those classes for whatever school that is, it can cost about ten thousand to fifteen thousand to do all that. We do know people—other Disney kids that have done the same kind of process. The odds of doing something like that and booking something aren't really in your favor. We would not have done that if somebody had charged us that much money. We just paid pretty much for our trip to come out there.

I think the younger you are to do something like that is better, because there were a group of talented kids—very talented kids—that were with us in our group, and it was mainly probably because of their age. I think when you're younger, it's easier to get an agent than as you get older, unfortunately. We were just really lucky that way.

Clark Trainor

In other markets, photographers charge a lot for headshots. But in LA, you can get a really good headshot for one fifty to two hundred dollars. With a lot of looks and everything. I went out and got [Tenzing] a headshot. Went to the SAG website and copied and pasted all the SAG franchised agents.

Not necessarily because they're better, but because they're SAG franchised and they don't want to lose their SAG franchise, so they're a little more legit. They're not going to send you to their photographer for special photos, where a lot of times they're getting kickbacks.

If they're not SAG franchised, I didn't even want to bother. I actually found a free program online. I don't remember the name of it, but I could plug in the website, and it would go and recognize an address based on the formatting. It would import it into a database. I used this program. I was able to download all the full addresses of LA's SAG agents in a minute through this program. Then I built a form letter.

I used a comma-separated database. I'm able to write really good form letters that don't read like form letters. So I was able to separate their first and last name, and I was able to write a form letter and then just do a huge mail merge.

I was very proud of my form letter. If the agent read my form letter, they probably wouldn't recognize it as having been a form letter. They probably would think that I actually typed it to them. Because their first name was merged here and there and there. Then we just did a big mail out. I think it was one hundred fourteen pieces. He got nine appointments, which really surprised me.

The only things he had on his résumé were the two summer-camp credits.

Which I think does show you that this town is, to a degree, based on youth. The younger you are, the less they expect on your résumé. So you do get a little bit of a pass there.

And then of course Tenzing's multiracial, so that meant he had a little bit of a different look.

And then, I will admit, one of the things I did was because I know people who were casting associates. I have friends who are actors, and they've worked as casting associates. They get a hundred résumés every couple days. Every week they get four to five hundred résumés.

And sadly, although CDs will probably never admit this to you, a lot of them probably wind up in the garbage because they don't have the storage, and they don't have the time to catalog these unsolicited résumés. So my thought was always the résumé that, if a casting associate's going, "Duh, duh, duh, duh," just flipping through, it's going to stand out.

So I actually picked out a really good picture where Tenzing was about eight years old. A really good picture of him doing a flying sidekick. And I had his regular picture on the headshot, the eight-by-ten. And then I did an insert on the side of the headshot, of the flying sidekick. The insert was maybe a two-inch-by-two-inch square, and I just laid it over to the side. I put it into the border so it wasn't lost in the picture. It kind of stood out. You never know what's going to get their attention. You never know what's going to make them remember you. I don't know if that was it. What I do know is, there were several agents and even later, on auditions, where after the audition was over or the interview was over, people asked about that one little flying sidekick. "Is that really him?"

Which I think is a clue in general. Don't hide who you are and try to be something other. The story I always heard, for instance, was Humphrey Bogart. One of the big reasons why he got one of his early roles was because of that lisp. I read an interview of the casting director. I can't remember who the casting director was, but the interviewer said, "He did a great job. We called in a lot of people, but we just couldn't forget that lisp."

Because a lot of people would try to hide that, wouldn't they? They would work to try to cover that up, whereas there's room in this town for everybody. They need big people; they need little people. They need skinny people; they need overweight people. They need all kinds of people.

I see these actors who come, and they try to be something other than what they are, and they don't even know what they bring to the stage.

He got about nine interviews, and he just went in for the interviews. And I probably overthink everything just because of who and what I am, but that's a terrifying decision.

Because you now have, like, nine people who are interested, and in LA, it's all about exclusivity unlike a lot of other smaller markets. In Miami you can have five agents—they don't care.

You don't realize the weight of that decision because it's one thing if it's you. But when you're making that decision on behalf of your child, who's too young to make that decision, you're really hoping you're putting them with the right agent. And that's just the business side of things.

There is an emotional toll when you have to split with someone who's not getting the job done because this is such a people business, and it's difficult to say the least. Because it's difficult splitting with someone or parting ways. Or, you know, the other thing we saw is, "OK, he got to this point. I don't want to mess with anything." Maybe it doesn't seem like this person is getting it done or that person is getting it done, but yet I don't want to disturb the formula because it's working. There's that element to it, and it's really tough.

There is a factor that factored into it in particular. The first audition he had with the agent he's with went terribly badly for Tenzing. Just bad. I picked him up from school. We drove him down; he fell asleep in the car. When he woke up, he was so groggy. I felt terrible for him. He never really kind of got out of the fog and everything. He just did really badly in the audition. All the other auditions went great, but this one audition didn't go really well.

Yet the agent came out, and it's who he's with now, Robin Nassif. She came out, and she said, "It didn't go well, but I see something, and I want him to go and take classes for a couple of months and then come back." That was huge for me because it told me that she was looking at the kid, not a one-time performance. She was looking at the kid, the person in front of her. And so we went, and I knew that he could do better. I knew he just had a really bad day. But she's meeting him for the first time so she doesn't know. She just assumed he needs classes. So we took a little time, and I did put him in a scene-study class because he needed to start putting up scenes anyway, because working in the industry and auditioning for the industry are two completely different skill sets. A lot of people don't realize.

Acting for camera is completely different than acting on stage, and auditioning is completely different than performing if you booked something. It's a completely different skill set. Everything's punched up a little bit more in auditions. You've got to be able to get something. You've got to be able to find those beats and find those moments and hit them in a way that you don't when you're shooting a real show. So we put him in classes, and after a few weeks, it turns out the guy who was teaching him the classes actually knew Robin on a personal level. She said, "Call us in two months."

After about three weeks, he called her and said, "You really need to bring him in again. He just had a bad day. Trust me." And we went back in about three weeks later and he auditioned, and she signed him.

The reason why I ended up going with Robin Nassif, whom we love to this day, is because of that. She didn't write him off. I felt like she never looked at him as just a commodity. "Oh, this kid's not hitting the moments, hitting the mark. Next." Because she had a hundred pictures on her desk.

She could have easily just moved on to the next kid. There's no shortage of anything in this town. There's no shortage of blonds or brunettes. There's no shortage of this or that. There's no shortage. They can move on and find someone who is hitting it, but she obviously saw something because she said, "I want you to come back," and she took us back. So it wasn't just lip service. And she signed him when he proved that he can stumble but get up and not quit.

And I thought that was as telling of her as it was of him. So she got to see Tenzing at his best and worst and realized that he just had a bad day. But I just thought that that spoke volumes about her.

Pat Fisher

Actually, at Red Mountain Theater Company, his current manager—and Jordan is one of the few that has had the same manager his entire career...While he was a year-round member, they also did a summer workshop for aspiring actors. So his manager from LA was one of the instructors at the summer workshop for Red Mountain, and she recruited him. And he was the first out-of-state kid she ever tried to work with. Managers and agents, as you probably well know, don't want out-of-state kids.

It's a difficult journey, especially when you are two thousand miles away. But she recruited him. It took us three years before we committed to even try coming out.

I was working. My husband was working. You know, it's just hard to make that decision. So the first time we came out, his manager set up a meeting for him to meet some agents.

And the very first agent he met with, he fell in love with, and she fell in love with him. And, again, we are one of the few families out here that have the same agent from the beginning of time till now.

We kind of had a leg up. [I've] talked to some families that never got an agent or a manager that have spent years out here. But because Lynn came to Birmingham and found Jordan and brought him out...And of course she already had the connections with agents. She already knew who was going to be a good match for Jordan. That was our first meeting, and we didn't take any more. That was it.

When you get a good one, you better keep him, because they are few and far between.

CHAPTER 15

Unions

Should your child join a union? Are they eligible? Which union? Until recently, a professional working actor in LA was likely to belong to either the Screen Actors Guild (SAG) or the American Federation of Television and Radio Artists (AFTRA) or both. Professional stage actors belong to Equity. Since Equity and stage work are outside the subject of this book, we'll leave that union largely aside for this conversation. In March of 2012, the other two unions merged to become one: SAG-AFTRA.

Previously, SAG was notoriously difficult to join, but one could simply write a check to become a member of AFTRA. That open-door option is no longer possible. Currently, the three routes to joining the merged union are as follows:

1. Be hired for a principal role under a SAG-AFTRA contract. In other words, your kid doesn't have to be a union member *before* they get a principal role—being cast will open the door to union membership. Thirty days after your child is "SAG-AFTRA eligible" due to being cast in a principal role on a SAG or AFTRA production, they become "SAG-AFTRA Must Join" and cannot work on another union job until they become members. Getting into the union because you were hired for a principal role is sometimes known as being "Taft-Hartleyed," which refers to that part of federal labor law. Dove got into the union this way.

2. Obtain three Background Vouchers: verified work for three days as a background performer or extra in a SAG-AFTRA background role *that is categorized as a union position*. Some percentage of background positions on union projects are union; most are not. If your kid is hired for one of the union slots, they will get one of the coveted vouchers. With three vouchers, they are *eligible* to join, though not required.
3. Be a paid member for at least one year in a sister union (ACTRA, AEA, AGMA, or AGVA) and have worked and been paid for a principal role in that union at least once.

Being cast in a SAG-AFTRA project is the easiest path into the union; a single role—if it's a principal one—can qualify an actor to join, and three roles can qualify them if they are smaller ones that fall under union designation and result in vouchers. Most background work is not going to lead to eligibility. Joining the union is a requirement if your child accepts a principal role in a SAG-AFTRA project.

If your child becomes eligible but is not yet required to join the union, what factors might affect the decision of whether or not to join?

- Cost. The current national initiation fee is $3,000 if you are in New York or LA (somewhat lower in smaller markets), with annual dues that begin at $198 plus 1.575 percent of covered earnings up to $500,000. So if your kid is still just getting smaller roles, this may not make financial sense.
- Timing. When your child doesn't have the experience to compete against more seasoned kids, joining may be a mistake because belonging to the union can keep them from gaining experience and building a résumé through easier, nonunion channels. If this is a concern, then don't join until it's required. Once you join, there is no doing non-union gigs and no going back.
- Pension and Healthcare. While it may feel a little early to think about a pension, health insurance can be an attractive piece of union membership. We saved money and Dove received better

coverage by switching to union health insurance. However, simply joining the union does not automatically qualify your child for the health-care benefit: members need to have worked a certain number of hours in the preceding calendar year before becoming eligible and must continue to work a minimum number of hours each year to continue to qualify. Check out the SAG Pension and Healthcare website and the AFTRA Health and Retirement website (at http://www.sagph.org and http://www.aftrahr.com, respectively) for current details.

There are many other benefits to joining the union, including higher pay, opportunities for residuals instead of a one-time buyout, access to educational workshops and contracts to cover student and nonunion films, business seminars, access to casting directors, health and human services, discounts, and more.

Joining the union is a big milestone, and to many it signifies recognition as a professional. If you are considering having your child join the union before they are required to, however, it may be wiser to wait either until they must or until they have worked enough to make the health-care option viable. Initiation fees are a large sum of money, and belonging to a union can cut off important opportunities for a novice performer to get work. In other words, just because your child *can* join, doesn't mean they should.

The merger itself has resulted in some amount of confusion, and the historical separation of the two unions has left some pieces still separate, even after the merger. For example, while your child will be a member of SAG-AFTRA if they join the union, each project they work on will either be SAG or AFTRA still. Health insurance under the unions is also still separate, at least at the time of this writing. Your kid would be covered under either SAG or AFTRA insurance (usually whichever union they have qualified for first). For example, Dove qualified to be covered under both SAG and AFTRA for health insurance in the first year she was qualified for coverage at all, but because she qualified first with AFTRA, that was the insurance we had to go with.

Finally, here are a few myths about SAG-AFTRA membership:

- Being a union member will help land an agent. (No, it will not. Talent and a good résumé will, however.)
- Being a union member will help your child get bigger roles. (Yes, most of the best roles are union only. However if you don't have the talent and experience to get those roles, belonging to the union will not make a difference.)
- Being a union member will make it easier to get roles in general. (Actually, it can be more difficult, as your kid is now competing against professionals.)
- Being a union member guarantees that your kid can get health insurance through the union. (Even if they belong to SAG-AFTRA, they have to meet a minimum number of hours worked on union jobs each year to qualify for health insurance.)

Tips and Takeaways

- It's easier for kids than for adults to get into SAG-AFTRA, which is one reason to help your child become professional while they're young.
- Your child doesn't have to belong to the union to get cast in a union role—they can be Taft-Hartleyed in if they are cast. This is how many young actors join the union. This route is more difficult for adults.
- Getting into the union via background vouchers is possible, but not typically recommended. It can put your child in the position of having to compete for union roles with kids who have much more experience.
- Joining the union is an exciting and serious step for a young actor. Take your time with this step.

CHAPTER 16

There are Always Surprises

No matter how hard you work to prepare yourself and your child for what you might encounter in the pursuit of a career in TV or film, there are always going to be curveballs. After five years in Hollywood, we are still encountering surprises, and they range from funny to scary. I was on set in Canada recently, watching Dove on the monitors as she filmed *Descendants* and checking messages on my phone. A little e-mail from her business manager stopped me in my tracks: he wanted to talk about insurance—specifically the fact that she was not covered for injuries occurring on the job.

What? My mind flashed back to the two months we'd spent in the snow for *Cloud Nine*, as well as the various hazards on any set. Didn't her insurance cover this? Well, no. Health insurance does not cover something considered work related and therefore coverable by workers' compensation insurance. But then didn't Disney cover that? Also no. As it turned out, no studio or production company would cover that exposure for an actor, as the actor is not technically an employee of that company. Dove may work on projects for the Disney Channel, but she is not officially an employee. She is an independent contractor, as are all actors, which means she would need to provide her own coverage, just as any self-employed person would.

Yikes! We swung into action, spent some more money, and took care of it. But I confess, it freaked me out. In the several years she had been in the business at that point, no one had ever brought this serious gap up, and I suspect few parents of young actors—or even adult actors themselves—are aware of their vulnerability. Work-related injuries require work-related insurance, which is not standard health insurance. Ugh!

Other surprises: for a long time, I was surprised by how capricious the casting process could be. If you didn't fit the look they envisioned, you would generally not even get in the door to demonstrate your talent. Is this fair? Maybe not, but film and TV are a business, not a meritocracy. Look first, talent second. And it is important here to understand that "the look" is not "looks"—in other words, it is not necessarily about attractiveness (though that can be a consideration) but more about whether the actor has the look the casting director is after, as suggested by the script and other factors, like the people who may have been already cast, and fixed issues like height, weight, age, complexion, and hair color. When you realize exactly how many hundreds, if not thousands, of actors are pursuing any given role, using "the look" as an initial sieve is simply the only efficient way for casting directors to handle the impossible task of sorting through everyone. Then, once they have a small pool of actors, all of whom look plausible in the role, they can explore the issue of talent. If everyone is coming in through reputable agents, there is an assumption of baseline talent anyway.

I was also occasionally surprised by how catty and mean some of the other parents could be. In my eyes, we are all in the same boat, and we can do a lot to help one another out by sharing information and supporting and encouraging one another. And most of the parents I have encountered at the more successful levels have in fact been great people. But I won't forget the words of one parent of a successful young (non-Disney) actor, spoken to me in a green room: "Oh, my daughter never wanted to be a Disney kid. She wanted to be a *real* actor!" Wow.

CHAPTER 17

Stories: Surprises

Hollywood Parents Share Some of The Surprises They Encountered on this Journey

Pat Fisher

Probably the last-minute callbacks, initially. You know?

We would get on a plane and get back to Birmingham, and literally the next day, we would get on another plane and come back to LA, which prompted us to get longer accommodations here. So, yeah, that was surprising.

I think, too, the parents surprise me. The kids seemed to be very compatible—don't have a lot of jealousy or competition for one another—but the parents...not so much. You know, there is a lot of competition. It's like, "Oh, your kid is working, right?"

It's very sad. One thing that Jordan and I talked about from the get-go was, "If you don't get a role, I hope one of your friends does. I hope somebody you know gets that role." You know—so the kids were able to remain friends. The parents had to keep themselves in check. You know, when the role is right and it's right for your kid, your kid is going to get it.

If the role is not right for your kid, your kid is not going to get it, so what difference does it make who does? Be happy for them. Everybody gets what's coming to them.

Kim Holt

I would have to say the time I had to put in for this. I didn't know how long it took to shoot a show. In reality, you watch TV, and you think, "Oh, they probably go to work for a few hours, and they shoot the show in thirty minutes. They're done." I don't really think I thought it was going to be that short, but I never knew that my child would be on set for ten and a half hours a day. Because she is so young, I have to be there because she is not really an age to work yet.

That was probably the most surprising thing to me. I didn't realize that it was going to be so time-consuming, and not just for me, but our entire family. When you've been on set for ten and a half hours and then it takes you an hour to get to work and an hour back, you've been gone all day long. You have another part of your family that's like, "Where are you? Are you going to be here for dinner? Or are you going to come home eventually?" That was the first year. It was really, really tough on us because it was a big transition to try to figure out how we were going to manage that.

I think before you get into doing all this, you should probably investigate the time that you might be putting in. I think for every age, it's a different time frame. The older they get, the more time they can put in. And there is school, if your child is still in school.

Amy Anderson

I was already pretty savvy about the business, fortunately, which gave me such a huge leg up. I often say to people who ask about getting their kids in this business, "I can't imagine going into this not knowing anything about the business." Just like, "I used to be a paralegal, and now my daughter wants to act." I can't even imagine being that woman. You would just be...My head is spinning, and I knew what to expect. And of course, not every kid is going to book a Modern Family *kind of job, so ours was pretty fast and furious immediately. But one of the things that has been kind of surprising and somewhat disappointing—and we even deal with it minimally on our set—is how children are treated in this business. And I knew that. I knew that children are traditionally not always treated well in this business. I'll start off by saying that our kids on our set are treated so well, and I think probably better than on most shows, because there are so many kids and it's just a great group of people. And most of the people—from the executive producers down to the other adult actors—are parents.*

They understand kids, and they are very respectful toward our kids. But businesswise, I'm kind of shocked...not shocked, but I guess I'm just kind of disappointed in how sometimes things are done to just...anything for the shot. I'm not saying on our set, but I've heard so many stories, because I have so many friends now in this business who are parents and have kids of business, and I've heard the nuttiest stories of how kids have been put in peril. Not in our set. Obviously never on our set. But this is something that does happen regularly. Kids who've been put in peril. Kids overworked over their labor-limit times. That all comes down to the studio teachers, and we are so fortunate that we have really, really good studio teachers on our show. But I have heard from other friends whose kids work on other shows that a lot of studio teachers, it seems to me, are just glorified babysitters, and they just sit around and watch their kids play on iPads all day, and the kids really aren't getting their education.

Yeah, and it can get really tense. I feel that often—and I've talked to people about this, too—that it can be so tricky for those good studio teachers where they're often put in very precarious positions. They don't want to lose their jobs, and they want to be there for those kids that they really care about, and they're constantly asked to compromise. It can be a very tricky situation, and of course there have been a couple of really bad stories that have surfaced, too, just in the last couple of years, of studio teachers.

Did you hear that story about that guy who was not actually a teacher? He wasn't certified—he had faked his credentials. There was no background check on this guy, and one of the parents whose kids had worked with him at one point on a movie that was shot in Palm Springs was watching a show...he was on it as the defendant, and there was a case against him because...something involving a strip club that he was partial owner of, and that he had assaulted these women who came in and interviewed to be strippers. He was supposed to hire them. And [the parent] was like, "That was our studio teacher. What the heck?" She alerted people, and then they researched him. He had no teaching credentials—because in the state of California, to be a studio teacher, you had to be a certified teacher of K through twelve. He had faked it. He was using an alias and everything, and he had taught several children on sets. Crazy!

> Author's note: This particular incident was covered in depth by *Deadline Hollywood* on September 21, 2014. It turns out that the imposter had worked exclusively on low-budget nonunion sets, including student film sets, where enforcement and oversight of studio teachers and other regulations in general is likely to be lax. This points again to the importance of working on union projects, even if your child is not yet in a union. The protections in place are taken seriously. Stories like this one are part of what led to the 2012 California Child Performer Services Permit, which requires just about anyone who works with artists under the age of eighteen to have a background check and fingerprinting.

Even with a really good studio teacher like ours...We have five minors on our set. She's busy; she has a lot on her plate. And then we have a separate teacher who works just with Aubrey on her schoolwork. Then she also works with the babies who play Baby Joe. That's kind of her role; she goes between the youngest kids. They have a lot to keep track of. And you do, as a parent, still have to be the number-one advocate for your kid and really watch for them. A lot is going on in those sets.

CHAPTER 18

School

There are probably about as many ways to manage the question of school as there are families trying to manage it. Parents whose kids are professional actors generally have to be a bit more flexible than those who are simply having a more normal childhood. Luckily there are options.

It's actually easier in some ways to keep your child consistently in school if they are working. This is because there are laws requiring set teachers for minors who have not yet graduated from high school. The studio pays for the teacher, who coordinates with the child's regular school on subjects and lessons. This is where your work permit comes into play: your child is only allowed to work if their grades remain acceptable. Working with a set teacher and work permit allows absences to be excused.

Conversely, absences are generally not excused if your child is auditioning (versus "working"). This can be really challenging. We were successful in having Dove's agent schedule most auditions for after school, but sometimes casting directors are not available in the late afternoon. In that case, you'll have to decide whether the opportunity is worth the absence. These can quickly add up and jeopardize your child's grades, ironically jeopardizing their work permit! Many kids who pursue acting are homeschooled for just this reason: the flexibility can't be beat.

Homeschooling is not for everyone, however. I love the idea of it myself, but I was not a very successful teacher when we homeschooled Dove in the seventh grade. In our case, her Dad and I were both working, and I was in graduate school, and we just underestimated how much oversight was needed. She essentially read whatever she wanted to all day with occasional algebra lessons from her Dad. At the end of the year, we administered the Iowa Test to check her achievement levels, and to our relief, she had very high scores. Emboldened, we had her challenge the eighth-grade Iowa test after a little more math coaching, and she scored even better! With test results in hand, she succeeded in skipping eighth grade, and we enrolled Dove in online high school.

Online high school is a great idea for a lot of kids. It tends to have more structure than homeschooling and is a popular option for those who are juggling auditions and acting gigs, but they have to be genuinely motivated and have consistent parental support. Still in grad school, working, and at that point getting divorced, I was not the most demanding parent when it came to making sure Dove was on top of her homework. She coasted through ninth grade online, again spending much of the year reading whatever interested her, which, luckily, seemed to be everything. There is an educational philosophy called "unschooling," and in some ways that is what those two years really were. For a naturally bright and curious kid, this can actually be a very meaningful way to learn.

When we arrived in Los Angeles, Dove was fourteen and entering her sophomore year. We both agreed that a normal high school experience was a good idea at that point. But by the end of that first year, it was clear that juggling regular high school and an accelerating acting career was not sustainable. She was missing too much school for auditions, and it was causing her a lot of stress and affecting her grades. Some private schools are much more flexible with young actors than public schools are, but we did not have that financial option. So we looked into some alternatives: a charter school popular with young actors, called Options, and the CHSPE.

Options for Youth is a tuition-free, accredited, open enrollment school with a very flexible program. It allows kids to work at their own pace under the guidance of teachers with whom they meet twice a week. It makes a lot of sense for a kid who is in and out of auditions frequently, which can be so disruptive to a regular school schedule. Still, it looked too much to both of us like homeschooling and online high school, the two other alternatives that had not been a great fit. So we checked out the CHSPE.

A CHSPE (California High School Proficiency Exam, commonly pronounced "chispie") certificate is the equivalent of a high school diploma. Having one makes your child a "legal eighteen," which can be magic words in this industry. Basically, it means that your child is no longer legally required to attend high school (since they have essentially graduated), and therefore they do not need a set teacher. They are also allowed to work adult hours, including overtime. The exam is offered three times a year (generally in March, June, and October) and is proctored like an SAT or other college-entrance test. In order to be eligible, your kid must be either sixteen or in the second semester of their sophomore year of high school.

Dove's agent told us that when she passed the CHSPE, it would transform her life. I thought that was probably an exaggeration, but it turned out to be true. The month after we had the certificate is when she started booking roles and getting auditions for leads, and she never looked back.

There are serious pros and cons to having your child take the CHSPE, and I wish someone had spelled them out to me. Ultimately we were glad that Dove took this route, but it is truly not for everyone. Here are some things to know.

CHSPE PROS

Passing the test allows your kid to work as a legal eighteen. This means, as mentioned above, they can leave school, avoid dealing with a set teacher, and work as many hours as any adult. Life gets simpler. Work permits are no longer necessary. Studios love this because it is logistically much easier to hire a kid who can work a full day, and it is cheaper to not have to pay a set teacher. There is a kind of sweet spot for kids who can actually play their real ages, or a little younger, in their mid- to late teens. You might have seen audition listings for "submit eighteen to play younger." This is especially likely for lead roles. If your kid is a legal eighteen, it increases their chances of being hired. They are now on an even playing field with the eighteen- to twenty-four-year olds who are going for those roles, but odds are that your kid looks a little more believable. To be honest, for kids who are sixteen or seventeen, it can be very hard to get work if they have *not* passed the CHSPE because they are competing with so many actors over eighteen who are simply easier to hire. Those two years can be pretty dry otherwise.

The CHSPE is often confused with the GED because both are tests that grant high school equivalence to those who pass them. But you can't take the GED until you are at least eighteen, so it is useless for kids who are looking to leave early. One nice aspect of the CHSPE is that if your child passes, they do not have to quit school. You can keep the certificate in reserve in case something great comes along but continue to stay enrolled in school until that time comes.

CHSPE CONS

What no one tells you: once your child begins auditioning as a legal eighteen, that's probably the only way the studios will want to hire them. This makes sense. But if you are trying to keep your kid enrolled in school just a bit longer, suddenly all of their absences are unexcused because the studio no longer is paying for a set teacher. Yikes! This happened to us: Dove decided to take one more year of high school even after she'd passed the CHSPE—largely because she was in love with the show choir program. But it made for a very stressful time as we skated right along the edge of the maximum excused absences all year.

This one is little more obvious but still bears noting: just because your child has the equivalent of a high school diploma, they do not necessarily have the high school credits to get into a great college or university! Leaving school early with a CHSPE certificate practically guarantees that they will need to spend some time in a community college or online making up some basic credits before they can transfer to a university. Many families make that choice already these days, as it is a much less expensive way to get a college education. But if four years in a university is important to your family, you may want to skip the CHSPE option.

You may also want to ask yourself and your child if your child really is ready—emotionally and physically—to work the hours of an adult. Kids at this age still need a lot of sleep, and there is a wide range of maturity between the ages of fifteen and eighteen. Are they prepared for the reality of this? Working adult hours in this industry can be exhausting, and you don't get this time back.

Finally, does your child have a strong drive to continue their education later? If education has been instilled as a high value, they will likely return to school when the time is right. But if you are concerned that this may not be the case, is it OK with you that their schooling may end before they finish four years of high school? If not, maybe they should stay in school and skip the CHSPE option.

In our case, Dove's career was looking promising enough and we had an agreement that she would begin attending either Santa Monica Community College or Fashion Institute of Design and Merchandising (FIDM) that fall if no big acting work had materialized, so we both felt comfortable with her choice to leave school at sixteen. Frankly, we'd left conventional school approaches behind years ago. As it worked out, she shot Disney's pilot *Bits and Pieces* about two weeks after completing her junior year, filmed a large guest star role on *The Mentalist* that August, and was cast in the movie *Cloud Nine* by September. Another guest star role, for *Malibu Country*, showed up in October. We found out in late December, just before leaving to shoot *Cloud 9*, that *Bits and Pieces* had been rewritten with dual roles for her and renamed *Liv and Maddie*. The Disney Channel series began filming a month after we returned from filming *Cloud 9* in Utah. At that point, it was clear that college would be a conversation after *Liv and Maddie* ended its run, whenever that would be.

One last personal thought on the CHSPE: I think that if we had started this journey earlier and Dove had a chance to get on a series or have a few movie roles before entering that difficult-to-be-cast period of fifteen to seventeen—in other words, competing with girls who were either actually eighteen and over or were a legal eighteen—that we might have made a different choice. I have talked to a number of parents whose kids had a name in the business by the time they hit that age, and they all expressed the opinion that they would be crazy to let their kid take the CHSPE, as all it would do is compromise their education and remove a genuine protection for their kid in terms of work hours and turnaround. All true. If your kid already has a role on a series or is working regularly, you have no real reason to give up their status as a minor in the industry. However, every family must make their own difficult choices, based on their own unique circumstances. Our choice worked for us, but it is not one I would recommend to most parents.

Legal Eighteen versus Emancipation

There is so much confusion over these two, even on sets, and they are entirely distinct. Industry people who really should know better use the terms interchangeably, generally saying, *emancipated* when they mean *legal eighteen*. Here are the basic differences spelled out.

Legal Eighteen (passed the CHSPE):

- an adult in the eyes of the industry in terms of work hours and education
- no longer required to attend high school or have a set teacher
- no work permit required

- still a minor in the eyes of the law
- cannot sign legal contracts
- earnings still subject to Coogan law

Emancipated (legally independent from parents):

- an adult in the eyes of the law *except for* education and work hours
- still required to be enrolled in school or have a set teacher
- work permit still required
- still follows work-hour guidelines for minors
- can sign legal contracts
- earnings not subject to Coogan law/Coogan funds available

There is an excellent chart at the BizParentz Foundation online (http://www.bizparentz.org/thebizness/emancipation.html) that spells out these and other related distinctions. I found it really helpful to have a few extra copies printed out to give to set production assistants, who were frequently confused about what my daughter's legal-eighteen status actually meant. It's conventional wisdom that emancipation is a choice of genuinely last resort, typically used when finances have been so mismanaged that the Coogan funds must be tapped to pay back taxes or when the relationship between parents and child has become so strained that the child wishes to be legally freed of them. Other than filing for emancipation with a court of law, getting married or joining the armed forces are the only other ways to become legally independent of one's parents before the age of eighteen.

Emancipation does not solve the educational requirement issue or the work-permit issue. And it leaves young people vulnerable to exploitation since they can sign legally binding contracts that they may not fully understand. Emancipation generally means that something has gone wrong. Try to avoid going there.

Work Permits

The subject of work permits—how they work, and how to get one—was largely covered in Chapter 3, "First Things First." But here you can see how entwined with the subject of school they are. If your child passes the CHSPE, they no longer need a work permit. But work permits can be great leverage to have your kid keep their grades up if that is an issue. And their very existence serves as a reminder that children are children. If they are working during hours when they would normally be in school, there are laws about how many hours are allowed and how much time should be set aside for education. Sidestepping those rules is an option that should not be taken lightly.

Tips and Takeaways

- Be prepared to be flexible in terms of how your young actor approaches education. Frequent auditions and acting jobs can be difficult to fit with a traditional school routine.
- Homeschooling, online school, and hybrid programs designed for professional kids are popular options for child actors.
- The CHSPE may be an option for your child if they are 16 or 17, but be aware that it has a downside as well as an upside.
- Regardless of the form their education takes, until your child either graduates from high school or is a "legal 18" through passing the CHSPE, they must keep their grades at a satisfactory level to maintain their work permit.
- Legal 18 and emancipation are two very different things, though frequently confused by many people.

CHAPTER 19

Stories: School

Hollywood Parents Share Stories of How They Managed the Question of School for Their Young Actors

Amy Anderson

That's one thing I wish I had—a book like this to know about. Because I really navigated the school thing like a blind person. I didn't know what to do. Our studio teacher is actually...she's a big believer in trying to keep kids in regular school. I think that's great if you can do it, but when your kid is a serious regular on a show and they work every week...She doesn't work every day, but she works every week. It got almost impossible for us, and so kindergarten...she was in regular school, but she didn't have to do studio school yet. She was in a small private school. I didn't like that school, and they were not being cooperative with us, so we left. Several reasons, but those are the two main reasons. Then we went to a really terrific public school. She had team teachers who taught her first-grade class, and they jumped through hoops to be accommodating to us.

But even with that, it was so difficult—the back and forth and the driving and the trying to get to work, and then her even being a bright kid and everything. If you're not in the classroom when everybody else is—even if you're doing the same worksheets in the same books, or whatever—if you didn't hear what the teacher said or how the teacher said it or learn it the way she said, you go back into the room...you still feel lost. Then, of course, there's the social aspect, where even the nicest kids in the room were just starting to leave her out, because if you're just not there, you're not there. Those social circles form without you. The last five weeks of Modern Family*—last season, season five—the last five weeks of production, she went to school three days, and it really broke her to pieces because the kids just weren't there. She went back, and some of the kids were mean to her, and, like I said, even the nice kids kind of just were leaving her out, and she was feeling really sad.*

Then, on top of that, that made her confidence plummet because she was in the classroom feeling left out. Then her work started to suffer even though I knew she knew the material. The studio teacher was frustrated because we couldn't always get the work on time. Then she would show up at studio school with nothing to do. Then I was frustrated because...You get the call time the night before. Like, at six o'clock the guy says, "Your kid needs to be here at eight o'clock tomorrow morning," which means, for us, it's going to take us an hour and fifteen minutes to drive there.

[At that point] you can't get the work from the teacher. I was paying my nanny to drive way out to get her schoolwork and bring it to the set, and I was having to pay her mileage, so it cost me like thirty, forty bucks just to get the work. Then, by the time she would get it all the way down to our lot, she would have already had an hour of schoolwork with nothing to do. "Well, we've put her in the studio school right away. That's why we called her at eight o'clock." And...it just was a nightmare. It was lose, lose, lose. Me losing, teachers losing, studio teacher losing, Aubrey losing—everybody was losing. I'm like, "There's got to be a better solution." Fortunately she is homeschooling. I started homeschooling at the end of last year, but she is homeschooling through a public district.

I think a lot of the Disney kids go there, actually. The school is actually designed for kids who have professional work schedules.

And they even have field teachers who go out and visit the studio teachers on set. Rico goes there, too. That's how we found out about it. He had started there last year, and he loves it. Literally it has changed our lives, and it's more work for me because the day she's not doing studio school, I set up that table, and we do school. But even though it's more actual work for me time wise, it has streamlined our lives in a way that makes our lives so much easier.

The stress and the chaos. I think homeschooling, overall, is a little bananas, and I don't understand why people who don't have to do it do it.

If she stays acting, I'm really curious to know if she would want to continue or would want to go to a school at some point. Ariel Winter goes to a prep school, a private school. Rico goes to the same school we do, a homeschooling independent school. Nolan already finished the high school equivalency [CHSPE]. We have a full range of what the kids do on our show, but there are a lot of options out there for people. Before you dive into things…I was so trial and error. I was like, "Oh no, this is stressful. Oh no, this isn't working. Oh gosh, this is stressful." It was a couple of years of really just so much stress for me, because there's nothing more important than your kid's education.

I have a lot of friends who are like, "I don't know if this is the right school for us. I don't know if this is going to be the best school. What school do you think I should send my kids?" They're switching schools, whatever. I really feel that the best school for your kid is the school where your kid is happiest.

It's not the one that costs the most money. It's not the one that other people are doing. And you just don't always know sometimes until you try something.

Kenda Benward

Luke went to three different high schools. They all worked with him. They were all willing to let him come and go, work with his on-set tutor. Come back, return the homework, and finish out the year and leave if he had to again. No one gave him a problem about it.

Actually, he was only at Burbank High, really, for maybe five out of nine months, honestly. And they worked with him, and, of course, he had to do his work. He had to get good grades. He was doing homework, and he was doing the stuff he had to do, but he just wasn't in the classroom. But they were so great to work with us.

And it was amazing. He got to graduate and go to normal school. And that was an important thing to us, just because I wanted him to work the hours that his age limit would allow him to work. I did not want him to work as an adult at eighteen. That was our personal family preference. That just isn't what I wanted him to do.

I think it's an individual choice, obviously, for each child. Because I look at some of Luke's costars. Kat McNamara is brilliant. She loves school. So whether she's working adult hours or whether she's working kid hours, she's going to get her homework done. Luke would not have got his homework done. He would have been like, "I'm an adult now. I don't have to do my homework." I just knew it wouldn't work for him.

So for Luke, I knew that if he was going to finish high school, he needed to finish it in a traditional setting. And it worked for us.

Allison Zuehlsdorff

I think the entertainment industry may be in a little bit of a crisis regarding the whole schooling issue. I've come to believe that what it takes to get a good education while being in film and television regularly is for both the child and the parent to first and foremost have a commitment to education. If there is not that understanding going in, it would end up that the actor-student couldn't care less about school. They're just so happy to be on TV!

There is already precious little time and atmosphere for study on set that without the intentional effort and focus, a good education is hard to come by. It really is, especially in the junior-high and high school years.

Most set teachers do their best to create an educational environment, but because of the chopped-up time blocks and the pressures that trickle down from the top, the only way it's really going to be meaningful is if the student makes a concerted effort when they are given the time to sit down and really focus. Also, the set teacher really helps when he or she makes the schoolroom a quiet area unless all the students are taking a quick break. After work, I always ask Cozi if the schoolroom atmosphere was conducive to studying, just to make sure she is able to get her work done.

There are a lot of the teens taking the CHSPE and opting out of just finishing school. For some kids, this works well because they are ahead in their work, but I do think that often it's doing a disservice to the average child growing up in this industry.

I feel for the actor-students. Especially in high school, how do you maintain a full school load while working five days a week? Even if they don't plan to quit school, once high school-age actors take the CHSPE, it's really hard to have the self-discipline to then go back. Also, many of the protections fall away once you're considered legal eighteen, which makes for longer work hours.

Kim Holt

We've never homeschooled Olivia before. She was already in school. That's one thing nobody ever really told us about. We didn't know where to send her or what to do with her. We knew she had to be taught on set when she couldn't go to a public school because she was on set for so long every day. We tried some different programs, and you would hear from other people.

There are so many different programs out there. There are programs online, and there are programs that you can go to. It was so confusing, trying to find the right one for your child. I knew Olivia didn't do really well just working off of a computer. I think she would have probably been on social media the whole time, and it would have been super distracting. That's probably not the case for a lot of kids, because I see them. They do a lot of their work. It's probably really great. They can take their computer, and they do it. Olivia is more of a book person.

We started her out on a program that, at the time...I didn't realize that when she finished, she would still get her high school degree, but she wouldn't be able to go to straight to college because she would be missing her labs. I didn't know all that. We were sending her to this school. She was doing really well, and then when I started talking about college to the school, they were like, "Well, your child is probably going to have to go to a junior college to pick up these classes to do that."

I was like, "Oh, wait."

So now I had to do some more research after her going to school for...I think she went two years there. I was going, "Oh, no. What have I done to my child?" Because before we moved out here, when Olivia was twelve, and we talked about this, I said, "School comes first, regardless. This is going to be like an extracurricular activity for you because you're only twelve now. You don't understand that you could be eighteen or nineteen and go, 'I don't want to do this anymore.' You've got to have a backup plan. College is first—or school, definitely."

She enrolled in a school. It's an independent-study program. So it's like a regular school that she goes to now. It's like a classroom that's separate from the school, and the teachers come to us once a week. She's had an amazing set teacher since she was twelve. She's had the same one.

I can't even imagine how we would have gotten through this without her. She comes over and reads to her when she is busy because Olivia doesn't even have time to read. So she'll read the book to her. I'm like, "Something is wrong with this picture. Why couldn't I have been taught like this?" (laughing). They do manage to get school done. It is challenging, I think, when you first start. It's super challenging for them to learn how to manage going on set for thirty minutes and then to come and go back to the classroom for fifteen and trying to focus right away.

That focus part is the hardest part because it's like going to recess every fifteen minutes and trying to calm yourself down to figure out how to focus back in school for fifteen minutes and get your time [logged in] and to get your schoolwork done, because you have to do school. You have to at least do three hours of school—good hours of school—a day.

Olivia took seven classes last year and three maths. The good thing is, she is a senior this year, and she only has four classes because she took so many last year. It's a lot easier for her this year. But, yeah, school is really challenging, I think, but it's super important at the same time.

Olivia wanted to try to attend NYU, but when this new show picked up…she is not going to be able to go to school right away because she'll probably be working at least until she is nineteen or twenty, but she is good with that. She loves what she is doing, but she definitely is going to try to fit college in there, even if it's online, doing a few classes here and there.

It's been her choice. Before we picked up and decided she was going to do this other show, we said, "It's going to be this or college."

She actually thought about it for a while, because it's a huge decision when all your friends are leaving to go to school and you haven't had that opportunity. She didn't want to feel like she was missing out on something, but I think that she is thankful for the opportunity and wanted to continue doing what she does. Because you never know when it's not going to be there. The opportunities…it's hard to explain that. Once it's over, it's over, and enjoy it while it lasts.

It's unpredictable, very unpredictable. It's one of those things that you live day by day, I think. This is a career that you have to live day by day. And enjoy it, but save your pennies for a rainy day.

We did talk about [the CHSPE], and it never, never even crossed my mind to do it, and this is why for us. I'm not opinionated about other ways. We already were on a show. I know a lot of people do it because sometimes they will hire you if you are legal eighteen. We have some on our show right now that are legal eighteen. It makes it easier because they can work longer hours, and they don't have to hire a teacher, which I understand. It's financially easier for people, and it's just a better fit sometimes to work with kids that are legal eighteen. We were already on a show. We didn't really have to have that.

I just looked at it as, if I did that, then she would just be working more hours, and then she wouldn't have that teacher anymore that she needs so much. I would have been kicking myself in the butt for doing that. That never even crossed my mind. I do have to say, if we had been not working and just sitting out here doing nothing, I think maybe I would have done it. Maybe, but I don't really know. I've not been in that situation. So I'm not sure. I don't really knock people for doing it. We were in a different situation.

And before we ever finished the other show, she was already picked up to do this show. There was never any question for me to do it. I know it makes it easier. I know that next year, they're all going… Everybody is going be like, "Woo. She is eighteen, finally." There will probably be a big party thrown here because she is the only one on our show right now that is not either eighteen or legal eighteen.

Victor Boyce

Well, the set teachers just administer the curriculum that comes from the normal school. Cameron is enrolled in a normal school. Well, I shouldn't say in a "normal school." He's enrolled in a school that's flexible enough to accommodate what he needs.

It is [a normal school], but the school is an independent studying school, so that's what it's for. Some of the kids who enroll in this school are athletes, some are actors, and some are singers. But they're all kids who are doing exceptionally big projects outside of school, so there's no way...Like, Gabby Douglas was in this school, the gymnast, and things like that and other actors. Some of the kids from Jessie *are also enrolled in this school. So it's something that we are very fortunate to have. Because before what we were doing was an online course thing. I thought it was cool, but none of the kids liked it. It was very impersonal, typing on a computer all day.*

So now they have classmates even though they don't go to a traditional classroom. And they have everything that a normal school has; they just do it on set. They have regular books, and the set teacher is here every day. They have two set teachers, so the student-to-teacher ratio is amazing.

Yeah, and they do all the regular tasks. All the regular things that my daughter in a regular school has to take, they have to do. So the only difference is the physical location of where they're doing it. Oh, yeah, and you can't beat the ratio.

Well, they are required to do a minimum amount of hours, but then they have to fulfill a certain hourly quota. So he might do more one day than the next. It's never, like, the same every day, but they have to get all their tests in. They have to get all their requirements in, including PE, including extracurricular, whatever that might be. He does Spanish; he has chemistry.

I love it. And the cool thing for me as a parent is, I can just go right upstairs and just check on them. I was in there yesterday. He got a ninety-seven, so I was teasing him. He got a ninety-seven on a test, and I'm like, "What? What is this? You're supposed to get a hundred."

I'm like, "What did you miss?" I'm looking at it...I say, "What's the answer to this one?" So I kind of gave him a hard time. I love a ninety-seven; that's fine. But so [school is] good.

Pam McCartan

As a family, we homeschooled. There's a lot more options today than there were even a few years ago. We did a lot through Brigham Young University, online-credited programming. We worked directly with our high school; they were phenomenal. And you always had six months to complete it, like, on your timeline. So while he was at the Guthrie, while she was at the Children's Theater, they didn't have to be schooling. They could finish that up and then kind of double up once they were back in mainstream school. Then they could double up with their online work, too, as long as they got it done. It was either six months or a year—now I can't recall—but there was some time to complete the courses that they missed. When we came to the Oakwood [for pilot season], I homeschooled them.

I will applaud all the teachers that gave us everything. I mean, it was just amazing. Every week they'd contact us with the weekly assignments. We just didn't have the electronic capability that we do today, but they would send packets to our Oakwood Apartment, and we'd send work back. It was phenomenal, the kind of support that we had with our schools to be able to do something like that. We'd disappear for four months and then come back.

Clark Trainor

It takes some logistics. It's a hybrid model, and we are lucky enough that we are not in LA Unified where we live. We are in a smaller school district. Which tends to be a little more responsive because it's a smaller ship. It's not the Titanic.

The Titanic *doesn't turn as fast, as we found out. Because we are in a more responsive school district, we're able to do a hybrid program [with the set teacher] and kind of keep [Tenzing] consistent with the classroom so that when he goes on hiatus, he can just slip right back in.*

You know what I thought was really a nice thing about it is when he does go back to school, for the few days, it's, "Ooh"—you know. But then all that wears off, and he just becomes Tenzing again to everybody, and he's just another kid.

Tenzing's got a great attitude because if someone posts something mean or something, he is like, "Haters going to hate. What are you going to do? Haters are going to hate." So every once in a while, you get someone who posts something not so nice on Instagram or Twitter—"He's one of those *kids," or whatever.*

And someone did that about six or seven months ago, and half of Tenzing's school flamed that person and said, nicely, "No, he's not like that. He's in my class. He's not like that. You have no idea who you are talking about." There is no publicist in the world who can buy that for you.

So that's the other great thing that we love about him just going and being a regular kid and other people seeing him as a regular kid—is that you have those friends out there. You know what I mean? They just silenced that person and said, "No, you have no idea what you are talking about. He's in my science class. He's in my fifth-grade science class, and he is not that way at all."

Pat Fisher

School is a big subject, and it's very critical. When we were still back in Birmingham, Jordan was so busy that he was getting sick. He was just wearing himself ragged. So we finally had to make a decision—it's school or work. And so we started looking into homeschooling opportunities, and that's what we decided. He was able to skip seventh grade by doing homeschool because the homeschool program we got into, they put them in their grades based on their abilities. But when he was in public schools, he was in all advanced classes. He was always a very good student, and so he was able to skip a grade, actually. Skipped seventh grade and went right into eight. But yeah, we homeschooled, and it worked for him. He was very diligent. But, you know, that again depends on the kid. Not every kid is meant to homeschool.

It's a great option. The CHSPE is as good as a GED or high school diploma, and the thing about it is, if they ever take any college courses, they never get asked about their high school again anyhow. They have college on their résumé. Jordan considered the CHSPE, but he was able to skip another grade later. And his last two years of high school, he actually did online college courses.

So by the time he was eighteen—he stayed in school so that he could get his high school diploma—he had his high school diploma and two years of online college courses.

But it's not for every child. It's just not. You have to have a very driven, self-motivated child to do the homeschool route, for sure.

A lot of people are like, "Don't you want him to go to college?" So we talked about it, and, yes, I did want him to go to college, and, yes, he does have two years of online courses. For me, it was more about wanting him to have the college experience—the being on campus, that education experience—rather than...you know...well...middle school is the last time he was in a school setting. But he said he might do that one day. But why would I want him to quit a career to go to college? That's just backwards to me. If he is already established in his career and still progressing and learning and moving forward, it would not be a wise choice to stop that to go get an education so you could get a job.

Not only that, but this whole industry and this whole experience and what they learn as far as real-life situations. And this is the college of hard knocks, really, because the education they get in this industry is...there is nothing to compare to it. And it's not only the education. It's the networking opportunities. You know, working with the real deal. You are not getting educated in a classroom; you are getting real-life experience, which to me speaks much louder volumes than sitting in a classroom.

And then, when Jordan was with Red Mountain, I would go in the seminars, and I would talk to the parents about their kids that wanted to get into the industry, and I would say, "You know, the thing about it is if your kid is really passionate about this and this is really something they want to do, then support them. Go for it. But if your kid is not really, really passionate about it and it's not something they want to do and it's something you want to live through them and do, or they are thinking maybe *they like it, this is probably not the right venue for that type of kid." But these kids...You know, Jordan can stand up... since he was ten years old, eleven years old, from his experience as an actor, he could stand up in front of anybody in any room and give any kind of presentation and give any kind of speech, and he could teach classes and tell people—exactly like you and I are talking—from the time he was a child. He could walk in a room full of people, make eye contact, shake hands, "Hi, I'm Jordan Fisher."*

And they're like "OK, then." So even the kids that don't end up really pursuing this as a career, the education and experience they get from taking this path in life is just incredible.

CHAPTER 20

Auditioning

I've talked about auditioning basics, but here we explore the subject with a little more depth. One of the major reasons to be in Los Angeles if your child is pursuing an acting career is being physically available to audition in front of casting directors. If the audition goes well, you'll be called back for another round (called "callbacks"). Flying back and forth from home—wherever home is, if it's not in the LA area—can be expensive and logistically difficult. Major roles typically involve several rounds of callbacks and ultimately chemistry tests, where the final casting choices come down to the exact mix of actors and how they look and feel together. Obviously this can't be done long distance. But the process can start long-distance.

Taped Auditions

Many auditions can be done on tape (digital now) and sent in for consideration. Even people who have relocated to LA have to tape some auditions—if a project is being cast out of New York, for example. So it is good to get proficient with this process.

I'm not a big fan of the taped audition. I personally feel that an actor's energy and charisma are much better communicated live. But I'll never forget talking one day with Kenda Benward, Luke Benward's mom, on the set of *Cloud 9* and discovering that she actually prefers them! Her position was that the downside of a live audition is that you only get one shot at doing a great job whereas in a taped audition, you can take all the time in the world to get a scene exactly the way you want it. This is a terrific example of the truth that there is no "right way" to do anything in this business. Luke in fact had a very successful career from the age of eight to seventeen living in his hometown just outside of Nashville, Tennessee, doing an average of one major movie per year, as well as pilots and other projects. The family finally moved to Los Angeles the summer he was seventeen, just before Disney cast *Cloud 9*.

Basic requirements for a do-it-yourself taped audition include some kind of camera that can tape digitally, some kind of tripod, and decent lighting control. You'll also need very basic digital-editing software and a way to send a large file.

Many phones now come with a good-enough filming function that they can do the job, but I'd still recommend a little tripod, just so your end result doesn't resemble *The Blair Witch Project*. When we moved to LA, I invested about $300 in a basic little Lumix with a Leica lens and a tripod. I'm sure you can spend less now and get an absolutely decent setup. The tripod is also useful if it's just you and your kid making the tape, as you are likely not only filming them, but also reading the other character's lines on the sides. It's very difficult to read, turn pages, and hold a camera still all at once! So get a tripod. They are not expensive.

A word on lighting: it can be amazing how awful basic home lighting looks on an audition video. Frequently your child is not well enough lit, or there are strong shadows, which can be distracting. Overhead florescent lighting is truly dreadful on film. We ended up using a couple of high-wattage halogens that we could aim toward Dove, and they were pretty good at lighting her well and eliminating shadows.

Finding a good place to tape can be a little challenging. We were living in a small apartment without a single blank wall to shoot against. You definitely want a backdrop that's free of distractions. We tried different things but ultimately ended up hanging a solid bedcover over a bookshelf to create a clean, clutter-free backdrop for most of the auditions we taped. Be creative if necessary.

Most computers come with a basic video-editing software bundle: Microsoft has Movie Maker, and Apple has iMovie. I find that iMovie is much easier to use, but either one can work. Get familiar with whichever one you have. You certainly don't need Final Cut Pro to do this!

OK! You're all set up. Your kid has memorized their lines and is dressed in a simple outfit that is not black or white or with tiny patterns. Maybe it slightly suggests the character they're reading for, but it is not costumey. Their hair is pulled back from their face, and they're well lit. Your camera battery is charged or plugged in, and you are ready to press the record button.

A few last-minute notes: since you are right behind the camera, your voice is going to be louder on tape than theirs unless you deliberately speak more softly. So do that, since you're not the one auditioning! And at the very beginning of each take, have your child "slate." This is where they say their name, sometimes their ages, and the talent agency that represents them. Sometimes the sides will come with more detailed requests for a slate: weight and height are not uncommon. But have your child do this at the beginning of each take so that when the casting director reviews all the auditions that are sent in, they know which one is your fabulous kid!

After you and your child have gotten the take that feels good, download the digital recording to your computer and save it. Do this before deleting anything from the camera. Then open up your software editor and select the take you like best. If you're feeling fancy, you can add simple graphics (your child's name in a title sequence, contact info at the end) or cross-fades between scenes if there is more than one set of sides in the audition. To be honest, we rarely did anything but send in a basic tape with a slate, so if that's all you can manage (and it's midnight on a school night and the tape is due), that is absolutely enough.

You'll discover that sending a large file like a video through your e-mail program is either impossible (the file size can exceed its limit) or can take many hours to upload. Worse, if you succeed in sending the file as an attachment, it may exceed the capacities of the recipient's server. Not good. This is where basic file-transfer software comes in. At the time of this writing, Wetransfer.com, Hightail.com (formerly YouSendIt.com), and DropBox.com are all good free sites that can help you send large files over the Internet. They're simple to use, and all the casting offices are familiar with them. Just follow their directions, upload your video, enter the e-mail address of the recipients, and press SEND. Done.

Callbacks, Chemistry Reads, and Screen Tests

Any day an actor gets a callback is a great day. If your child gets callbacks consistently, you know they are on the right track. A callback does not mean they have the role yet, but it does mean that the casting director liked what they did and wants another look at them.

Sometimes the news that your kid got a callback comes right away—even as quickly as the same day as the audition! More often you'll hear within a few days, and occasionally, depending on the scope of the project and the size of the search, it can be over a month. Often a callback will be in front of more people than the initial audition—the director might be in the room, or some of the executive producers. Or it might be the same people, but possibly new sides. Or all of the above. At any rate, a callback indicates that your child is on a relatively short list for the role, which is exciting.

Unless you are asked otherwise, it's generally a good idea for your kid to wear the same outfit to a callback that they wore for the first audition. This helps jog the memory of the casting director, and the fact that your child was called back means that the casting director probably thought the outfit worked. Some people photograph their kids as they go to auditions or make note of what they're wearing to which one, because if there are a lot of auditions happening and a few weeks go by before a callback, it can be difficult to remember what was worn!

The odds of being given direction in a callback are increased, and these auditions frequently take a little longer in the room. This is good news. The longer your child is in the room, the more the casting director is thinking about them.

Most roles will only go to one or two callbacks, but high-stakes roles like leads can have seemingly endless rounds, which end up in chemistry reads and screen tests. Before joining the Disney family, Dove did *seven* rounds of callbacks for the lead in a one-hour major network drama, including three screen tests. It was agonizing. Essentially there was a disagreement between the creative team and the executive in charge of the show. The writer, director, and executive producers all thought Dove was perfect for the role, even going so far as to rewrite the script to sound more like her and asking her to dye her hair darker. But the executive in charge—who never met her—thought she was too "mature"! After about a month of this, the executive pulled rank and insisted on casting another girl. It was one of the few times Dove actually cried after not getting a role. The loss of something that felt so real at that point was hard. But it was a very good learning experience, and two years later, the director of that show was an executive producer on *Barely Lethal*, a PG-13 movie where Dove was cast as the supporting lead. He remembered that experience as vividly as we did—a good example of how small this town can be and how important it is to get in front of as many casting directors, directors, and producers as possible.

Sometimes, if the chemistry between two or more roles is very important to the project, the casting director will hold chemistry reads, also known as chemistry tests or mix-and-match sessions. The casting director and producers will try different combinations of actors together to see which ones are the most compelling.

If your child has made it this far, congratulations—you know they are down to the final few for consideration. At this point, probably any of the choices would work—the question is now which choices make the most sense together, as well as any other considerations. This stuff is truly subjective and out of the hands of an actor. For example, it may be decided that the heights of the actors don't work together or that they are too similar physically. Even projects that cast "blind" or "non-traditional"—for example, ignoring ethnicity as a factor—will still seek to balance out looks. There is no way to deal with this except to show up and give it your best, knowing that if you aren't the final choice, it was something that was out of your hands.

Knowing how capricious the final casting choice can be makes it less personal, in my eyes. And if your kid is regularly making it to this level and still not getting the role, there are several things to consider. Is there something that they are doing or not doing that may be an issue? Sometimes your agent or manager can talk to the casting director and get feedback. Maybe a little coaching is in order. Or maybe it's just not their time yet. But if they are coming so close so often, you can be reasonably sure that one of these times will be theirs. Dove actually made it to screen tests for five different roles the season she finally got *Bits and Pieces* (which became *Liv and Maddie*). It was a crazy, frustrating season. But each of those experiences made her that much better—more confident, more fluid in a room full of executives and high stakes. And by the time she walked into the conference room on the top floor of the Disney Channel building for that final casting round, she was truly unattached to the outcome. And she got the job.

Screen tests are not always held before casting large roles, and they are never used for smaller roles. Now that pretty much all auditions are digitally taped by casting directors, a screen test is often redundant—every step of the audition has been a screen test! But they are useful when it's impossible for all the decision makers to be in the casting room. And it's important for a final decision on a large role to see how the actor looks on film. Interestingly, some people come to life on film while others seem to disappear. Finally, it can also be important to do a screen test if the actor needs to transform their look very much so the director and producers can see how the new look works. Most screen tests are done in simple casting offices, but some are done in wardrobe on a soundstage. In general, though, they are not as exciting as they sound.

If auditions are the primary activity for an actor, then rejection is the primary experience of this business. It's hard on anyone to feel rejected, but it can be especially hard for kids, who just haven't been around long enough to have much perspective. There will always be another role, another audition. And frequently, when you look back, it seems like everything happens for a reason.

Finally, you should be aware that the audition process actually is something you are part of, whether you know it or not. One of the considerations in the final choice of a kid for a role is their parent. Are you pleasant and easy to have around? Are you high maintenance? Do you complain a lot or make more demands than average? Are you generally positive or negative in your conversations? How you conduct yourself in the lobby of a casting office is noted, and how you manage yourself and your kid on set is too, and you will develop your own reputation after some time goes by. Make sure it's a good one!

Tips and Takeaways

- Basic setup for a taped audition need not be expensive. You need a camera or phone with video capability, tripod, decent lighting and a plain backdrop (a wall/ solid curtains, etc.) basic editing software, and simple file-transfer software (often free).
- Kids who consistently get into the final round for a role are clearly doing things right. But if your child consistently gets that close and never books, you might look into some coaching.
- Parents are definitely part of the casting considerations for important roles, so make sure your actions and reputation are positive!

CHAPTER 21

Spotlight Interview with Bonnie Zane

Casting Director, Principal at Zane Pillsbury Casting

Bonnie Wallace: *You're obviously an incredibly successful casting director. Did you always know you wanted to do this? How did you get started?*

Bonnie Zane: *No, I didn't. I moved to LA thinking I'd be a writer, but that was in the eighties. That never took off. I ended up working on music videos, back in the days when they actually made music videos. I then segued into casting when my sister got me into it. My sister's a casting director.*

She saw my natural knack for it because I would always want to help her out when she was doing projects. She suggested I try it out. There was a casting office that was looking for part-time help. I took a three-week job answering their phones and stayed for three years.

Bonnie Wallace: *Wow.*

Bonnie Zane: *Eventually I ended up leaving them to form my own company.*

Bonnie Wallace: *Inevitably you cast all ages as a casting director. Of course, I'm writing a book about parents and kids. What do you look for when a kid comes in to audition for you? What are you hoping to find?*

Bonnie Zane: *You're hoping to find the most natural actors. I just finished a project where I had a family—I went for the most natural, with the kids. It was a comedy.*

The little girl that we ended up casting came straight off a heavy, heavy drama. She's glorious because she's natural and she's talented, but she didn't come from the world of big live comedy at Disney and Nickelodeon.

Bonnie Wallace: *When do you feel like you know that you've found the right young actor for a role? How do you know?*

Bonnie Zane: *There have been a few times where I was casting kids, and it's just so apparent in the room. They're so natural; they're so charismatic. It's so effortless. You don't see them having to turn it on or off.*

So much of casting is gut feeling, and I think that's a big part of it right there. It's the kids that are the most natural. You know what it is, too? With little ones, I'll often give direction just for the sake of giving direction—to see if they can take direction. It was an interesting conversation I was having with my assistant while we were doing this last project because we're casting five and seven-year-old little boys. This one kid was doing a scene, and he took off his glasses and was cleaning his glasses in the scene.

I thought, "This is such a great character trait. I wonder if he was coached or if it was real." We did it a second time, and he didn't do the glasses. I thought, "See, that's what I'm looking for." When we give kids callbacks, the first note is always "no coaching."

Bonnie Wallace: *My kid was a lot older when we came down here and started doing this. I know that when they are under a certain age, memorizing sides is hard—even reading sides. What do you recommend with the whole sides thing for the younger kids?*

Bonnie Zane: *For the younger kids, it's best to have them memorize the material. It's also best for them to be able to adjust. When you're reading five-year-olds, you're going to have only a few lines. I'll say to them, "Read this like you're angry," just for the sake of variety to see what they can do. Obviously, the younger they are, the less they can read.*

They've got to memorize it anyway. It's the kind of thing where you want them rehearsed but not over-rehearsed for their auditions.

Bonnie Wallace: *Right. What do you wish the kids understood about the casting process? Is there a thing that you run into frequently that if people only understood it better, they would have an easier time?*

Bonnie Zane: *Personally, I want to see an extension of them. A little boy comes in, and his name is John. I say, "OK, I want you to be like John. I'm going to be just like your mom. Talk to me the way you talk to your mom," or "Just talk to me the way you talk to your friend or your brother." I don't want them to come in there and put on a show.*

Bonnie Wallace: *Have you ever seen a kid who was not right for a certain role that they came in for, but you then called them back for a completely different project later because you were just like—*

Bonnie Zane: *All the time.*

Bonnie Wallace: *You were keeping track of them?*

Bonnie Zane: *All the time.*

Bonnie Wallace: *How does that work for you?*

Bonnie Zane: *Well, this has just happened to me because I was casting a show in which [the producers] wanted no one that I liked. They picked all the wrong kids, in my opinion. But to me, that meant that all the right kids are still out there. Now I have seen all these kids—all the kids I wanted to cast.*

Many of them tested for my pilot. That's how good they were. I ended up testing three of them for my pilot, and one of them got it.

Bonnie Wallace: *What advice would you give to someone that's starting out? Is there something parents can do to increase their kid's chance of getting cast?*

Bonnie Zane: *In general, I think that parents need to follow their instincts. It has to be the kid's choice. It cannot be the parents' choice. That's a big thing. If a kid really shows interest in wanting to do this, obviously you can't stifle their dreams. But parents should not be doing this for themselves.*

They should let the kids do it for themselves. If they do it, get them in Improv classes. Get them in less traditional classes—not acting for television, but maybe Improv or musical theater or similar things where they can expand themselves and get comfortable. If they're comfortable, they're going to audition well. It's work that gets work.

Bonnie Wallace: *Any hot tips about headshots?*

Bonnie Zane: *You know, with kids it's tricky because you've got to keep them looking like themselves. You probably need to get headshots more often than you do when you're a little bit older.*

Bonnie Wallace: *Is there anything else you'd like to share for parents out there that you wish they knew?*

Bonnie Zane: *I think that it's important that they let the kids drive the career path. If your child is passionate about it, then that's what you need. So often we'd see that the parents are doing this for themselves and not for their children.*

When I see people like you and Ellen [Marano, mother of Laura Marano], who have these girls that are obviously naturally talented, and this is what they're meant to be doing, you guys sit back and watch it happen, as opposed to the ones that are classic stage parents.

It's interesting—the little girl that we hired on my pilot. We found a twelve-year-old girl, a ten-year-old boy, and a six-year-old boy for a Fox pilot. The twelve-year-old girl is a phenomenal actress that came off The Walking Dead. *She is wonderful. She's so mature for twelve. She's thoughtful; she's articulate.*

Her mom is so interesting in that she sits back and lets her daughter drive her career. She doesn't sit on set. She sits back behind the scenes. She's not part of it. Even when we sat at the table and read for the pilot, she didn't stay in the room, even though there were a hundred people in the room. She said, "This is her time. This is her thing." She lets her take the reins on the direction of her career.

The girl was offered a test on our pilot. She was also offered a test on an HBO pilot—it was the producer of Orange Is the New Black. *Obviously, this was a very high profile, cool HBO thing. The mom said to me that the girl read the script, and it didn't make her comfortable: "She feels that even though it's not her character, there's a lot of stuff in the script that made her uncomfortable."*

It made her uncomfortable, so she chose our project, to which she related. [The mom] let the twelve-year-old make a creative decision. Now, look—a six-year-old's not going to make a creative decision, but a six-year-old knows if they don't want to go into an audition or if they'd rather be playing baseball.

You don't want these kids being dragged around or being schlepped off to live in the Oakwood when they'd rather be home, playing soccer with their friends. I've said this all along. It's the ones that want to be doing this that are going to do best.

It's interesting because I talk to parents so much when I'm doing this. For example, you'll have a parent with twins. Obviously, twins are a good market for when they're younger because you get more airtime. But say one twin doesn't want to do it. I say, don't push him. Maybe he could be a photo double, which is always helpful. But don't push one to do it because it's what his twin wants to do.

So often you see the parents that are living some sort of a dream through their kids. You don't want that.

Also, when you go through the process, you do meet the parents and spend a lot of time with the parents. Parents can make or break the auditions, too.

Bonnie Wallace: *I'm so happy you brought that up. Can you speak to that a little more?*

Bonnie Zane: *Who wants to be around a crazy stage mom? All things being equal, if you have three kids that are equally talented, why not go with the person you want to live with for five years?*

Bonnie Wallace: *Yeah. Does that routinely affect choices that you make when it gets down to the last couple of kids?*

Bonnie Zane: *Crazy parents could definitely make or break it, because you also worry about the kids. Kids are more protected now than they were back in the day. But you still worry about the kids.*

Then I look at the little girl that I just worked with, and I said to her, "You had to kill people. It's The Walking Dead. *You had to watch yourself die. You're shooting people in the head."*

She said, "Yeah, but you know what? We work with a stunt man, and a special-effects guy. Nothing really affects us because it's kind of fun." The second the cameras aren't rolling, these people are not zombies anymore. The kids are anesthetized to it.

Bonnie Wallace: *Yeah, and we're having lunch together after that.*

Bonnie Zane: *And we're all going to craft services together. The kids are not going to be method at age ten.*

There are some kids just born with it. There are some kids that you just know that's what they're going to be doing.

Bonnie Wallace: *What kills an audition? What should kids just not do that they do a lot?*

Bonnie Zane: *When the kids are coming into an initial audition, they need to understand that they're in there to do their job. "Let me tell you jokes. Let me tell you this story. I have three jokes for you." I'll say, "Sorry, we're not doing that right now. There are twenty kids waiting to read, and we're not doing this right now." Now, when it gets closer to them getting the part, then that's what [the producers] are going to want to hear.*

They're going to want to sit down and get the real kid and get a sense of the real kid because you're living with this kid for five years, potentially. You want to ask questions. You want to hear stories. But for the initial part, don't come in and take up time.

Bonnie Wallace: *Any funny stories about casting kids?*

Bonnie Zane: *I think there have been times where I found kids and have just been blown away by them. When I know in my gut that it's going to be this kid.*

I remember I was doing a pilot, and there was a kid that I had not met before. He was about ten. His parents are both comedians. I actually knew them separately, but I didn't know that this was their kid because his manager brought him to us to audition. I had no idea who his parents were.

I first read this kid, and then we had him chemistry read with the two actors playing the parents. He was amazing. He's still amazing. I've hired him a few times since. When he left the room, the actors looked at me and said, "Are you kidding me? Where did you find this kid?" My producer said, "There's no way there's anyone but this kid."

We brought him to the network, and they also asked, "Where did you find this kid?" This kid was great. They basically wanted to give him his own show. When we got to the testing stage, and his parents walk in, I said, "What's going on? You're his mom? You're his dad?" I had known them for years. It was crazy. I had no idea that was their kid. The parents told me, "This is his choice. This is what he wanted to do. His manager picks him up at school and drives him around."

I love this. I love when it just feels so right, when you have this feeling that it all comes together. That's always, in any role—kids and adults—when you just know. That's the rewarding part of the job.

Something else that we should add is that kids need to go into this business as an art, as a craft. They should not go into it with only the hope of being famous.

Fame for the sake of fame is just BS. There are the Kardashians and all that stuff. To me, that's why I think reality TV, in general, feels like the downfall of civilization.

I feel that kids go into this now just for the sake of fame. What does that mean? You're famous because you take your top off on Girls Gone Wild, *or you're famous because you gave an amazing performance in a film or show. What's the difference? There's a huge difference.*

CHAPTER 22

Stories: Auditioning

Hollywood Parents Share Stories about the Audition Process

Victor Boyce

Honestly, the audition process wasn't really fun, especially the very first one, because we had no idea what to do. I'll never forget. We went in, they took him, and...First of all, as a parent you think you are supposed to go with your kid, but you don't, so right away I said, "What? I can't go in?" It was really weird. So they take him behind some curtain. They take a picture, he comes out, and I'm like, "That's it?"

Took off work, parked, drove around, had to find a place—all that drama, and then it would have ended up like that. And nothing happened, and so this goes on. Eventually you get used to that, but you are wondering, "What am I doing this for?" So the audition process, until you actually book something, is not very fun. But like I said, that first job was so much fun and so good in every way, including financially. It paid well, they fed us like kings, it was fun, and he ended up on all the pages [of the catalog], which is probably not typical, but it was very, very rewarding and great. And that's what got us saying, "Wow! This is great. We want to do this now." So that was extremely fun. So if you get into your mind that the auditions aren't necessarily fun but they are necessary, then I think that would ease parents into it a little better. But if you go in thinking auditioning is fun and great, honestly it's not.

It's not terrible. But it's not fun. Especially since I didn't have anybody in my ear saying, "Well, this is what you should expect," or anything, so I was just completely green. That was the thing. If I had somebody who could have told me, "Expect this..." But no. No one ever told me anything, so I was completely confused half the time. Even just signing in.

It was a trip, but the bottom line is, after a while I kind of became an audition expert. But we still didn't book anything. I knew how to park and keep the meter and not park in a tow-away zone. You tend to get sent to the same casting agencies, and, you know: "I can't park here after certain time" or "It's impossible for us to park. We'll walk and make time."

I watched people's cars get towed away in front of the 333 Library. You learn all those ins and outs, and then you still haven't booked anything. Then that's a whole other learning process with paperwork and all that stuff. I think that if someone were to have given me a little heads-up about what to expect, that would have really helped.

Clark Trainor

The first thing is, not every show is going for an award. It's show business. A lot of times...because a lot of people move to this town, and they think, "Yeah, it's all about the perfect performance," and everything like that. And sometimes it is. OK. If it is an artsy film that wants to go the awards route, then, yes, that's probably entirely what the focus is. But the overwhelming majority of product in this town is product.

It's entertainment product. They want someone who's going to show up on time, know their lines, get the shot in two or three takes, not be a problem when they are not working, not be running around the lot, and security is calling over saying, "This kid stole a golf cart." I mean, they just want to get the shot and stay on time and come in on budget.

Because it's show business. That's the first thing. The second thing, I don't care what casting associates or casting directors tell you—be off book.

Be off book. I don't care if your acting coach lets everyone take their sides out during the scene and read. You need to be the exception. Don't be the rule; be the exception. One of the biggest compliments I used to get with Tenzing is that—when we were doing the auditions, before this booked and everything—is that he listens so well. And I've always told Tenzing, "acting" is the worst thing you can call it. There is no acting because acting is fake. There's only reacting. I even tell Tenzing, "You are not an actor. You are a reactor."

Now, how do you react? You can't react unless you hear. You can't hear unless you truly listen. So your job in the scene is to listen to your scene partner and make your scene partner look good, not yourself.

But don't worry, because your scene partner's job is to make you look good. So at the end of the day, you both look good if you're both doing your job. But it's all about listening, and that's one of the biggest compliments I get. But, to close the circle, the only way you can listen is if you are not searching for your next line in the script—if you are off book.

And early on we would have arguments. I'm like, "You are not walking in."

(Tenzing):"I'm going to blow the audition."

There were a couple of days where I said, "Fine. Blow the audition, for two reasons. First off, I want you to learn your lesson. And second off, I want you to realize that there is no theater police. If you blow the audition, no one is going to come and arrest you. No one is going to hold you for contempt of court. Your patient's not going to die. You'll live, so you need to learn that there's consequences."

Pat Fisher

You know, in the early days of their career, before they are known in the industry, you don't have the luxury of putting them on tape and the casting directors and agents and people already knowing them. You're green. Nobody knows you. If you're going to audition, you've got to be in the room.

Well, you know, my take on that is, when a kid auditions on tape, the only thing the casting director gets to see is the audition. They don't get to see the sparkle in their eyes, the step when they walk, the smile on their face, the enthusiasm in their personality. All they see is the audition. They don't really get to see the kid.

And our trips just kind of started getting a little longer. You know, the first time was five weeks, the second time was probably two months, and the third time was probably three months. Needless to say, I had to take a different career path.

And then eventually sometimes we would come out for a week. You know, just come out and do an audition. And once the casting directors got to know him, he could do the first take on tape, and then sometimes the second take on tape. And then by the time of course it got to producers, he would have to come out and go into the room. But you save a lot of time and a lot of money when you get to the point that they'll even call him up or call his agent up and say, "Just have Jordan go on tape for this particular role." And then if they are interested, a couple of steps down the road, then you fly out.

But once we got to that point, we appreciated it. What, he can go on tape? We don't have to go the airport? We don't have to fly? I think it was about the second time out, we decided that every time we booked a return flight, he got a callback. One time we were actually on our layover and I checked messages, and he had gotten a callback. And that was really the only time we didn't go to the callback. We were like, "We are midstream." But many, many times we changed our return flights, to the point that we just started buying one-way tickets. Because it just was more efficient.

Allison Zuehlsdorff

We do have to drive up on almost all of them—I'd say ninety-five percent—and so we do. That's just part of what we've decided. But we do a lot of talking. We listen to books on tape. We listen to lots of music and share the things we love musically. iTunes is wonderful because I say, "Oh, buy this song," and she buys it for me, and then we take turns and we listen to each other's music.

We find it fun to work on an audition and then wait for it to see if it comes true for her. It's a fun cycle of getting an audition, digging into it, auditioning, waiting, and hearing something good sometimes. It's just a fun, creative cycle that we enjoy, and you have to enjoy that part of it. It comes with pain, too, because there's disappointment and endless waiting.

You've got to know that there are going to be those rebuilding times until you get to a high level, and you have to be able to be OK with it. You have to know that your life isn't the entertainment business—your life is your life. If you didn't do this, there are many other things you could do. Cozi...I love what she's come up with on her own. When people say, "Well, what's your fallback?" and she says, "I think we all should have more than one passion in our lives, so we don't call it a fallback. We'd say these are the things I enjoy doing."

And to really always work on the off times, to work on your craft. If you sing, work on your singing, work on your music, work on all your tools so that you are really never not working—you're just not being paid for it that moment.

I think some people get into trouble with substance abuse because they're trying to fill some hole that they didn't even know was there until they were done working and they didn't have other things to fill their lives.

One more thing that I wanted to share. Since it is almost a two-hour drive to and from auditions, she and I made a deal when she was just starting out. Out of respect for me taking the time to drive her to an audition, when we got back into the car and she had had time to process, she would tell me about the audition. That's the way we shared the experience. We actually became a really good team and ended up having tons of joyful, stressful, sad, and funny times over the years.

Kenda Benward

I will say this—it wasn't always easy because Luke was a very active child. And any kid would much rather be outside playing than learning lines and taping. It's not fun. It's really not. I don't care how much you love acting or how much you love being in television and film. Or plays, or whatever it is. It's just not fun to have to go through that entire process and most of the time be rejected.

They have to really want it. Or you have to kind of say, "OK, listen. You don't have to do this. You're a kid. If you want to go outside and play and kick the ball around for the next few hours, go do that. Go. Go have fun. Go do that. But what you're telling me is that you want to do this. So if you want to play soccer on a soccer team, can you just go out and play in the game without practicing? Of course not."

And it's the same thing with acting. You don't get to play in the game, which is the television show or the film or the commercial. You don't get to play in that game until you practice. And it just goes hand in hand.

And so, once he kind of got that in his brain, he thought, "OK, I guess as long as I want to do movies, I've got to do the prep stuff—the auditions and all that. It really helped put it in perspective for him. Then he was like, "Yeah." Any day, if he said, "I don't want to do this," then it wouldn't have just been for one audition. Because he has to realize that when you have an agent that works for you, you have an office full of people. That that is their job. That's how they're paying their mortgage. They're paying their bills by representing talent.

So your job as talent is to audition when they get you auditions—is to prepare and to go on those auditions. So I told him, "Listen, if you don't want to do this, no problem. Don't do it. But if you say you're going to do it, then you need to realize that there is a team of people that believe in you. And you can't just pick and choose when you feel like doing them and when you don't."

He auditioned from A to Z. It was just whatever came to us from the agency if we felt like it was appropriate for our son to do.

Every family has their own boundary lines. Everyone has their own set of rules as to what they will and won't do. And as a family, you need to discuss that before you move into this business. Because there are lines that some people will cross that other people won't. And you've got to know what that is. You've got to know what it is for you, what it is for your child. And it's OK to say no.

Luke would get auditions all the time. And I would say he would say yes probably seventy-five percent of the time. But he would say no twenty-five percent of the time. And it didn't mean his agent got mad at him. Never. Not one time did his agent get mad at him. He would say, "No problem. Let's move on." And no agent that is in this town that is a professional and that has your child's best interests at heart is going to insist that they do something that is out of their comfort zone. That is our experience.

For Luke, I believe it's been consistently steady in his career. Like you said, he's had one major project a year. Now that he's gotten older and kind of through the awkward stage of—yes, he had bad acne, and he was too tall for his age.

Kenda Benward on Taping Auditions

Taping auditions for us became an art form. We really got efficient at it, got the lighting down. We had the backdrop right. We were knocking them out.

Nowadays, even if you're in LA, you tape auditions. It's crazy. The casting studio can be twenty minutes from your house, but you're taping the audition and e-mailing it to them. The reason why I began to get a little more high-tech with my audition tapes was because I wanted them to be watched. And I really felt like being so far away, being two thousand miles away in Tennessee and sending these tapes in, they needed to look great. And they needed to fit the specifications of what were required. We needed to be shooting chest up. We needed to have great lighting; we needed to have a solid backdrop. The audio needed to be clear, and there needed to be no distraction around them. You needed to have someone that knew how to read off camera.

And those things were really important. You have to understand, these casting directors get thousands of audition tapes for maybe five roles. Thousands. And what's going to set yours apart? What is going to make them go, "Oh, yeah, I'm going to watch that," or "I'm not going to be watching that"?

I don't know if these facts are exactly correct, but I was in an acting class one time. And this was recently, like a year ago. The acting teacher was talking about the competition here in Los Angeles. And how much competition you are really up against when you go out for a role. And if I'm remembering the numbers correctly, I believe he said, "Say there's two pilots casting and there's twenty-two roles between the pilots. If the breakdown goes out on a Friday afternoon and the casting studio is receiving submissions by Monday morning, for twenty-two roles—getting submissions from A-list agencies, B-list agencies, managers, and maybe some self-submissions—they're getting close to twenty-six thousand submissions on a Monday morning."

You can't go through it all. And so that's why you need a good agent. They're going to start with the A-list agents. They're going to go to the people they have relationships with. They're going to go to the managers they respect. Those people are going to get those slots first, and they're going to work their way down.

We continued to live in Nashville for the next twelve years after we got agents here in Los Angeles. It was really important for us to keep our kids in a normal school environment with the community that they had been raised in. With their church friends, with their school friends, their neighborhood friends. We wanted them to be well rounded.

Luke actually ended up acting more as an extracurricular activity than a full-time hobby. Or a job, even. He was playing football; he was dancing on a hip-hop team. He was doing kid stuff. And then, occasionally, he would book something.

So what that looked like for us was we went back to Nashville, and Mitchell Gossett was willing to work with Luke. So he would send us e-mails with sides. And we would put things on tape. And back then, it was VHS.

So I literally made my kitchen my studio. I had a bay window, right? Necessity breeds invention. So I just used what I had. I had a bay window. And I would move my kitchen table out of the kitchen. I took the picture off the wall. And I would use that natural light until I realized one day, I had to shoot at nighttime.

So then I went to Home Depot, and I got one of those utility lights. I used that for a while, until I realized that it really blew them out, their face. It made it so bright. I thought, "Maybe that's not working." So then I went and bought a lighting set, which I think was maybe sixty dollars. I was just using a regular camcorder.

Not a big investment at all. It was maybe two hundred dollars with the camcorder and the light. But back then, I was taping the audition, converting it to VHS. And then I had to do VHS to VHS to edit it down. It was just ridiculous. Then I had to overnight it for forty dollars.

It's a lot cheaper than a plane ticket, and it's a lot cheaper than renting in Los Angeles.

CHAPTER 23

Pilot Season and Episodic Season

Just a few years ago, flocks of parents and their kids would come into LA for pilot season. They'd arrive in January and stay through April, the time of year when most TV networks cast and produced the test pilot, or initial episode, of a TV show. Most networks produce a pilot for a new show to run through test audiences before they commit to ordering more episodes. The fact that most new shows traditionally began airing in the fall meant that early spring was the right time to begin that process, and thus pilot season, a flurry of auditions and opportunity, was born.

But changes in technology, platforms, and viewing habits have led to changes in pilot season as well. Now many cable networks start new shows at any time of year, and emerging platforms like Netflix and Amazon are adding to this season-blind trend. Pilots are made whenever a green light is given for a new show. Pilot season still exists, but it is more diluted. Fox made news by declaring recently that it is abolishing pilot season altogether (though not pilots).

Getting cast in a pilot can be like catching the gold ring if the pilot is picked up, and this is why everyone wants to be in a pilot. Your odds of having a regular role in a series are good, though certainly not guaranteed, if you are in the initial pilot episode. But in fact most pilots are *not* picked up and never see a second episode. An actor in a project Dove was in told me he had been cast in thirteen pilots over the years, not one of which had made it to series. And even if a pilot does make it, sometimes characters are dropped, actors are replaced, and considerable changes are made.

Liv and Maddie is a great example of what can happen to a show between the initial pilot and the final product. Initially called *Bits and Pieces* and conceived as a blended family (think *Brady Bunch*) with four kids, it was structured in linked vignettes and did not have the typical storyline arc of traditional shows. The creators thought it would make sense to a generation raised on YouTube. But the concept didn't translate in testing. Audiences didn't get it. However, they did like the chemistry between the actors, and they especially liked what Dove was doing with her character, Alanna, who was very much like Liv in some ways.

So the creative team went back to the drawing board and reworked the concept, adding a twins theme and bringing back a more familiar story structure. Sadly, adding a twin meant dropping one of the original actors. It was thought that five kids were just too many. Our joy in hearing that the show was picked up was dampened by knowing that one of the original cast members was not going to be moving forward with the project. While difficult emotionally, this is not uncommon, and it serves as a reminder of how frequently decisions are made that have nothing to do with a young actor's talent. Rather, they are made for structural reasons. They feel personal but in fact are not.

Episodic season, the flip side in many ways to pilot season, is (very) roughly August through November, and its edges are similarly dissolving. This is the season when most costars, guest stars, and recurring characters are cast for the pilots that made it through testing and for ongoing shows.

If you think about it, an actor who is looking to get started in the business—whether a child actor or not—is much more likely to be cast during episodic season. Why? It is incredibly unlikely that a network would risk banking on a newcomer with few to no credits for a major role. It's just too risky. Episodics are an opportunity to get that experience, begin racking up guest star and recurring roles, and lay the track for that coveted larger role down the line. They can get you a legitimate page on IMDb. They are also a great way for your kid to get the experience they need to be up to the task of carrying a larger role later. If you are considering coming to LA for just a season to give your child a shot at getting cast in a TV show, I would consider aiming for fall instead of spring.

Of course this entire conversation about seasons only applies to television. Film is seasonless. And as time goes by, television is going that way too. Just about the only two months when little is happening in Los Angeles casting offices are July and December, when too many decision makers are on vacation!

Tips and Takeaways

- Pilot season is traditionally January through April, though that is becoming less relevant as pilots are increasingly cast year-round.
- An unknown actor with little experience is much more likely to be cast as a costar or guest star during episodic season, which is traditionally August through November, though like pilot season, increasingly year-round.
- Pilot season and episodic season are relevant for television only; film casting is entirely seasonless.

CHAPTER 24

Stories: Pilot Season

Hollywood Parents Share Stories about Pilot Season

Pam McCartan

Our situation was a little different than some, I think, in that I had two kids. Alison was actually discovered in a shopping mall. And I know we've all heard this story before, but in this case it was kind of a success story in that we were told that there was an audition at the Mall of America—that's where we were shopping—and that if she came to this particular area and performed, they would either yea or nay on her, but that she had this look and they wanted it. And at first we thought it was a little crazy, but we decided to do it. And Ryan really wanted to do it, too, even though he wasn't the person spotted.

She was twelve and had just come off of a show, and she ended up getting up there and singing "Tomorrow" from Annie. *And they loved her. And then Ryan sang something from* Oliver, *and they ended up giving us these cards and told us to come back to their agency and visit with them, and so we did. Anyway, as it turned out, there was a big competition—and I believe that it still exists today—called IMTA, International Model and Talent Association, I think.*

It was something that we chose to do for Alison but felt that Ryan was too young at the time. It was a week long, in New York

City; it was basically a competition in a lot of different categories—modeling, commercial, film, and television stuff. We participated. We had to raise some money to do it—we went through a whole little training program with our agency to get us ready, and it was parent and child along with twenty other kids and young adults. Like I said, Alison was twelve when we went through the training and when she competed that summer, and she actually ended up the recipient of a scholarship at the Young Actors Space in Los Angeles for the following spring—at the same time as pilot season—with representation.

She also had won I'm Ready for Your Close-Up, and she had won several other awards. So then we didn't know if we were going to do it or not do it. Because the scholarship was a scholarship, but we were still going to have to come out here and pay for lodging and all sorts of expenses.

We didn't know a ton about pilot season, but we had learned about it. And this woman from Hollywood, she gave out one scholarship, and there were thousands of kids participating. And Alison won it.

So we were really giving some serious thought to this. That summer, just literally two weeks after we had gotten back from New York, Ryan was called to our local casting director's office to be taped for a show—something about dogs, it's escaping me—and he ended up a finalist. They thought for sure he was going to go to network on this. Ended up not getting it, but ironically the boy who did looked just like him. And then a couple months later [the same boy] was cast in the Lemony Snicket movie (A Series of Unfortunate Events).

So our casting director in the Twin Cities, along with her associate, Nancy Kramer, were taking kids out for pilot season, and she said, "I don't know if you'd consider this, but he has been so close on a couple of things that were basically just tape. If he went out, what's the chance?"

And I was like, "OK, this is crazy because my daughter is also able to go for this Young Actors Space scholarship. Maybe I should bring them both."

Isn't that crazy? Like the stars were aligning, and they were coming from two very different directions. And so we studied up as best we could on what we were getting ourselves into, where to stay. And we had representation. That is, we came to Los Angeles with representation. Both kids landed in LA with representation, as opposed to other families, who come and have to go through that process. That is foreign to me.

It is always the hardest thing. That's what most parents will say—it's the hardest thing—and we came here with representation.

Alison won the scholarship, and Diane Hardin worked pretty exclusively with her very dear friend, Judy Savage, at the Savage Agency. And Ryan was with Nancy Kramer Management. She had moved out here years before; she had Josh Hartnett and Amy Adams. She was his management company, and she worked with Iris Burton.

And from the minute we got here, we had auditions. And then in the evening, we would go to the Young Actors Space for her scholarship. And then we just enrolled Ryan in some classes, so then he could go through classes, too. And, I mean, at that time I could name kids—AJ and Aly were both there at the same time and in her same class with her.

Alison was up for 13 Going On 30*, and she got sent a lot of things, but enough where that carrot kept dangling. It was like Las Vegas; that's what I always say.*

Because it wasn't the child with desire kicking and screaming to come out here because they really want to be on the Disney Channel. It was kids that had positive affirmations and a lot of acknowledgment, saying, "No, they're good enough that you should really give this a try." Affirmation, positive affirmation.

It went well. It went well in that it was a brand-new experience for us. It was a lot of learning. It was probably more learning than it was anything else. I had two kids auditioning a lot. Alison got called a lot. She would get called two or three times in a day whereas Ryan—fortunately, because it would have been really hard to manage—maybe got called out twice a week. And part of that was just because of who was representing them. That was really interesting to me as well.

Alison was being managed by Diane Hardin, and her agency was the Savage Agency. And they had an amazing reputation, and they called her out a lot. Ryan was being managed by Nancy Kremer Management and Iris Burton, who is now deceased. And Iris had a reputation. She had some big, big stars, as I'm sure the Savage Agency did, but it was a little bigger, whereas…I think, to be honest, I don't even know at this point how big Iris Burton's agency was, but she had some pretty special people. And she was more…I felt as though for Ryan they were more particular about wanting him out on big projects—specific projects—whereas Alison went out on everything: commercials, theater, movies, TV. They were looking for bigger projects with Ryan. And interestingly enough, they both had great callback rates. They both got really close.

We were only going to be there for twelve weeks. We ended up there four and a half months, to be exact. My husband came back twice to get us, and twice we sent him back. Because he would come, and then she would have an audition or he would have an audition, and then it was like, "Well, callbacks are next Monday, and we were going to leave that Friday." And then that Monday we would get the callback. And so that would keep us another…I always used to talk about it like it was Las Vegas. You put that in and then you win a little, and so you want to keep putting in your quarters because you just never know. And that's how it felt. It became a little bit addictive.

Alison had just turned thirteen, and Ryan was nine. Ryan met Kevin Spacey for a final callback for Beyond the Sea, *and Alison was up for a Gateway national commercial that was huge. It was about which girl with brown hair. It was down to two girls with brown hair, to match the family that they had already hired. I mean, when...you know, when you're that close, it may not happen this time. It may happen next week, so we'll stay another week.*

And in all fairness, we fully intended on coming back the next year. We fully intended. We said, "OK, we got this close. It went well. We learned so much." We felt positive about it. We did not leave saying, "We didn't meet the home run." We left saying, "The home run is still there for us to get." It was a really positive experience.

And to your point about staying at the Oakwood, that was the beauty of it. I probably learned the most. The kids had a lot of fun in addition to auditioning. I mean, auditioning is the work. That's what you do. You go out, and that's your job. Your job is to audition. But they had a lot of fun, and I had a lot of fun, too. I met some great parents. But for me, one of the nicest things about the Oakwood was that they provided a lot of seminars, and parents could elect to participate. And there were two things that probably stood out to me as really important factors in the decision-making process of who's going to get the job and who's not going to get the job.

Ultimately—you and I have talked about this—ultimately it is the look. It is the look. You have to have talent. I mean, this is the child now—the child has to be talented. The child has to have desire. The child has to have confidence. They have to be determined because you cannot bring them kicking and screaming. But lastly and most importantly, they have to be resilient. Because it is hard to be that person that gets no—when you get so far and then it's no. You have to be able to bounce back, and as a parent you have to be able to bounce back with them. You can't sit and say, "It's not fair. This isn't fair. What were they thinking?" Because when it boils down to their look, there's nothing you can do. This is how they look. The given is already there; the talent is there. All those other things are there. If it's not exactly what they're looking for, you just move on.

"You got so close. Good for you." You need to model, literally, positive behavior for these kids. And it's a big deal.

Finally I said, "We're going to leave. We've set our date. We're leaving. If this callback doesn't come back on Monday with Gateway, then we're leaving." And there were other things hanging out there, and it was just like, "But we have to go." So Monday came. We got in the car and said, "We will be back."

Clark Trainor

Yeah, it just sounds so bad, because I don't mean it to sound like this, but the truth is Tenzing got really hot really quick. When he got that agent, his first audition was for something—I don't even remember what it was. But I remember he goes in…and it's a little nerve-racking as the parent, because you're not allowed in the room, so you don't know what's going on.

It would be nice to at least see the tape, so you're having some idea. Because your kid may be great in one circumstance, but when he's alone in the room and there's a camera and two adults, do they shut down? Do they close up? You don't know, and you don't get to find out. And you don't get any feedback. I remember that first audition, the casting director comes walking out really fast: "You have to get over to the Warner Brothers lot right now. Are you busy? Are you booked? Do you have anything else going?" I'm not making this up just to be funny; I thought Tenzing had said something wrong. I thought something had blurted out accidentally. Yeah, like, "You're in trouble, and you have to go talk to someone."

I'm like, "Well, no. I'm fine on time. I can go."

"OK, you need to go right now. Here's the address."

I finally had to slow him down. I had to say. "Is everything OK? What's going on?"

He said, "Well, I brought you in for this, but they've actually cast a pilot for ABC, and they've closed the casting. They're actually having a director session today, where people are going and meeting with the directors. And they've closed the casting—a couple of weeks ago—but he's got to go in on this, so I made some phone calls."

So then we hopped in the car and we drove over to Warner Brothers, and he met with the director of a pilot. And then he had to come back the next day and read for producers and everything. Then, two days after that, he had to go to the ABC building, the one right over there on Burbank that shares the lot with Disney. That was just crazy, because this was literally his first audition, and three days later we go straight to network.

We walk in, and we walk in to the top floor of ABC for the producer session. It's got high twenty-foot ceilings, and there's a beautiful glass staircase. You feel like you're on the one-yard line in the Super Bowl, and right there is the goal. We look over, and half the cast from Modern Family *was right there. And they'd just won the Emmy. And you're like, "Is this really happening?"*

There were four kids—two had been flown in from New York for this, a local kid, and then Tenzing—going into this producer session. And you have no idea how your kid is going to react. They call them in one by one, and then they come down. They don't just call you in and release you. You're there for hours. It's a whole process.

They're calling you, and then another kid, and then another kid, and then you again. I remember the first time he came back, and I said, because it's all new to us, "What's going on in the room?"

(Tenzing): "Oh, there's just a lot of people in there watching."

I ask myself, "How many suits are in that room?" Because that's what I always called them, whenever we talked about it—"How many suits are in the room?"

He said, "I don't know, probably about twenty four."

I'm just looking at my little ten-year-old son, who is standing in front of twenty-four suits doing this. Obviously hitting it out of the park, because he's one of four kids after a nationwide search, and to this day...

That's the thing, honestly, and this is not lip service. Honestly, as a father, the proudest moment for me is not about my kid being on TV. There have been a lot of kids over the ages that have been on TV. It's seeing that he has the courage to do that. That blew my mind. I mean, as a parent we are going to raise them as best as we can to try to equip them with tools to go out and succeed. The courage to get up and try like that is the greatest gift you can try to give them. My dad used to call it "shovin' and lovin'." And that's what you've got to do.

You love them, but you've got to shove them a little bit. "Go, go, go." And then when that moment comes when they're alone in the room and there are twenty-four suits—forty-eight eyes looking right at them—and they still do it, that's the greatest thing in the world.

One of my favorite films is Defending Your Life. *You ever see* Defending Your Life? *Albert Brooks and Meryl Streep? You have to see that movie. They are trying to get into heaven, and they have to defend their life to show why they deserve to get into heaven. Meryl Streep is a shoo-in. Albert Brooks' character is not. Watch that movie. The entire lesson, the entire key to getting into heaven—which you'll find out in the last five minutes, what it all comes down to—is having the courage to try.*

Pat Fisher

When we came out, we booked a five-day trip just to get some professional headshots done for him, take an acting class with an acting coach out in LA—which is very different than taking an acting class anywhere else—and also to try and find an agent. While we were out here, he auditioned for a pilot, and they really didn't think...I mean, just them even getting him in—being green and his first trip to LA and no contacts—it was just not going to happen.

And they actually were able to get him seen. He got a callback. You know, callbacks don't happen the next day. They happen a week later. So here we are on our five-day journey, first journey out here, and Jordan gets a callback for next week.

We thought, "OK." So we made the decision to stay for the callback, of course. What are you going to do? We were just thrilled to death that he got a first audition, let alone a second.

It went on for five weeks.

Callback after callback after callback. Made it all the way to producers. He made it to the final four for one role and, of course, didn't make it at that point.

Five weeks. But we made good use of that time. You know, prior to coming out here, he had never had an acting class, so we kind of got his feet wet, you know? We did do the headshots, and we did all the preliminary...we got his Coogan account and all his work permits and everything that you need to do when you are out here.

And we just took really good advantage of that time. But, yeah, five weeks. My husband was like, "Are you ever coming home?" At that time Jordan was my only child, which made it a lot easier. When you do have other kids at home, it's a whole nother consideration, which I later learned.

Kim Holt

We didn't really know what to expect. The first thing, we didn't know where to go, and everybody had recommended that we stay at Oakwood. We did stay there. It probably wouldn't have been our first choice. I know there are other places, now that I've been out here to stay, but it is a great place to stay because it's conveniently located. It's furnished. It was kind of crazy. You go, and then you're out here for pilot season, and you wait. You wait for your phone to ring.

If you're just sitting around…I actually was like, "I can't sit still like this. If we are going to be out here, we're going to work this thing." Olivia would do fun things, like going to dance classes, where I would make sure that she kind of stayed busy doing stuff like that.

She never really went to any acting classes. I probably could have put her in some at that point, but I didn't. I wanted her to have more fun stuff, like dancing or singing or something like that. That's kind of what she did while we were waiting to be called. But then I would get online. I think, if I remember correctly, there is Actors Access and Casting Networks. When they weren't calling us, I was actually submitting her myself. I actually spent hours doing that. She actually booked two things off of that—two commercials, of me booking her.

I was really proud of myself. She went out a lot, commercially, because she was at that commercial age. We did not go out a whole lot for TV, but we did go out a lot for film. Olivia loved it. She loved everything about it. When she did start booking these commercials… We were out here for pilot season, but she only booked commercials. She had so much fun. I knew we were in trouble then.

One of the funny things is, when we got back home, she goes, "Mom, how much is it going to cost? How much do we have to pay to do another commercial?" She thought we were paying them to do the commercials. I was just…(laughs)*. Even up until probably about two years ago, she's never even asked how much money she makes, just because she loves it. It's not about the money to her. It's about the fun and how much she loves to entertain.*

When we first moved out here, when Olivia was ten, Olivia met Jordan Fisher. There was a group of kids, and they were all at the Oakwood, and they would hang out together. They actually would go to these dance classes on Friday nights together. I have some pictures of them. They're so cute. It's been fun to watch them grow up and do what they love.

CHAPTER 25

Background Work

Let me start this chapter with the admission that Dove never once went out for a background (or "extras") role. So my experience with this subject comes from seeing extras on sets—both film and TV—talking to them and sometimes their parents, and seeing with my own eyes the reality of those roles.

I'm going to say something here that may be unpopular, but it is my authentic opinion. I do not see much point in doing background work for kids who are looking for a professional career as an actor. At least not more than a few times.

As I wrote in Chapter 4, "Audition Basics," the upside to being an extra is that you can learn basic set vocabulary (and there is a whole specialized language on a set) and see if your child even enjoys being on a set before investing much more time and money in pursuing this career at a higher level. This alone can justify a few days working in background. And for those reasons it might be a great idea.

But after that is behind you—or even before that point—it is essentially a dead-end exercise that will only chew up your time and displace an opportunity for either something better (like a real role or an audition that might lead to one) or even simply school. Taking your kid out of school for a guest star role makes sense. This is something that will actually further their career. Taking them out of school to walk repeatedly back and forth behind the actors who have actual lines or to be in a crowd has very little value. It will do nothing for their career, and, worse, it subtracts precious school days that should be missed for more important reasons.

I think there is a persistent myth that having a lot of background work on a résumé will count for something in an audition. But all it says is that your child knows how to be an extra. Background roles by their very definition have no lines and no real camera time. In other words, they are more about one's ability to follow simple directions—"When I give the signal, walk from the locker through that door"—than any kind of indication that someone can act. So their value on a résumé is really nil. Worse, too much background work may lead to unconscious typecasting of your child as a background player rather than a potential lead. Most actors don't even list background work on their résumé for this reason. It's not a selling point for casting directors.

I also think that there are some persistent apocryphal stories about actors being "discovered" on sets as extras and becoming stars. I believe these kinds of stories are repeated because some part of all of us wants to believe that it might be that easy—like a lucky jackpot. If only it were that easy! Inasmuch as anything is possible, I can believe that it must have happened at some point to someone. But as someone whose kid has beaten tremendous odds and truly knows that almost anything is possible, I'd still not bet on that path. Do something where your child at least has a fighting chance at having their time and effort rewarded.

Pursuing extras work in order to rack up points toward getting into SAG-AFTRA also seems dubious, since any actor cast in a role that requires union membership will simply be Taft-Hartleyed in (instantly granted membership). This feeds into a common assumption that you have to "work your way up" to become a successful actor, which, if you look around at how the system actually works, you can see is not the case at all. No one is watching and noting how many times an actor "paid their dues" doing background work and then granting them a bigger opportunity.

A fairly common reason some people pursue background roles is that they think they might meet the stars of the show or film they work on. Sadly, this is highly unlikely. As I mentioned in an earlier section, leads are literally segregated from extras on sets. This isn't out of meanness, but logistics. Leads have a lot to be on top of: memorizing lines that may be changing even as they film, rehearsals, hair, makeup, wardrobe—even interviews jammed in between scenes. They generally have no time or energy to interact with anyone outside of their immediate work. And since extras don't have lines, they typically don't interact with or even get near the leads. Leads have private dressing rooms, and extras have common holding areas. Background players even eat in separate areas at lunch. Dove makes a deliberate effort, when she is able, to talk with extras on set, but she frequently doesn't have much chance to do it and still stay on top of her own job. Most stars, according to what I have seen and heard, don't even make the effort. Disappointing, but true.

Does the industry depend on the existence of extras to function? Of course it does. Think of any scene in any movie or TV show you've ever watched. All those people filling in the background were paid perhaps $100.00 per day (before deducting a decent percentage of that for agent and possibly manager commissions and of course taxes), so they might keep $7.50 an hour on an eight-hour day if they keep 60 percent of their gross. That's in the ballpark of minimum wage for many states, although meals are provided on set, which counts for something. Am I worried that discouraging you from pursuing background work for your kid (or frankly discouraging anyone serious about an acting career from pursuing background work) will destroy the industry? Not at all. There will always be thousands of people who are willing to do practically anything to get on film, in any capacity. But since this book is written in an effort to help your family navigate the often heartbreaking world of Hollywood and actually succeed, I must share my strongly held opinion that you should just say no to background work, except for a possible time or two for educational purposes.

Tips and Takeaways

- Background work can be educational, and a good way to see if your kid enjoys being on a set.
- Working background for a few days can teach important basics of set terminology.
- Other than the above two positives, there is very little upside to background work. It does not get your child any closer to being cast in speaking roles, and may in fact hold them back.
- Background work should never be listed on a resume, except perhaps under "education." Professionals do not consider it acting, and putting it on a resume is viewed as amateurish.

CHAPTER 26

Stories: Family Dynamics

Hollywood Parents Share Stories about How This Adventure Affected Their Family

Victor Boyce

(Cameron has a younger sister, Maya)

When Jessie came, that changed everything. So Maya basically had a conniption-fit breakdown season one because Cameron was getting so much attention, and in her little mind she was not getting any. Which wasn't true, but I can see her point.

Oh, yeah, totally. I didn't discount her feelings whatsoever, and it was a challenge to get her to understand: "This is something that your brother is doing; it's not something that you're doing. You're doing other things." Because what she was trying to do for a while was trying to be Cameron, so to speak. First of all, she's two and a half years younger, and she's a different gender. No matter what, you're never going to be Cameron, no matter what he is doing, good or bad.

And that was really tough. We've gotten past that, thank goodness, and the way to get past that is to make sure that your other children or your other child is involved and committed into their own endeavor, whatever it is. It's something that's only theirs.

Only theirs. And my daughter's thing is musical theater. Cameron doesn't do theater; he doesn't do anything like that. And Maya has gone from just kind of OK to better and better and better, to now she's doing leads.

So she, in her own little time of doing this, she has gone from "eh" to "I'm the lead, I'm going to voice lessons, I'm going to study my script." You know—she kicks butt.

Legitimately, and it's not candy-coated. She's earned it, which makes a difference.

Because I think what a lot of people do—and not to judge—but people overpraise their children, and they give them praise on things that they don't really deserve. Then when the kid gets out into a real situation where other people aren't their parents and are going to critically judge them, then the kid is crushed because they think, "Oh, Mum thinks I'm great." Well, everybody else thinks you're not so great.

It's really bad. So I've never been one to falsely praise my kids. You know—give them a hug, if they get a boo-boo, kiss the boo-boo—whatever. But when they don't do well, I tell them, "That wasn't that good. That wasn't good." Because if you lie to them, it's worse.

They know. So I never do that—I didn't do that with her; I certainly didn't do that with Cameron. We laugh. There's a video we found with Cameron. He's, like, three, and we had this little plastic basketball hoop, and he went up to do a slam dunk. Now, he did reach it because I had it really low. He does a slam dunk, and it kind of bounces off the rim and kind of goes in. And I said, "Cameron, that wasn't good." And he's, like, three.

Kim Holt

(Olivia has two siblings: an older sister, Morgan, and a younger brother, Cade.)

Olivia is our middle child. She definitely still—as much as she gets, still—has middle-child syndrome. She still thinks that, "What about me? I'm the middle child."

But she has always been my child that has been the busiest. She is an overachiever. They've grown up with her being like that. It doesn't matter what she's been doing in her life, whether it's gymnastics or whatever. She was the one bringing home trophies or doing what she does. That's been since she was little. So it's just been kind of gradually, "Now we're doing something else for Olivia." It's kind of how they looked at it.

My oldest daughter, she is in the business as well, on a different side. She went to college out here. She was out in California before we ever moved out here. We lived in Mississippi, and she wanted to learn how to make movies. She is a writer. She loves acting. She loves theater. She is the one that got Olivia interested in this whole thing, because it was she that had the love for it.

On the flip side of that, I think it was hard for her because it was her passion. It was never Olivia's passion. Olivia just has that gold mojo. Whenever she does something, she does it to the full extent, and she is talented. But Morgan is the one that had the passion for it.

At first, I think it was really difficult for [Morgan] but now she is really proud of her. My oldest just graduated from college. She has moved to the East Coast now. She is doing her own thing. I think that was a tough transition when it first started, but now she is good with it, and they feed off of each other. Olivia can call her for advice if she needs to about anything, even with acting, because Morgan has really a depth of insight into a lot of stuff.

My son, on the other hand, he likes the advantages of it, but he wants nothing to do with this business. He has been asked by Olivia's agents, and they've asked him even here at Disney if he wanted to do anything. It's not his thing. And my clear advice is, "If it's not your thing, don't get involved in it." He loves sports. He loves school. But he loves to hang out here on set. He loves all the kids. When we were on Kickin' It, *they made him a little junior PA, and he would go around with this little mic. He worked background, and they had him doing chores. I loved it.*

When he first started, he was at regular school, and then we put him into the same program Olivia was. We noticed that he really needed that social outlook with the kids his age. It's no big deal what Olivia does, really, to him. I think the main thing is when he is at school, people want to meet her. But he is his own person, which is good. He is just like, "OK. You want to meet my sister? OK, whatever." It's not that big of a deal to him at all.

Pam McCartan

(Ryan has an older sister, Alison, who is a successful stage actress based in New York).

I think, again, it goes back to the kind of person that Alison is. Because I'm going to give her this credit right now: Alison is so passionate. She went to college for four years at Boston Conservatory to study this art, to get her degree. She is so passionate and so focused on her goals to work in New York City, to live in New York City, to thrive in this business, to live paycheck by paycheck, if that's what it's about for her. I give her the credit for being able to say, "Great, I'm thrilled that my brother's got..." She calls him "my famous brother," with a smile and lovingly, "my famous brother." It's to her credit. They're very close.

Allison Zuehlsdorff

(Cozi has an older sister, Lacy.)

She feels really supportive. She really does; that's not just a line. She supports Cozi one hundred percent. I'm sure she has moments, and there are some family sacrifices that come into play, but overall I think she has enjoyed having a sister that is in this business. It's brought a lot of color to our lives.

Clark Trainor

(Tenzing has two younger brothers, Kalden and Yonden)

We take steps so that [the industry] doesn't change our lives too much. You know, when Tenzing's on hiatus, he goes back into public school. He actually goes back into school. And he has his soccer team. He is an adamant soccer player. So he's got to do that. He'll go crazy if he doesn't. So he's got all those friends who are not actors. I'm a big believer that all your friends should not be actors.

I don't mean to insult anyone who thinks otherwise. That's my belief system. All your friends cannot be actors because it's not a real world. It's not how the world functions. In the world, whether it's school or a job, you have to get up at a certain time, and you have to be somewhere. Yes, that's the way it is for actors when they've booked, but when they haven't booked, the rules tend to get a little lax, and I don't know exactly how healthy that is.

So he goes back into public school during the big hiatus between seasons. And he plays soccer, and he has all of that. So we try to keep it as normal as possible.

On Siblings

No, it hasn't been a challenge yet. But I'm sure when they get a little older, they might wake up to what's happening, and they might be interested. You don't know what's going to happen. Just because one kid books doesn't mean all your kids are going to book. This town is full of siblings where only one is working.

And it's really, really hard. I've spoken with parents who have one kid who books all the time, and they have another kid who goes out on lots of auditions and books occasionally. I haven't had to experience that yet because Tenzing's brothers are still at a younger age.

Tenzing's the oldest in the family. So I don't know. I can't really speak to that yet. But what we have always tried to do was to foster their own interests so that they can find what is important to them. I had a college professor who used to say that life's greatest tragedy is not having something to feel important about. He believed that that was why people get into trouble and do things that they shouldn't do or start drinking or whatever. Because they haven't found something to feel important about.

So my wife and I feel that our role is to help all three of them find what it is that they feel important about and foster that. And if we're really lucky, it will be completely different [for each of them].

We are in such a celebrity culture in the United States. We don't have a king and queen, so we take these people who are coming into our houses every day on the TV or film, and we put them...some people put them so high up. I see it on Twitter and Instagram, and it's crazy.

You know, Tenzing's a nice kid, but he is no different than any other kid. He is no different. He got lucky. He landed a great role on a great TV show with a great cast and crew and everything, but he's just a regular kid. [He has a] black belt in Tae Kwon Do, and he's belted in several other forms. He's working on Tang Soo Do now, which was Chuck Norris's form. And he's working up through there.

Pat Fisher

(Jordan has two younger siblings, Cory and Trinity.)

I mean, it's very common to have a houseful of celebrities at my house. You know?

The kids come over, and they eat. And I wake up in the morning, and there are kids crashed on the couch. And I've always been the Kool-Aid mum of the block since my kids were little, so it's really nothing different. And these actor kids are just kids just like anybody else's kids. They're just kids; they are just people.

And the ones that we're around are awesome people. They are great. They are grounded. They have good families, and we hang out with the families, and it's just normal.

It was a little hard for my kids to figure out that they couldn't go to school and talk about Jordan and his friends. It only took one experience. Trinity was actually at a summer camp where Jordan was working—you know, teaching—and she said, "That's my brother."

And she got called a liar: "That's not your brother." And the kid was like, "Well, that's OK, because Will Smith is my dad."

And Trinity didn't know who Will Smith was and didn't care, but it did hurt her feelings. And so she went and got Jordan, and Jordan made everything OK. And all is well that ends well. It was fine, but from that point forward, I said, "You guys can't go to school and talk about the people you hang out with. You know, you just can't."

And so when Jordan would go pick them up from school or something…and other kids see Jordan, and they are like, "Why didn't you tell me Jordan was your brother?"

And they say, "Well, you don't tell me who your brother or sister is. Why should I tell you who mine is, right?" So to them, it's just normal, everyday life. But they definitely like the celebrity opportunities. They like when the limo picks us up to take us somewhere, and they like getting to go the Disney events and things like that. They love riding on his coattails. But other than that, he is just a brother.

Kenda Benward

I have two younger daughters, Gracie and Ella. And they are very supportive of their older brother. But it wasn't always like that.

And I remember specifically when Luke was shooting Because of Winn-Dixie*. That was his first film that he had done with a cast of kids. And any actor knows, any set mom knows that when you are on set for a period of time, the people that you're working with—the crew, the cast, catering, wardrobe, everybody—you guys become a family.*

And if you're working, if you're in a cast with a bunch of kids, those are your best friends. Well, when he was shooting Because of Winn-Dixie*, Gracie and Ella had been at home for the first few weeks. Aaron brought them out later and met us on set.*

By the time they got there, we had bonded. We had bonded with these people. We were family with these people. And I could tell…Ella was a little too young, but I could tell Gracie felt that.

It wasn't that she was being excluded. She just knew she wasn't part of it. But it wasn't because anyone was making her feel that way. She just was feeling that internally. And we had to have a discussion about it. And I said, "Listen, honey, you are going to have experiences that Luke doesn't have. And Luke is going to do things that you're never going to be able to do. But as a family, we show up and we support each other, regardless. If you have a dance recital and it lasts for eight hours, Luke is going to be there."

And he does—he does go. And he has been. And he has sat at so many dance competitions and so many recitals. I can't even tell you. It's actually pretty cute.

And so she realized, "OK, this is Luke's thing. This isn't about me right now. It is about Luke right now, and that's OK. Because we love him, and this is something he's been gifted in. This is an opportunity he has. And we as a family are going to come around him. We're going to give him the love and support he needs to soar right now. And then, when it's not his time—when it's my time—my family is going to do that for me, too."

And even now, Luke is nineteen years old, and he went to Ella's volleyball game yesterday. And he sat there. And some of the girls on the other team would come up and be like, "Does anyone tell you, you look like Luke Benward?"

He goes, "I am *Luke Benward."*

They're like, "Wow."

He goes to her games and supports her. And he'll be at homecoming in three weeks to support Gracie on homecoming court. They're just...they're close. And I'm so thankful for that because I saw in that moment on Because of Winn-Dixie, *when Gracie was feeling left out, that it could have gone bad real quick. And we needed to nip that in the bud.*

There were times where I'd be on set with Luke for two or three weeks. We always made it a point to bring our younger kids out with us on set, or Aaron and I would flip-flop, and he would come on set, and I would go home to be with the girls.

But that was a sacrifice that we made as a family, and our girls did have to make that sacrifice. But at the same time, it was reversed and made the other way as well.

And when you're making a film, it may not seem like it's the same as going to a dance recital. Because one feels so much bigger than the other one. But if you make them a big deal, if you give them the same amount of weight, then it feels like the same amount of weight.

I couldn't look at Luke and the opportunities that he had...I didn't think it was right to say to him, "Well, your sisters can't do this, so you're not going to." That's not fair. That is not right. That would have been poor parenting on my part. So I had to figure out a way that he could do it and everybody could be OK with that.

PART 2

Hollywood Kids 102: Advanced

CHAPTER 27

The Team, and Incorporation

The first two years we spent in LA were in many ways about building the foundation for the career we envisioned for Dove rather than the one she actually had. It can be a good idea to have the team in place before you need it, rather than after. What does her full team look like at this point?

- agent
- manager(s)
- music manager
- lawyer
- business manager
- PR company

That is a *lot* of people! And each of them takes a cut of the paycheck, though each one is worth it. Looking at that list, it becomes apparent why actors frequently get paid what they do—most of it goes straight out to the team, the Coogan account (if they are under eighteen), and taxes! Thankfully, most actors will never need a music manager or a PR company. But even so, can you see why being a stage parent is essentially a full-time job? You are basically the center of a wheel with many spokes. And until and unless you have some of these people on the team, you are essentially performing these roles yourself.

Most of these roles were discussed in chapter 5, "Basic Players." But here we address them with a little more depth, in the context of the team.

Until your child is making regular and significant income—say around $200,000 per year—they should not need a business manager. When you are approaching that point, if you are fortunate enough to—and let's be honest, most actors, child or adult, never do—begin your search by talking to people already on the team, and see whom they recommend. You want someone with a sterling reputation who specializes in entertainment business management, as this is a very specialized field with complex tax rules. Ideally you can find someone who will not only manage your kid's financial assets and taxes but also eventually be able to advise them on investments and career strategies.

A music manager made sense for us because Dove is as much a singer as an actor, and we knew that she would eventually be recording as well as writing and co-writing songs. Music is a very different business from acting, and few regular talent agents or managers are really equipped to deal with it properly. We were very fortunate to find a great one. She has been invaluable in bringing Dove together with experienced songwriters for co-writing sessions as well as finding top-notch producers for her to work with. The question of whether to sign with BMI or ASCAP, if your child is writing or co-writing songs, can be guided by a music manager. Signing with a record label—or deciding to go it on your own—is a high-stakes process you would need a music manager for. Music can be a much rougher business than even the acting world, and it is changing so rapidly that there is little money in it for artists unless their contracts are very carefully written. In fact, it can resemble indentured servitude if you are not careful.

Each time you add a member to the team, you change its dynamics. It is critical that everyone has complete trust and very clear communication. It's amazing to me how frequently the team consults in little phone calls and e-mails. So building the team one member at a time is a process you want to take some time doing. Make sure that the existing team approves and is comfortable with every new team member. They will be working very closely together—hopefully for years—and ideally will be able to step in and take over your role of mission control completely at some point if and when your child continues their acting career into adulthood.

A publicist is another member of the team that is only necessary after a certain point. Don't waste your money thinking that one will catapult your kid to the front of magazine covers before they have the roles or success to warrant that attention. Fame does not make a career—it's the other way around! If your child is getting major roles in film or television and routinely being interviewed and making regular red-carpet appearances, then it may be time to invest in the services of a PR company to help shape their image and get them the kind of press that will support their career growth. Good PR people are like gold. No one knows how to manage an image like they do. But until that time, should it come, save your money.

The best lawyers are more involved with your child's career than merely reviewing contracts at your request. The ideal lawyer works synergistically with the rest of the team to protect and support your kid. We had an experience at one point where our lawyer stepped up and drew a line in the sand for us that we would not have had the courage to do ourselves. It was hard and scary and frankly the right thing to do. Were some good people upset? Yes, unfortunately. It felt awful. But not as awful as watching my child's health and joy compromised because she didn't get the break she needed. And that is why I love this attorney. She fights for the best interests of my kid.

This takes us to the difficult subject of what to do if it becomes apparent that someone on your team is *not* most driven by your child's best interests. Maybe they were originally, and something changed over time. Maybe they got lost as the stakes got more promising. Good people can lose their way and lose their judgment. If everything else feels right and there is simply a question of a single decision or two, then obviously a conversation is in order. Hopefully that will set things straight. But if it becomes a matter of lost trust or if the driver of their decisions has consistently become their own best interests (usually finances or power) rather than your child's, then you will have to fire them from the team.

Firing someone is painful, but not as painful as operating in an environment that is potentially unsafe for your child or that doesn't feel safe for the team. Before you set changes into motion, consult with your lawyer to make sure you are proceeding appropriately in terms of your actions. And know that unless something truly egregious occurred, your child will still typically be paying commissions to their previous agent or manager for some period of time—usually until the money stops coming in for any projects that team member was around for at inception. And that can be quite a while in some cases!

Since firing someone from the team is so difficult—emotionally as well as financially—it makes all the more sense to proceed slowly and thoughtfully as you build your child's team. Listen to your gut instinct, but go beyond that: ask everyone you know what they feel or have heard about someone you are considering bringing on to represent your child. Don't be swayed by a big name or a flashy office. Most of all, be sure that every person on the team feels comfortable with your choice, starting with your child. Ultimately, the results belong to them.

In a different but related vein, if your child is fortunate enough to build a very successful career, they can begin to receive the attention of competing agents or managers who want to poach them. It can be flattering to receive the attention of big-name reps and tempting to move to a "big-time" agency or management house. But frequently these moves result in your child being represented by someone who may not be as passionate about them, and they can get lost in the shuffle of a very big agency. These are difficult decisions that can affect your child's career and the quality of your lives for a long time, so think carefully before making changes. And if a change is necessary, act with the advice of your lawyer, and be as professional as possible.

Incorporation

Incorporation is another issue that will only come up after your child gets to a certain level of success, if they are fortunate enough to do so. But sometimes you have to move quickly, so it's good to understand the basics ahead of time. We had been told that the point at which an actor was bringing in a gross of perhaps $200,000 per year was the time when incorporating (creating a corporation, also commonly called a loan-out corporation) for tax purposes was advised. Dove was making nothing like that, so we weren't paying much attention to the question. However, in a completely random conversation, we discovered—the week before she signed her contract for *Liv and Maddie*—that whatever your child's legal status is at the time of signing a contract is the status they will have for the duration of that agreement. In other words, if Dove was not incorporated on the day she signed a contract that might last three years or more, she would be taxed at the personal rate rather than the corporate rate for that entire length of time.

For a kid making less than you might think to begin with and seeing much of her money go straight out to her team and taxes after that, this would have been financially disastrous. We jumped fast and with the help of her lawyer and brand-new business manager, expedited the process and got everything set up within the week. It was nerve-racking. So be aware that even if your child is not yet making the kind of income that would warrant incorporation, if they are about to sign a contract that will eventually get them to that place, you need to have them incorporate before that contract is signed, not after.

Tips and Takeaways

- A strong team is critical to a young actor's success.

- Add members to your child's team slowly and carefully. The whole team works together closely and each member must be comfortable with the others.
- It is much easier to hire than to fire—one more reason to be very careful with the people you choose to represent your kid.
- Be aware that incorporating your child (creating a corporation for them) is not necessary until they are making around $200,000 per year, but that it can be critical to make that move before a contract is signed that puts them into that bracket.

CHAPTER 28

Set Etiquette and the Set Experience

Where do I even start with the subject of set etiquette? From the moment you step onto a set until long after you leave, your behavior, as well as your child's behavior, affects every person on that set. Sets are like little worlds of their own, and they have a delicate ecosystem. If you are fortunate, you will primarily be on sets that are run by good-natured and strong leaders. If you are unfortunate, you can find yourself on a set run by someone who is impatient and immature. Worst of all might be the sets where it appears that no one is in charge. These sets can be dangerous, because in the vacuum of leadership, things get unpredictable. The people at the top—the director and the star—generally determine the tone of a set. Executive producers come right behind them. From there, most people will follow the lead for attitude and behavior.

We have been largely very fortunate in our set experiences. But whatever the tone of a set you step onto, you can make a difference for everyone by what you do. Stay positive in every interaction. Everyone on a set is working very hard and is frequently under some amount of pressure. There may be a hierarchy on set (and there is), but every single person there performs a critical part of the whole. No one is unimportant. And no one should be treated as though they are. You are also providing a direct example to your child for professional behavior. Be unfailingly gracious to every person you encounter, and they will pick that up. Make sure your child arrives before their call time and arrives prepared.

As in all relationships, first impressions count for a lot, and you don't always know what you are walking into. Relationships on sets can go back years and have many layers. Assume that you know absolutely nothing about everyone you meet, and do your best to suspend expectations of all kinds. Remember that everyone is there to work, not to become friends. Genuine lifelong friendships are born on sets every day; just don't assume that any one particular experience will bring that. That way, you can be pleasantly surprised when it does and avoid disappointment when it doesn't. This is also a good thing to remind your child.

If your child has a decent-sized role in either a film or a TV show, odds are they will be invited to the "table read" before filming begins. This is where the actors literally sit around a large table and read the script out loud. This gives the writers, director, and producers a feel for how the script is sounding while there is still time to make changes. It also gives the actors a chance to get a sense of the dynamics and arc of that script, which is helpful because it will invariably be shot out of sequence. As always, aim to be at least fifteen minutes early. Parking can be confusing, and gates can be backed up while the guards check everyone's ID. Some lots are huge and resemble small towns. Getting to the lot is one thing, but getting to the room where they are holding the table read may be something else!

A note about dress: people tend to dress casually on sets. Everyone is working hard, conditions can be less than pristine, and temperatures can vary wildly. During rehearsal days on the *Liv and Maddie* set, the air conditioning makes it so cold that many of us wear Uggs and down jackets—even when it is ninety-five degrees outside! Shooting days typically begin frigid because the AC has been on, but since it must be turned off during shooting and the lights are so warm, the temperature rises steadily during the day until it can be incredibly hot in the afternoon and evening. Dressing casually for comfort is the standard. Bring layers!

Also bring books, games, and whatever activities you and your child might find useful in dealing with what are generally very long days with a lot of waiting and downtime. iPads can be great. Sets can be incredibly boring places, and a child that is especially young will need help in staying focused while they wait to be called. Snacks are a good idea. Even though Craft Services should have you pretty covered for food, you may not always be able to get to it when your child is suddenly hungry, or they may have special dietary needs. And bring schoolbooks and assignments if your child will be working with a set teacher.

What should you *not* bring? Friends, siblings, your spouse, or anyone else. Production knows that a minor child will (and must) have a parent with them, but there is no space to accommodate other people. This can be hard to explain for family or friends who are excited about the prospect of seeing your child on a real set or possibly meeting a star, but sets are complex workplaces that are not designed for spectators. If you have younger children that you need to watch, you'll have to either arrange for a babysitter or hire a guardian over eighteen to accompany your child to set. Obviously a sitter is the better option, as your young actor is likely to be nervous and do better with a parent there than with a hired guardian.

You should also know that filming, both video and still, is generally not allowed in any way. Use your call sheet or other paperwork as souvenir. Sometimes you can take a photo with no flash, with the permission of the 1st or 2nd Assistant Director (1st or 2nd AD), but understand that production often has very strict rules about posting photos on social media. Important plot points and key publicity information are generally tightly controlled, and it is not cool if a careless Twitter or Instagram post spoils a big surprise.

The structure of the shoot will vary according to the project, but there is a common distinction that is helpful to understand: single-cam versus multicam. Single-camera shoots are generally used for dramas and film. These are also projects that use more locations and fewer sets. Because they shoot all over the place, it makes more sense to rehearse as you go—in other words, to rehearse a scene for the first time, shoot it immediately, and then move on to the next one. In comparison, multicamera shoots are typically used for sitcoms or shows that are largely if not entirely shot on a single soundstage. Because the show is filmed in a controlled, contained space, it's easier to set up multiple cameras that can catch the action from several angles, which saves a lot of time. It also means that the entire show can be rehearsed before a single moment of filming is done. Many multicam shows will rehearse for three days (starting with a table read the morning of the first day) and shoot for two. However, your child may not be there for the entire run of rehearsals and filming: they will only be called to set when they are needed.

When exactly will your child be called to set? You may not know until the night before filming in many cases, as the call times for most productions are set at the end of the day for the following day. This may seem stressfully last minute, but in fact the schedule for the next day really can't be determined until the current day is near completion. Call times are based on many things, including how much was shot, how many hours certain actors worked, and what time they finished shooting (turnaround can be a factor, especially when minors are involved). Just stay relaxed, and your child will take their cue from you. And when you finally get the call sheet e-mailed to you—either from production or your agent—double-check all the information, and see if you have any questions. If you are shooting on location, you may need extra time to travel or to drop your car at one location and be shuttled to another.

When you walk onto a set for the first time, assuming your child is not an extra (I can't speak to this experience since we didn't have it), the set PA, or production assistant will greet you. They will show you to your kid's dressing room or trailer and likely hand you the call sheet and shooting schedule. You should be prepared to sign contracts and come with all required legal documents:

- passport or birth certificate
- work permit (unless they have passed the CHSPE)
- social security card or photocopy
- All Coogan blocked trust account information
- CHSPE certificate if applicable
- Articles of Incorporation (if your child has incorporated)

You should keep photocopies of all of these documents in a set folder that automatically goes with you whenever your child is working. Your child will not be allowed to work if you can't produce these documents at the start of a job.

You will need to fill out paperwork and let the PA photocopy whichever legal documents they need. It's not a bad idea to bring extra photocopies. I often brought a copy of the excellent Emancipation Grid downloaded from BizParentz.org after Dove had passed the CHSPE to help educate PAs and sometimes even producers on the fine distinctions between work permits, the CHSPE, legal eighteen, and emancipation. There is *so* much confusion around these subjects.

The PA works longer hours than almost anyone and is usually a smart, educated person on a track to joining the DGA, or Director's Guild of America. Meanwhile their job is like being an interning physician and cat herder: impossibly long days on their feet and doing a thousand things at once. So be nice! They are also the first line of communication between you and the rest of the set. When you have basic questions about anything, you should start with them. And if for any reason you need to wander off, be sure to tell the PA where they can find you. It's part of their job to know where you and your child are at all times.

The next person you are likely to meet is the 2nd AD, or second assistant director. This person is generally charged with dealing most directly with the actors and will likely be the one who communicates the requests of the director to you and your child, as well as the one who lets you know when it is time to go to set. Generally, unless your child is actively in a scene, they are encouraged to stay in their dressing room until called. Sets are busy, crowded places, and they function best when only occupied by the people who must be on them at any given time. Every additional person on a set creates an opportunity to have a cough, sneeze, accidental laugh, or cell phone disrupt a scene and cost everyone time and money. The 2nd AD will also let you know when your child needs to be in the classroom with their set teacher and keep track of when they will hit the "pumpkin hour" (i.e., when they have worked the maximum allowed hours for their age that day). These things are closely monitored.

Sometimes there is a second 2nd AD, and that person fits in the niche between the PA and the 2nd AD. They typically are charged with wrangling the background players.

Next you are likely to meet the wardrobe team. These guys are miracle workers. They clothe everybody on set despite tight budgets and often-tighter deadlines, having to change course whenever the script changes. Possibly your child will have a fitting with them before the first day on set. The bigger the role, the more likely this is. Or maybe all they have had a chance to do is get your child's measurements over the phone and pull some possible wardrobe options. At any rate, they will likely have already delivered your child's wardrobe to the little closet in their dressing room or trailer or be ready to present final fitting choices when you arrive.

Some notes about wardrobe: it's not important that your child like what they have been assigned to wear. It's not about what might be flattering or make them look good—it's about the character and the storyline. So unless it's actually physically uncomfortable (and every wardrobe person I've ever met has bent over backward to be sure their actors are as comfortable in their clothes as possible), no complaining! You also must be careful that the wardrobe remains clean. So generally your child needs to either change out of it or wear a protective smock of some kind (which wardrobe will provide) when it's time to eat. Obviously playing outside in wardrobe is not recommended. And, finally, should your child be lucky enough to actually like their wardrobe, they do not get to take it home at the end of a job. Sad but true.

The hair and makeup artists are likely the next people you will meet. The star of a show or movie typically has their own dedicated hair and makeup artists, and the rest of the actors generally share the services of several more artists. Your kid will be taken to the hair and makeup trailer or room to have their hair and makeup done before shooting. Again, as in the case of wardrobe, it's not actually important that your kid love the way they are being "done"—what matters is that the look supports the character and story line. So trust that these hardworking, talented professionals know what they are doing, and encourage your child to leave their ego at home. If you are lucky, you might both learn a few tricks from these guys. Many of them are gifted communicators since they are essentially in the people business. And they work so intimately with their actors that close relationships often form if enough time goes by. Dove is deeply attached to the people who do her hair and makeup on *Liv and Maddie*, and we love them like family. One more aspect of their job is watching the filming for continuity issues with hair and makeup. Was the hair over the left shoulder in the last take, or was it pushed behind the ear? Encourage your kid to be mindful of that aspect of the job; this means they should try to avoid changing the way their hair is falling or adjusting their makeup while on set!

Once you and your child are taken to set by either the PA or the 2nd AD, you will meet the 1st AD (first assistant director), who operates as mission control on the set. The 1st AD is the liaison between the director and everyone else, and they also are charged with designing the complex shoot schedule, translating a script into minute-by-minute blocks of time where the story is shot out of sequence but in the most efficient means possible, taking into account many elements, including locations, actors schedules (including shorter work hours for kids), and camera setups.

The director is likely to be in a chair in front of a monitor, wearing a headset and talking to several people at once. This is the person charged with the final result of the episode or movie, and the buck truly stops with them in terms of anything on set. Whether a scene moves on after three takes or twelve is up to them. The best directors are gifted at communicating to their actors what they are looking for in terms of performance and still allow the space for a little improvisation to happen. But ironically, a fair amount of control and structure is necessary for the sense of safety that an actor needs to take those chances that can make magic on screen. And it is the director who creates that sense of safety—or lack thereof—by the way they run a set.

Where are you in all of this? If your child is in their dressing room, then you are there too, maybe helping run lines if they need it. If they are in "school" (i.e., with the set teacher) you have a little break, but you must stay nearby. If they are on set, you are legally required by state law as well as by the union to be within earshot or sight of them. This is for everyone's best interest, but especially your kid's. It's a safety and liability issue. This also means that you can't drop your kid off on set, go to work yourself, and pick them up at the end of the day. A parent or guardian *must* be on set with a child. Most sets are more than used to dealing with parents, even if you are new to being on set.

There will be an area for you to sit and watch their work—usually at one of the "video villages." A video village is the area of chairs set up in front of the various camera monitors where the people whose job it is to watch the filming can do so. Typically there are two—one for the director and producers and another for hair, makeup, wardrobe, props, and set dressers. The editors frequently have a small one tucked away in a corner as well. You can likely sit in either one, as long as you do not sit in front of someone whose job it is to watch! Be mindful of this. You may see other parents of child actors here too, and hopefully they will make you feel welcome. But remember to be utterly silent when filming is happening, and do not be that parent whose cell phone goes off and ruins a take.

It can be tempting to sit around and talk all day with other parents (between takes of course), and to some extent this can be useful. I've learned a lot by asking questions of people whose kids have been in the business much longer than mine, and I've saved us some grief with what I've learned. But it's easy for this kind of sharing to devolve into gossip, and ultimately that's a toxic activity. You are on set to support your child, and keep an eye on them: to give them feedback when they ask for it (and generally not when they don't—no backseat directing!) and to see if they are doing OK. Literally. Their safety is ultimately in your hands, and even though union regulations are in place and no one on set wants to do anything to compromise the health or well-being of your kid, you'd be surprised at how easy it can be to go just a little too far—even when everyone has the best intentions.

Two examples: when shooting *Cloud 9*, we had numerous "night shoots"—when the script calls for shooting in the dark, and the filming can go either all night or very late into the night. It was far below freezing (as it was every day of that film, up on a snowy mountain in Utah) and getting very late. I could tell that Dove was just about at the end of her very long rope and getting dangerously tired. Every person on that shoot was challenged by the brutal weather conditions, and the scene was taking longer to shoot than anyone wanted, just because it was so difficult. When everyone is just doing their best to do their job, then that is what they are focused on. And it's your job to stay focused on your kid. Only you can read the look in their eyes that says, "This is it—I have one more take in me, and then I'm going to collapse." So you watch them carefully, and when you see that look, you step up to the director or the 1st AD, and you tell them that your kid has one more take in them and then you have to call it a night. It's hard. Frequently you only have that location or that setup for that day, and if you can't get a shot you lose it forever. This can be potentially disastrous, for a film especially. So you don't want to ever step in unless you kid's health or safety is really on the line. But if it is, you must.

At the other extreme, during the season one Christmas episode of *Liv and Maddie* (which was shot on a soundstage in Hollywood in July) the soundstage became almost unbearably hot. Air conditioning on most stages has to be turned off during filming because it is too noisy, and this was one of those stages. The heat was rough for everyone, but Dove was in a heavy fake-fur dress, vinyl boots, a long wig, and a fake-fur Santa hat. During the sequence where she was singing and dancing (in all these layers) in the living room, one of the writers came up to me and said, "Does Dove look OK to you? She looks to me like she might be about to faint." And sure enough, she did look woozy. I had been watching the monitors but hadn't noticed. He was actually watching her directly and saw something I missed. We asked for a break and pulled her off the stage and into her air-conditioned dressing room and got her some water. After about ten minutes, she was in much better shape. Sometimes it only takes a little break to make a big difference. Again, you want to be very careful to not be the parent who is always asking for special exceptions for their kid. Time is very precious on a set, and falling behind on the schedule can wreak havoc on a shoot. If you are consistently a pain, it can affect whether people are willing to even work with your child. But you also are your child's ultimate protector and the only one whose sole job it is to look out for them.

Speaking of well being, food on most sets is plentiful and pretty decent. Basic food and beverages are generally available at all times at craft services (fondly referred to by many as "crafty"), the little area near the back or side of a set. It is absolutely OK for you to go there and get what you and your child need to keep body and soul together. There are strict union rules about how many hours can be worked between meal breaks, and lunch is typically a one-hour affair when everybody gets to eat a proper meal and have a true break.

When your child's day on set is finished, make sure you leave their dressing room in good shape. Hang their clothes back up in the closet for wardrobe to collect. It can be hard to leave if people are still shooting because your kid will probably want to say goodbye—but shooting often must continue. On some sets, it's a tradition for the director or 1st AD to call out, "That's a wrap!" when an actor is finished with the job. And for a moment, everyone stops work and applauds. I like this—it acknowledges the person and feels good to everyone.

When your time on set is finished—whether it is a one-day job, a one-week job, or a two-month job—make sure you thank everyone who made your time there a pleasant experience, and leave with as little disruption as possible. If your child was a costar or guest star, they have entered a world that existed before them and will continue to exist after they leave. If your child was fortunate enough to bond with some of the other actors on set, leaving can feel very sad. One of the downsides of having an especially wonderful experience is wondering if you'll ever have that feeling again after it ends. I think just about everybody cried at the end of the *Bits and Pieces* pilot. The bond between cast members felt so special, and we weren't sure if it would go forward. When it did, even in a modified form, we were ecstatic. When *Cloud Nine* wrapped, there were a lot of tears. That experience was like a two-month summer camp, and truly lifelong friendships were formed during that project. Sets where there are a lot of other kids near the age of yours can be particularly magical. When that magic is caught on film, it shows.

I've seen a few kids get overly attached, to the point of obsession with a set or a cast they were part of for just a short time, which can be unhealthy. Try to help your child have realistic expectations about the relationships they form on set. Some will carry forward outside of work, but most will not. And that can be especially hard for a young guest star who falls in love with a cast and believes their character will recur but then is never called back. Generally this has nothing to do with their performance, but with the writing direction. Some characters are really meant to show up only once. Others recur a few times in a season. Only a few guest stars go on to become heavily recurring on a given show. Remind your child of this truth, and help them look forward to the next project instead of looking back.

Tips and Takeaways

- The actions of every person on a set, including you and your child, affect everyone. Be extra thoughtful with how you speak and behave in that little ecosystem.
- Enter each new set experience with an open mind and no assumptions, and encourage your child to do the same.
- Keep a file of required paperwork to bring to set so you are always prepared and don't have to scramble for documents at the last minute.
- Even if you are on a professional, union set, you are ultimately responsible for your child's safety and wellbeing. Keep an eye on them, as you may catch something that others miss.
- You not only have a right to be within sight and sound of your child, but you are required to be by law. Production is accustomed to parents on set and they will have a place for you.

CHAPTER 29

Stories: Arriving in Hollywood

Hollywood Parents Share Stories of What it was Like to Finally Arrive

Pam McCartan

It was just a week before Christmas, and I was Christmas shopping, and I got the call from Ryan. He said, "You're not going to believe this, but Lynn wants me to run in and do a quick tape for a pilot called Zombies and Cheerleaders.*"*

And I said, "OK, when is it?"

(Ryan):"Well, it's, like, today at four o'clock." So off we went. She sent the tape—this is the casting director from Minneapolis who we loved—and the next day we're taking him straight to network.

This is the week before Christmas, but they are on vacation for two weeks as well. So right after the holidays, they said, "We need to see him." And sure enough, he reconnected with Nancy Kremer. She picked him up at the airport.

Then I got this text message from him that said, "I need to be here." And he's eighteen. "I need to be here."

School hadn't resumed. In fact, he had an obligation. He was going to participate as an alumnus in Young Arts, and he had a decision to make. Was he going to Miami to speak of his success, or was he going to this network call at Disney? That's an adult decision to make. He had made the first decision because Young Arts had done so much for him but then (finally) made the decision to go to the screen test, to Network.

So out he came. But prior to that he said, "Mom, I'm not sure how this is gonna go, and I'm not sure if it matters. But what matters is I think I want to leave college and go out to Los Angeles. Do you think I'm crazy? Would you support me?"

And right after he'd won the Jimmy Award, there were a couple big talent agencies in New York—Abrams was one of them—who'd contacted him and said, "If you're interested, we would really like to see you. If you are thinking about moving to New York, we'd really like to represent you." And he took their names and numbers and put them on a bulletin board at home, basically. And I remember thinking...But [I] didn't say anything because you pick and choose, and I always say no regrets. Everything happens for a reason. No regrets. So he didn't contact these agencies; he went to school. And I always said, "Do you walk in the doors that are wide open?" It just kept chasing him down.

It just kept chasing him down, and this was almost the ultimate sign of, "Wait a minute. I can go to college. I will go to college. I will be that English teacher someday." That's all he kept saying: "I don't have to go to college right now. My door is open; it's time to run through it." And we were super supportive of that.

(Author's Note: Ryan was actually nineteen when he was cast in the role of sixteen-year-old Diggie on Disney's *Liv and Maddie*.)

I believe everything happens for a reason. I said to the kids when we couldn't go back the second year—we chose not to go back the second year; it didn't seem right—I said, "I know for a fact—my heart, my gut said—that what we experienced was for a reason, and that reason will be crystal clear in the future."

We drove back, and everything was familiar. How many years later? Everything was familiar; all the streets were familiar. We checked back into the Oakwood for the first thirty days, until we could find an apartment for him. Everything was meant to be.

Amy Anderson

For me as a parent, it's just been so amazing watching her development. She has come so far since the time she started and what she's doing now. Any parent knows that there's just no greater joy than watching your kid take joy in what they like to do, and to do it well—to just really work hard at something and then to execute it with pure joy. There's nothing better. That's all you live for as a parent, like, "Wow, my kid is happy." Seeing what it has done for her life and her confidence—her skills and everything that she really enjoys—that's been great. On, like, the fun, fun side, it's so exciting to get to go to places and to get to go to these events. To get to meet different people, to go to the Emmys—all those things are exciting. They're not one hundred percent cracked up to what you think they're going to be all the time. Like going to the Emmys is not actually fun, but it's interesting.

Oh, gosh, it's exhausting. People are going to turn on the TV at five o'clock, and they watch for a few hours. But your day starts at eight in the morning, and then you don't get home till after midnight with the five-year-old. You're like, "Oh my God." Then you have this...I don't know if you saw—I was tweeting it, because it was so funny, because I always am the one who has the youngest kid there at the award shows, and I always bring this giant, ugly purse. Everyone else has got their cute little clutch, and they're like, "Oh, look at your clutch; ooh, your cute little..." I'm like, "I don't care. I'm bringing the mom purse."

I have to. I am with a small child for twelve hours straight. They don't give you food. You're literally in the Nokia Theatre, and they have popcorn and pretzels. You're like, "We're at an event, like a baseball game," and I've got granola bars, gum, and candy, and I bring the iPad mini.

Yeah, because during the commercial breaks, it's "Can I play with the iPad?" and "Now we have to put it away. Now you can."

It's funny, because every year, the moms with the older kids know that I have snacks, and they're all, "Do you have another granola bar, Amy?"

I'm like, "Mm-hmm."

[The mom will] look at you like, "My kid's fifteen—I can bring a clutch," and now you're just coming to me for snacks. They know every year that I have the snacks.

I know: "Amy, she's got granola bars in that giant bag, the biggest, ugliest bag this year."

I'm like, "I don't care," and it weighed twenty pounds. Oh my God (laughing).

*The other thing, too, especially with Aubrey's show being an ABC show, is all the Disney stuff is so fun. It's kind of good that she doesn't understand how special this stuff is, because then she might get a really inflated ego. But we really do get the royal treatment when we go to the Disney parks, as you know, and it's just magical for her to get to experience those things in such a way. I kind of tell her, "*Modern Family *goes away, we're never going to Disneyland again."*

It is amazing, and I try not to let her be so spoiled, but this is a business that really kind of caters to you like you're royalty every once in a while. I try to keep her normal by keeping her around her regular friends, and she does this community theater, which is great for her because she is the only professional actor in that thing. They don't even like to audition the kids; they just let anybody perform who wants to perform.

And she loves it. She just loves it, and she's excited for the other kids and really proud of the work that she does, and she takes it very seriously. It's hard keeping that balance, but the fun parts really have been amazing.

Pat Fisher

Well, again, it was a journey. I think the first time we kind of kept a dual residency for about four years, with my husband back home and us out here. And so we'd come out and we'd take a three-month lease. We'd come out, and we'd take a six-month lease. And finally, you know, I called my husband one day, and I said, "Well, I signed a one-year lease today."

And you know, he's like, "That's great."

So Jordan and I actually moved out about three years before my husband did. We were probably coming out for about three years, and, you know, he was getting enough little things. He was getting, you know, the short shoots, the one-day shoots, the guest spots. The promo things, the student films. You know—enough to keep him busy. When you are building up a career, you can't pass up opportunities, and you have to be very selective of your opportunities. You don't say yes to everything, which I think is a mistake a lot of people do make. They say yes to things that can actually hurt them, build a reputation they don't want to live with.

So you have to be very selective. And that's a parent's responsibility, to be selective. Just because it's a dollar doesn't mean it's in your kid's best interest. But he was getting enough stuff that warranted us being here. I mean, we would go home for two or three days, and we'd get that call: "Jordan has got a producer session tomorrow."

One time we came out...we got a call on a Wednesday night. He had an audition not the next day, but the next. We needed one travel day. We actually bought one-way tickets to LA, and I got a rental car. That's all we had when we got here. We didn't have a place to stay. We didn't have a return flight. We didn't have anything. But we got him to his audition on time and figured out the rest when we got here.

The first time we came out, when we ended up staying five weeks, after a week of getting hotel rooms each night, we did go to the Oakwood. And we stayed there. We took a one-month lease, and we stayed for the month. And I think for our first time, that was really a good choice for us, just because of all the things they gear themselves toward for the acting child. I don't recommend it more than once, but the first time, I think, it's very beneficial. It's not some place that we want to live, but we learned a lot. Good, bad, ugly, indifferent—we learned a lot that month.

It's very valuable. And then after that, either we would rent a guesthouse or we would get short-term lodging, which is very difficult to find. We did do Craigslist a few times. We did have good luck. We didn't have any bad experiences. I was very careful with that, and then once we started coming out and making friends and meeting people, we would even share with other people. I had a friend that would rent us her master bedroom, and we'd stay in the house with her, and I would rent from her. People out here don't do things for free. They really don't.

It's hard. It's very expensive. Guesthouse, short-term leases, apartments, motels—whatever. Whatever worked at the moment.

Kim Holt

It's not like you can get an agent and then just go back home and live, especially if you're not working, but Olivia was doing some things to work. So they kept her on. She was able to go back home with the promise that she would come out in the summertime or whenever. She had to at least commit to do something during the year.

We would put stuff on tape. I would have to say, we would do one to two auditions a week on tape, which would sometimes cut into football time—like if she wanted to go to football games or if she wanted to go hang out with her friends for pizza or something like that. Because when they wanted an audition, it wasn't on her time.

That was a good starting point—to know how committed she would have to be and how much she really loved it—because she still had to sacrifice a little bit. She loved doing all that, I think. Olivia has always had really good self-esteem. I think it's really, really important to have that if you're going to be in this industry because it's going to be knocked down regardless at some point, a little bit. If you don't start out with it, then it's probably not a good fit for you because you want your kids to be happy and healthy, and this isn't really the industry that's going to shape that for you. It can break you before it makes you.

We didn't know if the pilot was going to pick up. I think our family was still in denial about the whole thing. I know my husband was. I know when Disney called and said it picked up, he didn't pack one thing. He was in denial because we had told her—that was just the hard thing...we had told her, if we had to move out there, we would.

That's a challenging thing, I think, when you have a family. I think it's super challenging because you want your child to follow the dream. It's an amazing opportunity. It doesn't happen...it's not something that happens every day. It's like winning the lottery, kind of. It's not just luck sometimes, but it is sometimes being at the right place at the right time. And other times it's just you having the ability and the talent to be able to do it and then love it.

It was hard. My husband had a business. He has an ad agency, and he can move his business, some of it. He does have an office out here.

He still has one back home. We still have our house back in Mississippi that we keep, even though we get there maybe one week out of the year. I don't know if we'll ever move back there, but all our furniture and all our stuff is still there.

I think we kind of thought that...We didn't want to make any rash decisions, because I think it's exciting when you get a role, but you have to also see that it's not for a forever job. Your job only lasts as long as that show is going to last. It's exciting for that time, and then you have to realize that life will go on after that show. We didn't want to pack up and say, "What if it doesn't go a second season? What it doesn't go a third season?"

We didn't want to throw all our eggs in a basket and move out here. My husband still has a job, trying to support our family. We've kept to that. Now we know that we're probably going to be out here awhile. We even thought that after Kickin' It *was going to be over, we may go back. We didn't know, and then she picked up* I Didn't Do It, *and then her music stuff picked up. We do know now that, regardless, we are probably going to be here for another five years, and she is probably going to never come back home because she will be eighteen now.*

Clark Trainor

OK, I have a little bit of an advantage because I lived in LA from '98 to 2005, and I was pursuing acting while practicing [law]. When we moved back from Florida in 2010, I knew exactly what dominos had to fall and in what order. I know that sounds arrogant, but I did. I did. Because I made all the mistakes on me.

We moved to Los Angeles when [Tenzing] was ten. But not because of acting. He was born here. We actually lived here. We moved back to Florida for five years and then missed LA so much, so we just wanted to come back out.

My wife and I adore Los Angeles. We love LA. We were coming back because this was where we wanted to raise our kids. But of course, you're here, and he had done the theater camp, so you're like, "Well, what the heck. Let's just see where this goes."

And this town is so much about youth that is he's very lucky we just happened to be in LA because we love LA. But, I mean, you can act anywhere. You can just go out, and I don't know of a single town in this country that doesn't have some form of community theater or something. There's really no excuse, if you want to do it, to not just go out and do it. In this town, the acting can definitely go someplace, you know, but you can act anywhere. And in that regard, if you do ever want to come here, just never forget that chance favors the prepared.

Because you have to get lucky in this town. There are a lot of incredibly talented actors and actresses, but you do need a little bit of luck on top of it. That's where just going out and doing it is very useful, because you never know. I mean, I think that's why people stay in this town for as long as they do—because your break literally can be four days away.

For all you know, your agent is going to call you right now saying, "Hey, I've got an audition for the next Marvel film for you, but you've got to be over at Seraphim Casting by this afternoon." And then next week you are on set!

Then, boom! It can literally happen just like that.

CHAPTER 30

Some Notes on Disney

Disney is an extraordinary company, and its reach is global. But more than that, it delivers magic to millions of homes, and its stories and characters are an integral part of childhood for generations of people. It's no wonder that it is the dream of so many to be on Disney Channel!

It's fascinating to me how many kids who don't really aspire to be actors otherwise want to be on Disney. I think that says a lot about how powerful the brand really is. However, it is a big red flag if your child wants *only* to be on Disney Channel and does not dream of being an actor otherwise. If this is your situation, I would not pursue that particular dream. Disney wants professional kids who are actually experienced performers with track records. When you consider how much they invest in creating and producing a show, this makes sense. From a business standpoint—and despite the magic, Disney is ultimately a business—why would you bet on someone with no previous experience?

Most of the kids who have been cast in series regular roles on the Disney Channel or starring roles in Disney Channel Original Movies had actually been paying their dues for years before Disney brought their work to international attention.

- Miley Cyrus was born into a showbiz family and appeared at the age of nine in three episodes of the TV series *Doc* as well as the movie *Big Fish* before being cast in *Hannah Montana* at age thirteen.

- Demi Lovato began as a series regular on *Barney and Friends* at the age of ten, followed by a number of TV guest star appearances before getting cast in Disney's *As the Bell Rings* at age fifteen, followed by *Camp Rock* and other Disney projects.
- Selena Gomez also began as a series regular on *Barney and Friends*, at age nine. She then went on to have two small film roles and several guest star appearances before Disney picked her up for guest star roles on *Suite Life* and *Hannah Montana*. She starred in two different Disney pilots that were not picked up to go forward before *Wizards* was written for her.
- Debbie Ryan began her career in film at fourteen and appeared in several films and national TV commercials before landing her role at sixteen in Disney's *Suite Life on Deck* and then her own Disney series, *Jessie*, when she was nineteen.
- China Ann McClain appeared in her first film at the age of six and was cast in a handful of films and shorts before Disney cast her at nine as a guest star in *Hannah Montana* and then her series regular role on *Ant Farm* at age eleven.
- Bridgit Mendler began acting at the age of eight, began guest starring in TV shows at thirteen, and had numerous TV shows and animated features under her belt before Disney cast her as a major recurring character in *Wizards of Waverly Place* at seventeen and then *Good Luck Charlie* at eighteen.
- Zendaya began as a model and dancer and performed in a local Shakespeare theater where her mother was house manager before Disney cast her at fourteen in *Shake It Up*.
- Bella Thorne appeared in many commercials, guest star roles and short films starting at the age of nine before Disney cast her in *Shake It Up* at thirteen.
- Ross Lynch was originally a musician and dancer, playing guitar and singing lead vocals in the band R5. He was cast as a guest star on a TV series as well as two short films before Disney picked him up at the age of sixteen for *Austin and Ally* and, later, *Teen Beach Movie*.

- Laura Marano began acting in local theater at the age of five. She continued on to *many* television roles as well as national commercials before Disney cast her in *Austin and Ally* at sixteen.
- Maia Mitchell was cast at the age of twelve as the lead in her native Australia's television show *Mortified*, followed by another Australian TV series, *Trapped*, at the age of fifteen; she did other work before being cast as a lead in *Teen Beach Movie* at nineteen.
- Olivia Holt began singing and acting onstage at the age of three and appeared in local theater productions, national TV commercials, and an indie film before Disney cast her at twelve in *Kickin' It*, followed by *Girl vs. Monster* and *I Didn't Do It*.
- Luke Benward appeared at the age of five with Mel Gibson in *We Were Soldiers* and then continued to film an average of one TV appearance or film a year. He was also cast in a number of national commercials and starred in two different Disney pilots that were not picked up before getting his recurring guest star appearances in *Good Luck Charlie* and lead role in *Cloud 9* at seventeen.
- Cameron Boyce had many commercials under his belt, several movies, and a number of guest star roles before he was cast as a guest star in Disney's *Shake It Up* and then *Good Luck Charlie*, which preceded his series regular role on *Jessie*. He completed 4 seasons of *Jessie* before he was announced as the lead in Disney's *Gamer's Guide to Pretty Much Everything.* Disney cast Cameron as Carlos in *Disney Descendants* between seasons three and four of *Jessie*.
- Dove Cameron began steadily performing in local theater at the age of eight and had two guest star appearances on Showtime's *Shameless* before Disney cast her in *Bits and Pieces* at the age of sixteen. That pilot was eventually reworked to become *Liv and Maddie*. She then guest starred as Simon Baker's daughter in *The Mentalist* before Disney cast her in *Cloud 9*, and she filmed a full season of *Liv and Maddie* before they cast her as Mal in *Disney Descendants*.

I researched and shared this list (largely sourced at IMDb) to demonstrate that the kids that Disney bets on are not typically "discovered" and brought into that dreamed-of world out of nowhere. These kids worked for years at their craft and did projects—stage, film, television, commercials, dance, music—in many different arenas before they landed in the casting room at the twenty-first floor of the Disney Channel building in Burbank. And for every role they were cast in, they auditioned for many more with no results.

Most, if not all, of these young stars were not aiming exclusively for Disney. They were putting themselves out in the world because they loved to perform. Their agents sent them out for every project that looked appropriate, and if they were fortunate, they were cast. And one day, for each of them, it was a Disney project. When Dove and I arrived in LA, we were expecting her to end up in films and dramas because we knew this was her strong suit. She actually made it to callbacks on several different Disney pilots—none of which resulted in being cast for a role—before we asked her agent to stop sending her out for Disney projects because they didn't seem to get her, and she didn't feel comfortable in comedy. But one day a script showed up that was compelling, and she auditioned for a set of casting directors who had never seen her. *They* seemed to get her and think she was funny as well. And then everything changed.

If after reading this it still makes sense to you to directly aim to get your kid onto a Disney show, there are a few more things to know:

- *Disney does not charge a fee for auditions.* Anyone who says otherwise is scamming you. Scams for Disney casting are rampant. Please be careful.
- Disney Channel casts its shows almost entirely in Los Angeles through independent casting directors. The corporation only gets involved when casting for leads or regular characters in a new series or for a DCOM (Disney Channel Original Movie, such as *Disney Descendants* or *High School Musical*). Then it is the executives like Judy Taylor who engage at a supervisory level. Once a year or so, they will hold an open casting call. The

only website where this information is reliably posted is http://disneychannel.disney.com/open-call.

- *Disney is not affiliated with any acting workshops, schools, or boot camps.*
- Anyone who has worked for Disney in the past, been on one of their many shows, or knows someone who works at The Walt Disney Company or Disney Channel has no special ability to help your child get an audition. Including me!
- While it is true that casting for a new show happens only once—and then the leads and series regulars are essentially set—there is ongoing casting for guest star and costar roles when a show is filming. This process happens very quickly—generally within a week or less of shooting. The following week's script is sent to the show's casting directors, who create the breakdown for whichever additional character(s) are needed that week. Then the call goes out to agents, who submit their clients who might fit the description(s). Auditions are held in LA at the offices of the independent casting director (here is an example of where remote auditions won't work), and the process is finished within a day or so. In other words, to be a guest star on a Disney Channel show, you essentially must be living in the LA area, have an agent who will submit your child for the appropriate auditions, and be able to jump quickly.
- Legitimate casting director contact information for Disney Channel shows—as well as *all* current television and film—can be found at CastingAbout.com for around forty dollars per year per region (Los Angeles, New York, and so on) or ten dollars per month. This gives you an opportunity to send your child's headshot and résumé directly to the right people. However it still does not tell you what they are looking for in a given episode, so the normal channels are still recommended.

Tips and Takeaways

- Disney almost exclusively casts kids with some professional experience. It is very rare for them to cast young actors in large roles without some kind of track record.
- The major stars on The Disney Channel were not necessarily aiming for Disney; rather, they were aiming for a career as a performer, and one day they were cast in a Disney project.
- Disney does not charge a fee for auditions. Ever.
- Disney is not affiliated with any acting workshops, schools, or boot camps.
- Most casting for Disney shows happens in Los Angeles.
- The best way to prepare your child for a chance at landing on a Disney show or movie is exactly the same as for any other success in Hollywood: acting classes, theater training, and as much experience auditioning and working as possible. Dance and voice training are a major plus for Disney, which does tend to favor triple-threats.

CHAPTER 31

Stories: The Disney Channel

Hollywood Parents Share Stories on Their Experience with The Disney Channel

Kenda Benward

After High School Musical, *Disney Channel created a pilot called* Madison High. *Luke was playing the equivalent of the Zac Efron character in that, and it was a musical.*

It was amazing. It was full dance—it was just incredible. It was so good. And I don't really know why it didn't work out. Things just work out for a reason. Or they don't work out for a reason. And you just go, "OK. Again, I put it out there. I did the best I could. And now, we'll see what's next."

The very next pilot season, they came up with another musical idea called Zombies and Cheerleaders. *And Luke was to play the lead zombie in that, named Zed. And that one was super fun—great choreography, amazing characters. He actually met some of his very best friends in both of those pilots, that are still his best friends today.*

But it didn't go. It's so hard because you're in this mind-set of, "I just did a pilot for the Disney Channel. And this is a no-brainer." They were so much fun. And honestly, they could have been on the Disney Channel and done just fine. But for whatever reason, they decided against it, and so it didn't happen. He cried on those. Those were huge.

The Disney Channel has been so good to Luke. Judy Taylor at Disney basically had Luke on her radar from the time he was probably...I would say around eight or nine till present day.

We would always come in—maybe once or twice a year—bring her a new headshot, sit down for ten or fifteen minutes. She talked to Luke about what he was doing and to get to know him. And then when they would have a project that would fit him, he would either tape for it, or—if we were in town—he would go in for it.

He was just always in the back of their mind. And I so appreciate her for believing in Luke. And I appreciate the channel just for how much they supported him and how many shots they gave him. It was a really great experience.

In my opinion, Judy Taylor is one of the best casting directors. She's probably the best of the best, in my opinion, for the genre. She's just crazy good, and she's done so many amazing films. Back to the Future, Goonies*—are you kidding me? I love* Goonies.

The list goes on and on with her. I'm a huge Judy Taylor fan. But, yeah, they have a long-term view, and they're patient. They are patient, and they have the memory of an elephant—they don't forget anything.

And so, they meet these young actors, and they just kind of file them away until they have a place to put them. And then if it works, they bring them in. And when they bring you in, it's like a family. It's really sweet. Disney Channel was a great experience for Luke and our entire family.

Oh my gosh. He and Dove together in Cloud 9*, their chemistry was so great. And it's amazing, too, because they're really great friends. They're like siblings; they're like brother and sister. But at the same time, they have great chemistry to play love interests. It was just great. There's a freedom in that because you're friends. There's nothing expected. You're always safe. So you really can go there and know that it's a safe zone.*

Victor Boyce

The way we got onto Disney was the same way we got onto anything else that we did. We auditioned. We went on a lot of Disney auditions before we ever got the first one. I believe the first one was Good Luck Charlie.

I had never been on a big set like that for a camera show, number one. Number two, it was an audience show, which was exciting. Number three, when I watched Cameron doing it, I just saw the light go "Ping!" in his eyes because he had done some commercials. He had done...at this point he had done, I don't know...ten or fifteen commercials, maybe more.

He did a lot of commercials before he did that, and some other stuff, but he'd never done a TV show like that. When I watched him I knew, "Oh, his little brain is spinning." And the thing was...you know after the audience show, the actors sign the autographs. It was Bradley and all the stars, and they are out there signing, and I was watching Cameron. And people came up to him, a couple of people. They didn't know who he was, but they saw him earlier in the playback. He was not on the live show; he was only on the playback, of course.

He was only in the playback, but a couple of people recognized him, and he signed a couple of autographs. And I swear he denied it, but he was so excited, like, "This is cool!" This was cool. Like, wow!

And I had fun and I said, "Cameron, if we could ever get on one of these shows, that would be so cool."

He was like, "Yeah." And then we auditioned again, and he got Shake It Up. Now the Shake It Up thing was a dance thing, and he danced on Shake It Up. Which was really cool, but again it was natural for him. It wasn't so much acting. Both episodes were dancing.

His dance skills totally opened the door, because even on Good Luck Charlie he danced. He tap-danced. He was fake Gabe, and the mom did a talent show. I remember the kids had no talent, so she got a fake family to replace them all. The husband, the daughter, the son—everybody—and Cameron was fake Gabe, and so he danced on both shows. But what happens is now he's on Disney's radar.

Now he's on the radar, so we are auditioning for all these things, still doing regular commercials and whatnot. Then when Jessie came up, they knew him. And later on I found out they had been watching him on YouTube videos—all this stuff. So if you attract enough attention through other means, you could be on Disney's radar, and you might not even know it.

So it's not a question of "How do I get on Disney," because there's no magic formula to getting on Disney.

It doesn't work that way at all. It's a lot of work. It's a lot of hard work; it's a little bit of luck. But if you do have the opportunity to audition, don't miss that, because it could be something big later on. I mean Good Luck Charlie was two years or a year and a half before Jessie. Time went by, and then we ended up on Jessie.

Again, it was just a regular audition. Now, like I said, I know that he was on the radar, but I found that out later. So we just went in as a regular audition. And I knew it was a possibility when they kept calling him back. I mean, when you get one callback and you don't hear anything, you know it's done. But when you get one callback, then another callback, then another callback, you know. You know it's looking positive.

So that was good. And then there is a funny story with him and Karan [Brar]. He and Karan were actually going after the same role. And, yeah, the role originally was supposed to be for a Korean kid, and the character's name was Hiro. One day we were driving...I picked him up from school, and we're driving home, and there was a pickup truck in front of us; it was a Chevrolet. You know people peel the letters out to make it say something else? It was a Chevrolet in front of us, and they had peeled off most letters, and they left H-E-R-O.

And I said, "Cameron, look." The character's name was H-I-R-O.

But I was like, "That's a sign." And they changed the name to Luke. He is a kid from Detroit, and the rest is history. But with Karan, because they were both funny and interesting, they were trying to figure out which one to pick. It's like, "Forget it. Let's just pick them both." Yeah. They took them both, and it's been all good ever since.

Kim Holt

We'd never even been on an audition for Disney, and actually we had only been on maybe two Nickelodeon auditions. Most of our stuff was feature film. We had never done a lot of TV. You try to explain this to somebody—that you have an agent or a manager, and you just go on the auditions that they've sent to you, which means they submit your picture, and if you look like a role, then you're called in for that. It's not like you get a choice of what you go out for. It is totally random.

That is a big question that people ask. They want their kids to be on Disney. It just doesn't really happen that way. You don't really knock on Disney's door and say, "We would like to audition."

[Olivia] had done a lot of commercials. She had done some independent films, and she was still doing some theater stuff at home. She was staying busy with all that. It was pretty exciting.

We'd come out for our six weeks in the summer, and I think how it all kind of started is we came out for a producer session for a Nickelodeon show. Olivia was only twelve at the time. They said she was too young. She looked even younger than twelve because she was so tiny.

We had never auditioned for Disney before. That's when we went in, and they said she actually was too young for that show. But when we came back out in the summer, they wanted her to come audition again, for Kickin' It.

We started doing it when she was ten, and she was almost thirteen when she booked again. She was twelve when they shot the pilot, but she was thirteen when they picked it up at the end of the year.

Clark Trainor

Remember how long that audition process was [for Bits and Pieces, *which became* Liv and Maddie*]? Oh my gosh—like seven callbacks to the twenty-first floor. Again and again and again.*

I remember meeting Kali at one of the callbacks because they kept pulling in moms. And I remember meeting Dove at one of the callbacks. But even meeting them, you didn't know who they were looking at. Tenzing is a mixed race, and we go in one time, and all the mothers were Asian. They called all Asian women for the moms, and for all the fathers, they called in whites. So then we got really excited. I remember driving home thinking, "Tenzing, they are really considering you!" Because they are trying to make the parents work now. They were trying to make it.

Getting cast is never personal. They've got to literally make all the planets align. The mother and the father...and then the last two or three callbacks were probably less about callbacks and more about chemistry reads. And I'm like, "What are we doing here? Are they just pulling in Tenzing to try to get ideas? I mean, what are they doing?"

I gained so much respect for Disney at that point because—let's face it—they cast the show where they said, "Just hire the best people for the job. Just forget this whole family look-alike structure." I think it's so humorous, because—I will admit—every once in a while, I go online and I see what people are posting about the show and everything. And there are still people who say, "They don't even look alike."

And I think, "Yes, but are you laughing?" Because at the end of the day, that's all that matters, isn't it? It wasn't about looks.

I'm glad that this is where we landed, but no. When you're starting out, you take what comes. Student films and whatever—just anything to get in front of the camera and practice. But, no, we were not specifically targeting Disney.

Work is work, and I still tell Tenzing that to this day, even though he's landed a show. I tell him, "Work is work." Even if it's one line and something, it's still just work-is-work at this point. If you've got time and you're not booked, just go and do it.

Pat Fisher

Well, Jordan is a triple threat. He sings, dances, and acts, and he loves to do all three. It's not like he prefers one over the other, so we tried to open up doors in all three avenues for him. He and I would even talk about it and say, "We are going to pursue the opportunities that come along. We are not going to set our sights on one thing and try for that, because it's a tough market out here." If you come out here and just set your eyes on Disney and you don't do the other things and you don't earn your stripes and you don't get the experiences, you are never going to end up with Disney.

So, no, it was not our goal to end up with Disney. It was our goal to open up all the doors and see, you know, really what worked out for him.

You can't know. Now, if you have a kid that is only interested in one of those areas, then obviously that's the area you want to pursue. But at the same time, getting a little training in the other areas is only going to help with auditions and things like that.

And, you know, most kids on the Channel, I would say, have to know how to do all three to a certain extent. You may have a passion for one and be really good at one, but you kind of need to know how to sing a little, at least "Happy Birthday." And you [should] know how to move around a little bit, just to give yourself the advantage.

Allison Zuehlsdorff

No, we didn't intentionally go that way—not at all. We have a set of parameters, because I think every family has a line they draw. We are very material-driven. I remember sitting with someone in the business, and they were talking about, "Are you money-driven, are you fame-driven, or are you material-driven?" I think it was a publicist. He was talking about that because they deal with image all the time. They deal with how to build. We realized we are material-driven.

Also, being Christians, there's a whole lot of material that isn't in our comfort zone, and that Cozi doesn't want to audition for. That narrows the field, but it's a choice we've made. We're just trying to get more efficient with what she wants to achieve professionally and balance it with our goals spiritually. As she gets older, she is starting to assert her own thoughts into the equation, which feels very healthy.

I think because of our values, some of the roles she's auditioned for have naturally ended up being for the Disney Channel and Disney XD.

Besides that, what we've come to realize is that there are not a whole lot of roles for young people, from ten years old through sixteen, in movies and film. In fact, there are precious few, along with a whole lot of already established young actors who are first in line to audition for them. It's super competitive, but, then again, so is Disney Channel. We feel grateful that she was seen as right for the roles she's had on Disney Channel. It's been a blessing and perfect for that transitional time from being seen as a teen into being seen as an adult. I guess you could say that though Cozi didn't start out with the goal of being on the Disney Channel, we're happy that it's turned out that way.

CHAPTER 32

Finances

If you are starting to wonder how to make a living while either being on set with your child all day or running all over town to get them to auditions, you are getting in touch with one of the central challenges of being a stage parent. I know a few who somehow manage to make a living while their child works on a regular basis—say on a TV show—but these people are almost all self-employed in ways that are exceptionally flexible, and all of them admit that it is incredibly difficult. The ideal situation would be a two-parent family: one parent can support the whole family financially while the other one devotes themselves to what is essentially an unpaid full-time job. Do not gloss over the financial realities of this. Countless families go into deep debt or even bankrupt themselves because they are not realistic about what it can take to actually support the fledgling career of a young actor.

I've talked to a number of actors in their twenties who are wistful that they had to go the more "normal" route to acting (i.e., waiting until they were eighteen to head to Hollywood or going through a university or professional training program first, arriving in LA at twenty-two or twenty-four). They wish their parents had been willing to uproot the family and support them in pursuit of their dream. How much easier it is when someone else is paying the rent and other bills, and even managing all the confusing aspects of a career! But that just is not realistic or appropriate for many families. Los Angeles is expensive, and the uncertain schedule of an actor (and the parent of a young actor who must drive them to every audition and stay with them on set when they do get a job) makes earning a living exceptionally difficult.

We were fortunate that I had a large chunk of savings (from cashing out my half of a house and business in a divorce), and that is what we lived on while Dove established herself. It took much longer than I expected for her to get her first job—a full year from the moment we landed. And then it was another eight months before things began to *really* happen—eight months filled with near misses. Granted, she could possibly have gotten some commercial work, but that wasn't what we had come to LA for, and I didn't want to go that route unless we had to. Every family is different. Some people aim directly for commercials, some of which can be incredibly lucrative.

Whatever you do, I recommend having a plan that both parents and kids agree to *before* embarking on this adventure. In our case, Dove and I agreed that if she didn't "make it" (whatever that means—looking back we clearly should have been more specific) by the time she was eighteen, that she would enroll in college and try a different direction. Arriving when she was fourteen, that seemed reasonable. Somehow we made it to eighteen, and she has, fortunately, clearly broken out into what probably anyone would call a successful career. Whatever follows her current projects, I suspect Dove will be able to make a living as an actor as long as she cares to. Which is all you can hope for, I think, because making a living doing what you love is really the dream. That and a healthy, grounded life.

I think it is much more difficult for the people who have just a little success but not enough to be clear in terms of whether to hold on a little longer or to fold and go home. This is dangerous financially and emotionally as well. It can be so hard to let go of a dream. But if you remember that this is not just a dream but also a business, you will realize that all businesses must close when enough time goes by and demand is not high enough to sustain them. This is why having an agreement made long before that point is crucial. Talent is only one component of making a successful career in Hollywood; luck is another huge part.

This town is full of talented people who won't ever make it because the odds are simply stacked against *anyone* making it. What matters ultimately is that your family stays intact and your kids stay healthy and happy. No career, real or hoped for, is worth sacrificing that.

Some people keep their hometown residence and add on a second small apartment in LA. If you are here for very long, a basic apartment will be cheaper than a motel. But carrying the expenses on two households can quickly get expensive. What if your child actually lands a regular role on something? Are you prepared to stay? Can you afford to? Remember: California state law says that a child's earnings belong to them only—not to the family. This can make things really challenging financially. I did not have the financial resources to keep one foot in our old life while attempting to create a new one, so we simply made the full leap and moved here.

Some factors affecting your decision on how to manage supporting your child in their dream of becoming a professional actor are listed below:

- How old is the child (or children)?
- What exactly is their goal?
- Could this be accomplished from home?
- Do you have objective, professional support for the decision to pursue this? In other words, is there anyone relevant besides you and your child who believes that this is a risk worth taking? Do you have credible mentors? By this I mean people who have no financial interest in telling you to go for it.
- What are your resources, and how much of them are you willing to sacrifice for this effort?
- Is the entire family in agreement that this is a good direction to go in, whether it entails a temporary split or a full move?
- Can you create an agreement about what should trigger a retreat, either temporary or permanent?

There are many creative ways to get yourself and your child to LA and give them the opportunity to pursue their dream. Some people have friends or family that they can stay with temporarily. While I doubt that most people can crash with someone else long enough to get their child actually established, it may be that you can couch surf long enough to know whether or not to commit further to the pursuit.

Some people use their summer vacation as a time to try to get established in LA and see if staying might make sense. This works for a child's school schedule, but it's less than ideal from an industry standpoint. Yes, things are casting year-round now, but June is a pretty quiet month, in July much of the town is on vacation, and August is the just the beginning of the episodic casting season. You could actually spend much of that summer break just trying to get a meeting with the right agent!

On the other hand, if you are highly organized and connected, you could set up a series of appointments before you even arrive and have your child signed with an agency (hopefully a good one, not just any agency) within a few weeks. If you are really lucky, your child might be sent out on enough auditions for you both to know whether that is an activity that you are willing to make sacrifices for to continue. Remember, for most actors at any age, auditioning is their primary pursuit. Is it fun? Is your child learning and improving? Or is it more stressful and unrewarding than you had anticipated? Making some kind of a trial run before committing more deeply might be prudent.

Some kids even end up living with their agents or managers for a time while their families remain back home. This can happen when one or both parents have a job that can't be moved or other children who can't be brought out to LA without tremendous disruption. I've talked to a number of people who have done this, and the stories range from sweet and really impressive to outright horrific, one ending in prosecution. Really.

Every family is different, but I can't imagine leaving my child to live with someone else. I know a few kids whose parents ran out of time and money and needed to go back home when the kids were sixteen or seventeen, and the kids stayed to make it on their own. While fending for themselves in this town can work for a small percentage of incredibly mature kids, many end up with serious scars or worse. Even eighteen is very young to be on your own here. Think long and hard before leaving your child in a vulnerable position, either on their own or with someone else.

If you believe you can make a living off management commissions from the work your child books, I would encourage you to reconsider this fantasy. Taking a part of your child's earnings—if they have any—can help defray expenses, but it is very unlikely to be enough to support your family.

Finally, a quick breakdown of the standard distribution of an actor's wages for a typical guest star contract, just as a financial reality check:

The rates paid to performers are governed by a complex set of rules negotiated by the union. If your child is employed as a principal performer on a SAG-AFTRA contract for a half-hour show, (not as an extra, but as a performer with lines), they will gross approximately $860 a day. (See SAG-AFTRA Network TV Code). This sounds like a lot of money, but remember that this is not a salary they are making regularly. How much do they get to keep?

Gross	$860.00
Taxes*	-$172.00
Agent (10%)	-$ 86.00
Manager (10–15%)	-$108.00
Coogan account	-$129.00
Approximate net	$365.00

*Yes, children have to pay taxes and file tax returns! Their rates depend entirely on how much they make and can range from 10 percent to 39.6 percent of their earnings, depending on their bracket at the end of each year. For illustration, I used 20 percent here. I also averaged the difference between 10 percent and 15 percent for a manager's cut. Note too that the money deducted for a child's Coogan account ultimately ends up back in their hands, but it can be years before those funds are available, and most families use the Coogan as a way to save for college.

For bigger stars, that is just where the deductions start. Subtract another 5 percent for the attorney on retainer, another 5 percent for the business manager, and a hefty flat monthly fee for a publicist, and you will see why successful actors get paid the rates that they do. Then of course there are union dues and all the expenses directly incurred through this career. An entire ecosystem is living off of these salaries.

Tips and Takeaways

- Being a stage parent to a young actor in LA can be a full-time, unpaid job.
- Regardless of how much money your child might make, you are extremely unlikely to make enough off management commissions (if you go that route) to support your family, and it is illegal to use your child's earnings as "family money." Your child's earnings belong to them alone.
- It's a good idea to have an agreement in place about what would trigger a retreat before you come to Los Angeles. A specific event—an amount of time, or financial threshold—is better than something difficult to define like "success."
- Discuss your child's specific goals and dreams around acting. Could they be accomplished where you are? Even if you eventually go to LA, it's good to get some experience and training before spending the resources to move, either temporarily or permanently.

CHAPTER 33

Stories: Challenges

Hollywood Parents Share Some of the Challenges They have Encountered on this Journey

Victor Boyce

Mirrors *was a humongous commitment because* Mirrors *filmed in Romania. I'm a dad.*

I've got another kid. I've got a wife, got a job.

They said, "OK, you're booked."

Then we were like, "Yes! Awesome! Amazing!"

"And, by the way, they shoot in Romania."

"What? Romania?" First of all, Romania is a real place? Like, isn't that Transylvania? What the hell? So, OK, Romania. OK, well, so how long are we going to be in Romania? A week? Yeah, well, I don't know anything. Still Mr. Green. I don't know that will be, like, eight weeks.

So this is when as a parent...Like I said, he had done a few commercials at this point. This was obviously going to be the biggest thing by far he's ever done. This is when I jumped in with two feet, and I said, "OK, I'm just going. I'm done." I walked away [from my job]. It's terrifying. I walked away. But at this point I'm thinking, "OK, even if it doesn't work out, I can go back."

At this point, there's no going back. No, there's no going back. But back then I thought, "OK, I'm just going to see what happens." So we go to Romania. There's total culture shock, but it was amazing. It was amazing, and that was the big thing.

So Grown Ups *was a comedy. It was great. This movie...OK, so how long are you going to be on* Grown Ups*? Four months. Four months we went to Boston. I literally felt like I moved to Boston.*

I had to open a new bank account. I'm with Wells Fargo; there's no Wells Fargo in Boston. I had to pay bills. I had to run my household from Boston. I had to drive around there. I figured out where to go—I found my Trader Joes. I mean everything...it was like I moved to Boston, and, I have to be honest, it puts a strain on our marriage because we were away, and you can't really...things don't work out the same when you are that far away.

Everything's different. So the way we worked around that, a little bit, was my wife and my daughter flew out for a while. They stayed with us, but, I mean, that's a visit. It's not the same. And you're tested by being away.

I would say the most challenging thing for us at this moment, after all that's happened, is the uncertainty of what's next. Because this TV show [Jessie] has changed the way we do things. Before, we were always going out on auditions, and book here and book there, and it's not consistent. It's not a steady thing.

It has peaks and valleys, but now we've had the stability. That's really kind of nice. This is season four. So when that ends, now what? Go back out onto auditions? Or what's going to happen? So that's probably the most challenging thing right now, even though I think in the back of my mind I feel like he's been steady since that first print job. There's never been a huge low. And now it's just like I said before—one thing begets the next. I think there'll be a Descendants 2, *I think there'll be a* Grown Ups 3, *and I think there'll be something else in TV for him to do.*

(Author's note: shortly after this interview, Cameron was cast as the lead in the new Disney Channel Series, *Gamer's Guide to Pretty Much Everything*).

Clark Trainor

(From Tenzing's *Liv and Maddie* dressing room): *You are sitting in the law office of Clark Trainor right now. I'm lucky—because of the type of law I practice and the way I've structured my office, I'm able to do this. So, we're very fortunate, very lucky.*

You definitely have to get creative, and you find ways to make things work. You just do. You just find ways to make things work.

Because you don't want to just walk away from the opportunity. I have no idea what tomorrow holds. All I know is that Tenzing is on a show now, and he's having a lot of fun, and it's a great opportunity. So you're going to do everything you can to make it happen. And I think almost any parent would. So you just figure it out.

Kim Holt

I think at the beginning, it's just the not knowing. There is no handbook, which...this is an amazing thing that you're doing, because there is no handbook. It's kind of like when you have a child. There is no handbook how to raise a child, but you just kind of figure it out. It's kind of the same thing with this.

You would think that somebody would guide you. You come out here. They say, "Hey, move out here," and then nobody tells you what to do. You can't expect your agents or your manager or anybody. Sometimes they don't really know, which blows me away—that you ask them, and they don't really know. Maybe they just don't want to give you the advice because they don't want to give you the wrong advice or tell you something that may not work for you.

This is a great thing that you're doing, because it was really hard. I think that was the hardest thing. We didn't even know where to get a Coogan account or...We knew the basic rules. We did have a great agent that told us the basic rules about going on auditions or just... work permits, which—I didn't realize you could go pick one up when you moved out here. I was still mailing stuff forever, and I was like, "Really? We can just go pick that up? That would be so much easier than when I'm at the last minute, trying to get it done." There are a lot of things.

I think even just knowing to focus on what your child's doing is one of the most important things, and not worrying about what everybody else is doing. Because I think you can get really down. You can really beat yourself up about stuff. So if you're focusing on what you're doing and the positive stuff that's going on in your life, then you're going to have a much more successful...Because it already is a tough, tough business.

We still are having challenging moments. People starting out may not have this right away, but finding business management...there is no guide to it. You don't really need that when you first start out, but eventually there are certain things, as you go down the road, that you need, and you are kind of lost because you're just like, "Who do you go with? Who is going to be really good? How do you know your manager is really good?"

We are on our second manager, which isn't an easy thing, because you can like somebody all day long, and they're a great person, but is it going to be a good fit for your team? Is that going to be the right person for you? You should be super wise on who you put in your camp—who you hire—because that person is going to be growing with your child, and you need somebody that you can trust one hundred percent. We've had to let people go that I really liked, personally.

But if it doesn't fit and it doesn't work, and they're not doing what we need them to do for the moment that's going to fit for my child, then it's not going to work. What's really hard—and people don't understand—is you still have to pay that person until that project is finished. It's super important to know who you're hiring because that's just the way it works. And that's your kid's money.

You watch your child work really hard, and somebody is getting paid for something they're not even doing any more. Especially hiring a manager you should be super careful about, because you don't really need one if you have a really, really good agent.

I do have to say, our manager at the time worked ruthlessly for Olivia. He is the one that got her out here. But once she started working, we never saw him again. I'm so thankful for all the hard work that he did, and he definitely got paid for the work he did. The other part of it is that you don't know sometimes until it's too late.

When we first came out here, we didn't even know you were supposed to have an attorney. When we first signed our contract with Disney, we had no idea. Those were things that we learned along the way. Because you don't really understand all the fine print, and you're excited that this is something cool that your child is getting to do, even though you probably should have somebody read and go through everything and explain it to you. It's super important.

Pat Fisher

For me, it was the rejection, you know? Because no parent wants to see their child go through that, and Jordan...he was, like, the king of coming in second. He would just make it through so many rounds of auditions. You don't just walk in the room, audition, and book a role. When you are new, especially, and, like, that first time out. And he made it so far—five weeks of auditions and the challenges that my family went through to make all that happen, to just come out to LA. It's not cheap here. Your family is separated and in different directions. My job had to go on hold. Jordan's education went on hold. I mean, life went on hold to come out and see what LA was all about. And, you know, it's a challenge.

Well, at the end of that five-week journey, and he didn't get that part, that was five weeks' worth of a whole lot of work and emotion and dedication and drive and determination. And then to get a no at the end was kind of devastating. And so that's kind of when you figure out really if your kid's made for this. Because Jordan had to shake it off and go on another audition and start all over again. And I would tell him, "You are going to get a hundred no's before you ever get a yes. And then, after you get your first yes, you are going to get a hundred more no's before you get another yes. Don't think just because you come out here and book something that you are set." Because when you walk into the audition room with your kid to audition for something, the kids you see on TV every day are sitting in that same audition, and you are auditioning for the same role. And that's tough. It's really tough, right?

And then when you are out here, you are kind of trying to live your life. But at the same time, it's like, "Yes, I can have lunch with you tomorrow, unless Jordan gets an audition. Yes, I can come in for that job interview—unless Jordan gets an audition." And your whole life revolves around the kid's getting an audition.

But the hardest thing for me personally was the rejection part. You know, eventually, Jordan got to the point where he could just shake it off. And he just goes and puts it out of his mind. And if it comes around again, it comes around again. And if it doesn't, it doesn't. And as a matter of fact, some of the things he's booked, we had written off months before.

Yeah, three months later, they say, "Oh, can you come back in?"

And we're like, "You hadn't secured all those actors for those roles yet?"

And you know what's happened before, too, is just because you booked a pilot and the pilot gets picked up—gets green lit—it doesn't mean you are necessarily going to keep the role that you had in the pilot. And so Jordan...that happened to him more than once.

Not that he shot the pilot, but he auditioned for the pilot, didn't get the role. They shot the pilot, and then [the producers decided] it didn't work for one of the actors in there, and they would call him back in to fill that role that he didn't get to shoot the pilot for. I mean, how disappointing for somebody to shoot the pilot only to find out, "Yeah, you did the pilot, but we don't want you for the show."

And that's just like Jordan getting down to the final two so many times. Once they get to the final two—or the final four, even—you know, as far as that goes, any one of those kids, four kids for one role...any one of them at that stage of the game is worthy of that role. They are very talented, you know. They've worked hard, they've given what they can give for the role, and, as you know, it usually boils down to a chemistry read. It's either your nationality, the color of your skin, do you blend with the family. If it's a boyfriend-girlfriend situation, is the chemistry just right? I mean, when you are down to the chemistry read—better known as screen testing, or whatever you want to call it—that's when it's out of your control. I mean, I've told Jordan a hundred times, "You can be a lot of things, but you can't have blond hair and blue eyes."

I mean, there are just certain things that, when you are down to those finals, they are looking for a particular fit.

Amy Anderson

I think probably the biggest issue that would affect parents—since your book is really geared toward the parents, like, "Here's how to do it"—is that when your child is really young, and if they book something...even on a small thing...they book a commercial shoot...that they're going to be there eight, ten hours, or maybe a couple of days or something, your primary job is...I always tell people this, when they ask, "So what do you all day when you're there?"

I'm like, "I'm pretty much her bitch all day long. I'm her bitch."

And when your kid is very young, it's even more so—like, the bitch you have to be. Because when she started, she couldn't even wipe her own butt. And it's constant.

It's better now that she's seven as opposed to four. She's somewhat more independent, but she couldn't change her own clothes even, and the costume changes were my least favorite part of the day because, one, kids hate putting clothes on and off—they just hate it. There's not a child in the world...They like doing it when they're playing with their friends and they dress up, but when it's like, "Now you have to put on this outfit, now you have to put on that outfit. You have to put on this thing to hold the microphone pack, and you have to put on these shoes that maybe aren't very comfortable, and you have to put on these skinny jeans that aren't comfortable and wear things that you might really not want to wear."

Yeah, and it was just like a chore every time. Then, also, she's sort of the bottom on the totem pole on her show because she's the youngest, and she's been there the least amount of time. Our trailer, of course, is the farthest away from the stage.

It always is. People don't realize that, and when you're four, walking the equivalent of a block is really different than walking like a fifteen-year-old. It takes a second when you're a kid—a teenager—because you can walk an adult pace. A four-year-old is going to trip over their shoe, and they want to sniff this flower. Then they want to do ballet in the middle of the road, and you have to literally watch that they're not getting hit by a golf cart. It is exhausting. And just the changing of clothes, the "Now we're going to take you to get wired. You have five minutes; you should probably have a snack right now. Don't eat candy all day and craft services." I have a roller bag of her schoolbooks that weighs forty pounds that I have to schlep around with me. Stuff like, "Bring a sweatshirt. We're going to be on location." You have to be ready. When they're little like that, your job is so constant. It's like you never get a break. Because she wasn't in studio school yet when she started. So I didn't get that three-hour break. [With school], you can take a nap. You can get your own work done—whatever.

That's what I do now—I use that time. Because I do some freelance writing, and I usually use that school block to get my writing done. But she didn't have school. So before it was constant: "Just bring her here, now bring here, now bring her back, now change her clothes, now take her to the bathroom, now get her a snack, now order her lunch." It was just, like—wow! People think the parents just sit around on set and eat craft services all day. You really don't. And I think the smaller your child is, the harder the job is for the set sitter or the parent who's there with them. Because they really need you every minute of their day that they're not actually shooting the scene. And you have to really, really keep an eye on them. You have to really be there, because sometimes they need something but they're not going to say it, and you have to see it in their face. Everybody else is busy doing their jobs, and they're not likely to catch that stuff.

Pam McCartan

Alison grew five inches—I mean five inches between the ages of thirteen and fourteen. And one of the things you learn about this business—there's a lot you learn about this business—but one of the things you learn about is acting at sixteen and acting at eighteen and then acting pre-sixteen. Well, if you can get a sixteen-year-old that's five feet to play thirteen or twelve or younger, they can work an hour longer. If you can get an eighteen-year-old to play fourteen, and there are no hour regulations, you can't be five five or five six and compete with an eighteen-year-old who's five one and looks fourteen. So when I called her team and said, "Here's the deal. We want to come back," the first thing [her manager] Diane said is, "How tall is she?"

It was the first thing she said because she knows her business. I said, "Well, she's five five and a half."

"Pam, it's going to be tough for her. The chances of her at fourteen going out when there's eighteen-year-olds that can work all hours...I don't think it's worth it to you." And I appreciated that. I appreciated that straightforwardness. Obviously, there's not much in it for them, either, if their client's not going to work, so why do that? As for Ryan, he had a huge growth spurt as well. Not that year—a couple of years later, and he's currently six one.

And so we really couldn't go back until they were adults because until they were adults and they could work all hours, they couldn't compete for those ultimate roles where you're eighteen and you can play fourteen. And I can name the kids that they hung out with that are still huge stars today that lived in the next building at the Oakwood, that swam in the pool with our kids but never grew a whole lot taller than five five or five six, and they're in the business to stay.

So then Allison did some print. Ryan did several commercials. That's about best as we could do in the Twin Cities. We also submitted tape. We had a nice relationship with the greatest casting director in Minneapolis as well, as they both were in two agencies. Because you didn't have exclusive contracts in Minneapolis, so you can be with multiple agents. We continued our relationship between the casting director and Nancy Kremer Management a little bit, where if Lynn, the casting director in Minneapolis, had a project come through and breakdowns that—you know, like a movie—that she thought Ryan was right for, she would go through his agent, and they would tape him and send it in. He was doing more local commercial work than he was sending the tapes, really. A few here and there.

Alison's primary theater was the Children's Theater. I think, including intensive work, she was probably in seven main stage shows and three intensives. Ryan had two primary theaters, the Great American History Theater in Saint Paul and the Guthrie in Minneapolis. But they both were at the dinner theater and stages in some of our local theaters. The Children's Theater and Guthrie Theater are both Tony Award-winning regional theaters, and [Allison and Ryan] both had the great fortune of working in those theaters. And really, they both had a passion for theater. And, as you know, Allison has continued on the theater side. Ryan has pretty much focused on the film and television side but took some time off this year to do Heathers *in New York City.*

Allison Zuehlsdorff

Well, I will say that the very first agency we met with sat us down at the table first thing and told me as a parent that I needed to completely get out of the way, that they knew what was best for my child. Mind you, they had spent exactly ten minutes with Cozi at that point. She was ten years old at the time, so of course that didn't sit well with me. I get that they wanted to be aggressive on behalf of my daughter's career, but I didn't appreciate being intimidated from the get-go. Even as green as we were, we knew right away that it was not the right fit for us. First and foremost she was our daughter, and her well-being and childhood innocence were our first priority.

Looking back over the past six years, it has been a lot of work to keep from compromising along the way. As parents, we have had to self-evaluate many times to make sure we were not using or pressuring Cozi and that she was indeed enjoying the work and happy to go on all the auditions.

By the grace of God and with much effort by Cozi—and our whole family, really—we have stayed pretty close to our original plan. It's been interesting because there have been many, many things we've learned and needed to grow in the knowledge of. The trick has been to learn the difference between growing and compromising. We've found that that can be a very slippery slope.

The hardest thing about this business so far is the in-between time. The in between: between the up of being in a movie and being able to do what you love to do on a day-to-day basis and all the perks that go with that to coming home and having, all of a sudden, nothing.

Nothing for a bit, and then having to audition. The truth is, there are only a few actors and actresses that go from one thing to the next like that. Only a few, if you think of it. Sometimes I encourage us all—like friends that are in the business—let's think of how many of the people really are able to work all the time. It's a very elite group.

I would say also the time away from each other. When you go do a movie, of course, it can be three months plus, and it's not realistic for all the people in the family to go usually. And so it has meant separation. It's usually Cozi and I that go, and then Cozi's dad and sister stay at home. But there are benefits, too: the premieres and the fun—all of that stuff they share. But just the day-to-day...it's separate, and that can be a hard thing.

Kenda Benward

With both of those pilots, Madison High *and* Zombies and Cheerleaders, *we had been in a limbo state for two years because we thought we were moving.*

At the end of Zombies and Cheerleaders*—when we were at the six-month mark of finding out whether it was going to go or it wasn't going to go—the very last minute, we found out it wasn't going to go. And at that point, we had kind of already detached from Tennessee.*

And we were ready. We were like, "You know? Let's just do it. Let's just go. We've wanted to move for ten years. We haven't because our kids have been involved in things here and our life here. But we can always move back. No one says you have to move there and stay there forever."

We can always turn around and get a U-Haul and come right back. And so we sold our house, and we did it. We made that jump permanently. We sold our house; we sold most of our things and put the rest of it on a U-Haul and hitched up our car and drove another car behind the U-Haul and drove out to California two years ago.

Luke was starting his senior year. Gracie was starting her sophomore year in high school. And Ella was starting her sixth-grade year. That was a really hard transition. That was probably harder than anything else we've done as a family.

Because coming from Tennessee to California is just culturally so different. And the diversity is great. Because when you're in a bubble for so long, it's nice to get out of that bubble sometimes and see that there's a big world out there. That's good. But at the same time, it's shocking to your system because you don't really know how to acclimate to it. And you don't have friends that you've been friends with since you were a child, since you were a baby.

And because we came in the summer, a lot of auditions had been missed, like for cheer team and dance team and whatever else there is that they auditioned for in the spring. Those had been missed, so going into the fall, they weren't involved in anything. They had to start brand-new schools not knowing a soul.

It was hard. And Burbank High School is a big school. I don't know how many kids. Three thousand kids? And I could tell that my kids were depressed. It was hard. I was praying, "I don't know what to do. Oh my gosh." We got through that first year and then ended up changing schools for them to another school. And they are thriving now. And doing so well. And I'm so thankful.

It's interesting. I look back on that time at Burbank High School, because I know a lot of kids go there and they really love it and they have a great experience. And I kept thinking, "Why aren't we having a great experience here? What is it we're missing?" And as I'm looking back now...hindsight is always twenty-twenty, right? I just know it's because we weren't supposed to stay there. Seriously.

We weren't supposed to be there—that's why it wasn't fun for us to be there. We were supposed to continue to evolve and move somewhere else. And now they're at a place that they're supposed to be at. They're involved in the community; they're thriving in the community. It's great. It's just been awesome.

Pam McCartan

Probably balancing—trying to balance it all. Ryan got to a point where the Guthrie Theater would call and say, "You know, we're going to do Lost in Yonkers, *and we're looking for two thirteen-year-old boys, and we'd really like you to come down." And I say that because he did some great shows at the Guthrie Theater. And then you have to balance school with work, and he loved school and social. He loved social. And then he was a drummer and a guitarist. He was a musician, and he didn't want to miss those lessons. And he took voice lessons. How do you balance school? Because he loved school. That's the hardest thing, is the balance.*

Pat Fisher

You know, besides being separated as a family, as I was mentioning as a challenge, the finances were incredibly tough. I wish I would have known that I would go through my retirement funds and refinance my house and my life savings. And, you know, you hear all the horror stories about the parents spending the kid's money, and I'm like, "What money? We're going through all our money. What money are we spending here, exactly?"

But really I wish I would have been better financially prepared for the journey. We knew from the first time we came out here that it's very expensive. The cost of living out here is tremendous. Plus we went from a two-parent-working family and one home to a one-parent-working family and two homes. So there is no way to predict that. And when you see the talent and you see the possibilities and you see him getting to number two over and over and over again and the callbacks and the interest level of people, you just can't give up. You want to give up, but you can't. And so you do what you have to do to make that happen, and then you just work toward recovery later.

Amy Anderson

Yeah, it has been hard because, like I said, I write freelance. I do a biweekly column for IAmKorean.com—they're an Asian American publication. They have a printed magazine, and they have a website. I write for the website, roughly about my experience in Hollywood, and that involves Aubrey. I recently just had written in there—I was kind of addressing some of this—and I said, "Aubrey likes being an actor; she doesn't like being famous."

People really...when you try to address that—even in a really polite way—they think that you're being a jerk. I have been called the worst things by trying to protect my child from creepy strangers: "You're a bad mom. You're bad for her career."

I'm like, "She is five," or whatever she was at the time. I literary have had people, in public, yell at me because they were trying to get her autograph. You know those weird autograph collectors who have a stack of pictures, and they show up at a red carpet? Then they talk directly to your child as if you're not there.

They're like, "Aubrey, come here. Sign these."

I say, "You know what..."

Aubrey looks at me like, "I don't want to do any more."

I very politely say, "I'm sorry, but she's tired, and we have to go inside now."

I've had more than one incident where they tell me, "You know what? You're going to ruin her career. You're a mean mom." This one guy said to me, "You should let her talk to her fans. We're not talking to you."

She was six years old, or five. You really have to bite your tongue. If it was somebody dealing with me and my kid wasn't there, I'd be... Especially me as a comedian—I'm very used to just saying whatever I want—I would rip that person a new one. But when you're there in front of your kid, I'm trying to be the best example and somebody that she would want to be proud of. So I'm just like, "OK, just walk away with your child. Don't look at that person," but, man, the part of you that's a mom just wants to go feral. But you just can't because that would be on TMZ immediately the next day: "Lily's mother goes crazy at the red carpet."

Oh, yeah. It has been challenging for me in that respect, and it's been super challenging for her in that she is...People always think when you are an entertainer—in any kind of way—that you're an extrovert, and I find a lot of us are not. I'm very much an introvert, and my daughter's personality is just like me. She is social with people she knows and social with people she likes. She does not like talking to strangers—nor should she—because she is a small child. People expect...well, it's that phenomenon that everybody who's been on TV for more than five minutes knows—that when people see you on TV regularly, they think they know you.

Yeah, because they think you're that character. And they think they know who you are, and they think they know about you. So they feel really comfortable. People who are extroverts feel really comfortable walking up to you and just start getting in your face—talking to you and saying cool things to you—and it's scary to her.

I always tell her, "I will always protect you. Nothing bad is going to happen to you. I will never let a scary person come up to you. It is your choice if you want to take a picture with somebody, your choice if you want to sign an autograph. But you never have to. If it's a red carpet—that's one thing you have to do, some of the red carpet. But when it's just strangers coming up to you or weird people on the side of the red carpet, you never have to. If you want to, that is OK. I will make sure that you are safe, but it is up to you. And if you don't even feel comfortable saying anything, you just tell me, and I will handle it."

She feels pretty confident when she's with me, but my fear for her was she would become agoraphobic, because there was a point where she would just say, "I don't want to go here. I don't want to go," because she knew. "We're going to be a target. Every third person is going to come up to me and go, 'Are you Lily?'" Right in her face. They bend down, and they get in her face. People [actually] put their phone in her face.

Are you kidding me? Like, behind my back, if I turn my back for a second. I turn around...when Aubrey was four, it was the first year she's on the show. We were in a hotel going to an event. I was checking in with the woman where we were supposed to go in, and I told her, "Just sit on this little couch." We're in the lobby of a very nice hotel in Beverly Hills.

That's where the people are craziest, right? There was a lady...I turned around...This is kind of funny, but it was an Asian lady. I heard her behind me go, "What are you doing here?" I didn't know she was talking to Aubrey.

I finished checking in, I turned around, and she was talking to Aubrey. Then when I saw her, I thought, "Is this somebody that I know?" Because I know a lot of people through the Asian American community. I was like, "Is this someone I know? I feel really embarrassed that I don't recognize them." Then I realized, "No, that is just a weird lady attacking my kid."

She was saying, "Here, smile. Hold on, smile."

And Aubrey didn't know what to do. She was just going, "What the hell?"

I just walked up to her, and I said, "Excuse me, but we have to go upstairs now." That was one of the earlier incidents that we had. If that happened right now, that lady would have gotten a piece of my mind. Because you just don't treat children that way, no matter who they are.

Yeah, we've kind of got it down now. I have my list of responses, and I also am very good at scanning. Because she's so little, she doesn't really see it all yet, which is different when your kid is older. I can kind of see stuff that she doesn't see, and I will steer clear of it or position myself to block the people doing the pictures because I don't want her to see all that right now. Because then she will get afraid of going out, and she shouldn't have to feel that way. My next column that I wrote is all about this, actually. It gets really ridiculous. And not to say that we don't love our lives and we don't love everything that the show has brought—not everything, obviously, but the great things that we do love about what her being on the show has brought to our lives. It's been the greatest experience of my life in many ways, and I'm sure probably for her because she's only seven.

It's been half of her life—over half of it now—those parts that are really, really wonderful. But that definitely is some of the hardest, and it's the kind of stuff that you know is lasting.

Some of the worst incidents have been in airports, actually. But the other thing, too, when kids are really little like that...that was another thing that reared its ugly head the first season she was on, because she was little—she was four. Four is a hard year. A lot of tantrums happen around that year.

Three into four was a really difficult time for us, and that's right when she was starting the show. That was another thing that I had to be aware of, was her behavior in public. Because if she throws a tantrum or starts crying about something or has a meltdown, people are going to watch it. And people are going to judge me, and they're going to judge her. And it's going to be on the TV, and there will be GIFs.

Yeah, the memes will be there. I had to really make a conscious decision about what kind of parent I was going to be in public. And as much as people really like to criticize Kate Gosselin, I have to say, there was a moment that I thought, "You know what? Good for her." Because there was a time when she went super under fire for spanking one of her kids in public. She'd swatted her child on the bottom for doing something naughty, and people went ape shit. They attacked her. She made a statement. She said, "I am a mother first and foremost, and it is my responsibility to discipline my children as I see fit, and I am not going to make any apologies for it."

I was like, "Absolutely not." She has to be the right kind of mother that she feels is right for her children. She didn't go bananas and start beating her kid in public. Her kid did something naughty, and she reprimanded her with a swat on the butt. And people saw it and went crazy.

Yeah, now I agree with that. You can't compromise your parenting responsibility just because people are looking, but...

CHAPTER 34

Self-Care for the Hollywood Parent

It's easy when you are a parent to spend all of your resources—time, money, and energy—on your kids. This is simply instinctive for most of us, and it can be difficult to consider what it might mean to take care of ourselves as well.

However, like the flight attendant's classic line about air masks, if you don't take care of your own needs, you may not be able to take care of the ones who depend on you.

Hollywood parents face every issue that most parents of active, ambitious kids do in terms of being stretched in all directions. We juggle the needs of the family while doing whatever we can to support the passions of our children. But there are some special issues that can pose extra challenges.

Some of us are separated from our spouses and possibly other children if we are staying here temporarily to help launch the career of one or more of our kids. This can be profoundly stressful.

Those of us who have not made a permanent move may be covering the cost of two households. This can add tremendous strain to everyday life and to our marriages if we are married.

Many of us are isolated—new to this town and away from friends and family, who may or may not support or understand our decision to make the move to give our kid a shot at their dream. Even if we are lucky enough to have supportive friends and family, it can be difficult to share the details of this world since few people outside of it can really relate. This causes further isolation. Sharing triumphs can feel like bragging. Sharing difficulties can actually feel worse.

If you are not careful, your world can get very small. And you can find yourself looking to your kid for company and friendship when they need you to be their parent.

I am no role model in this department, having been guilty of spending way too much time either alone or just with Dove, who is excellent company, but not a peer. I think I did a pretty good job of keeping my personal concerns firewalled from her (kids have enough of their own concerns and are usually acutely aware of the sacrifices you are making). But I do have a few suggestions and thoughts to share that I hope will help you stay happy and sane while on this adventure.

First, remember that this is your adventure, too. Look for ways to have fun with what you are doing. This will help your kid, too! Stressed-out parents lead to stressed-out kids.

Find ways to stay connected with the people you love, even if they are far away. When my older daughter, Claire, was in Indonesia and India for a year, we had a standing weekly Skype call. Not only did we both look forward to that all week, but it was amazing how connected it allowed us to feel. If you are intimidated by technology, I can assure you that this is pretty easy. Many new laptops have cameras built in now. If your computer does not, you can easily get a simple one from Target or Best Buy or many similar stores for under twenty-five dollars that plugs into a USB port. Even easier may be using Skype or FaceTime or a similar program on your phone. Being able to look into the eyes of someone you love who is far away is priceless.

Simpler than Skype, of course, is staying in touch with your own support system via phone. We are the primary support system for our kids, and we need support ourselves if we are to be able to sustain that role. A long talk with a friend or close family member can make a huge difference, restoring perspective and sanity!

Parents of other kids in the business can become great friends if you are lucky. As someone who likes to assume the best of everyone, I have had to learn the hard way—to my disappointment—that not all parents of kids in this industry are natural allies. Some are deeply competitive and genuinely crazy. Happily, most are grounded, good people who simply want to do the best they can for their kids. Take a little time getting to know someone before sharing too much, just to be on the safe side. At this point I can say with real pleasure that some of my favorite people in the world—true friends—are fellow Hollywood parents. And because we have shared so many of the same experiences, it feels like we are members of an accidental club.

Even if you are successful in finding ways to combat isolation, money can be a huge source of stress. I know a number of families who have sacrificed decades of assets and sold their homes or added second mortgages—or all of the above and then some—to finance this dream. This is a very personal set of decisions to make, and I can't tell anyone where to draw the line, but do remember that it does not do your child any good if you actually go broke or sacrifice your own future security for this dream. No child should have to bear that guilt.

I encourage honesty and whatever level of transparency you feel comfortable with in conversations with your child about what you are and are not able to do in terms of committing financial resources to this pursuit. Obviously this is somewhat dictated by the age and maturity of your child. But most of us do not have unlimited resources, and this is a fact of life. Even if you end up returning home without having conquered this town, you will have learned so much that your time will not have been wasted. Yours may be a story like the McCartans'—one pilot season in Los Angeles when your kid is young, and then a return to LA when they are a young adult that comes with success, the foundation having been laid years before.

Los Angeles is a relatively expensive town, but there are still many things you can do that are cheap or free. There is no reason to stay cooped up in an apartment waiting for the next audition. Getting out, even if just for a walk, can make a difference in the quality of your day.

Finally, a note for those of us who end up doing this for years: there will come a day when suddenly your child is able to manage their career without you. Or at least enough on their own that you are free to start to turn your attention back to your own path. Part of the reason I spent so much time and effort putting together a great team for Dove was in anticipation of when she turned eighteen and would no longer need me constantly on set. Again, this is different for everyone, but I knew that she was mature enough that she might want to be reasonably independent at that point. Over the course of the last year, her managers and she have handled more and more of the communications I used to field. I am incredibly proud of how well she is dealing with the very adult demands of her professional life. And I am also still part of the team, though less hands-on than I was for the four years it took to get to this new phase.

I have seen parents—single moms seem to be especially vulnerable to this—literally at a loss as to what to do with themselves when they get to this place. Many have sacrificed their own careers as well as personal assets to get their kid up and running in this business, and when that chief organizing element is gone, they are in many ways starting from scratch. Don't let this be you. The day is coming when your child will leave, whether to go off to college or to assume the reins of their own career and move out, and the more both of you are prepared for this, the better. Have a plan in place for yourself. Lay some track for your own future while you are busy doing this for your kid, and you will both be in good shape when that day arrives.

Tips and Takeaways

- Make sure to take care of your own needs as well as those of your kid/s. Reach out to friends and family, and look for new friends.
- Get out of the house, and not just for auditions. Many of the best things to do in LA are cheap, or free. Remember: this is your adventure too!
- Prepare for the day when your young actor is ready to be independent. Set up the best team you can for your kid, and be ready to turn your attention back to your own life when it's time.

CHAPTER 35

Some Notes on Success

If your child is lucky enough and talented enough to find what anyone would call success as an actor—steady work, a growing positive reputation, and increasing opportunities—this opens up a whole other host of issues. Many of these issues fall into the "first-world problems" category, but they can be problems nonetheless. Some are easy to predict: jealousy from friends and strangers, decreasing privacy, questioning whether people value you for you or for your fame. It's one thing for adults to have to grapple with these issues, but it is not easier for a child, who may already have the normal insecurities of a young person to deal with. One nasty comment on social media can erase a hundred nice ones. Once someone hits a certain profile level, they can become objectified in the eyes of many people, even if they are still just a kid or teen. Online bullying is something many kids have to contend with, but it can be greatly magnified with fame. A healthy sense of self helps here. As do regular breaks from social media.

If your kid becomes extremely successful, the pressures can sometimes become intense. Finding ways to create boundaries to protect them is important, as is good coaching for the unavoidable difficulties. Here is where it is more important than ever to have a strong team in place to keep your child's career and life on track by guiding them toward good choices. This often means passing up the quick money in favor of a slower but longer career arc. Sometimes it means saying no to work that is not in alignment with the future you envision. A "small" but high-quality role or project might be a better choice than a bigger one that takes your kid's image in the wrong direction. Every time you see a young artist do something questionable in terms of a performance or endorsement choice, realize that an entire team of people thought it was a good idea. And frequently money was the deciding factor instead of the child's long-term success. Don't let that be your kid.

CHAPTER 36

This Is a Small Town

I lived most of my life in a genuinely small town—an island, in fact. Moving to LA, I assumed that running repeatedly into the same people and having a sense of community was something I would lose. I could not have been more wrong.

Los Angeles covers a truly vast expanse of real estate, but somehow it is still a small town. I think that's because in Hollywood, the law of six degrees of separation works especially well. In my experience, it's been more like one or two degrees of separation.

Everybody seems to know everybody, and the examples are endless. When we were introduced to the new costume designer for season two of *Liv and Maddie,* we realized we had met at a backyard party at a mutual friend's house the previous summer in Burbank. Our mutual friend is not in the industry, nor is her husband. But their daughter babysat the costumer's daughter for years.

If someone is not in the industry here, they know a ton of people who are. And since all of these people work on different projects constantly, their networks are large and ever changing. If you step back and trace the links between all of us, it is kind of breathtaking. We are all connected.

Why am I talking about this? Because that is what we do. We talk. Everybody talks. And talk is an equal-opportunity medium—it can make or break reputations. Is someone great to work with? Are they hardworking and professional? Or are they a diva and difficult? What about the parents, if the actor is a child? We all have opinions on the people we've worked with, and it's not even necessarily gossip. If someone is a joy to work with, we want to work with them again, and we would definitely recommend them to our friends. Conversely, if they were a nightmare, we'd try hard to avoid a repeat of that experience, and we'd want our friends to escape that too. It's natural.

Every project has a lot at stake in its success—often years of work and deferred rewards, as well as small or large fortunes on the line. So this information is relevant, maybe even vital to know. Why stack the deck against your livelihood when another choice could make things so much easier? Here you see the critical importance of keeping a sterling reputation.

I know that people outside of Hollywood love to tell stories about how outrageous certain actors can be—how difficult to work with, how demanding and diva-like they are. But in all honesty, my experience is that the vast majority of people at the top—whether actors, directors, producers, tech people, wardrobe, hair, makeup, agents, managers, or anyone else—are smart, thoughtful, hardworking people. I think it's hard to get to the top without those qualities; frankly, there are just too many other good people to choose from. No one wants to work with someone difficult if they have a choice—and there is nearly always a choice. Keeping your reputation, and that of your kid, sparkling is one of the easiest things you can do to make sure the role goes to your child instead of someone else when the choice gets down to two actors. And it makes for a better life in general.

CHAPTER 37

Faith and Resilience

Even with all the pieces in place—a supportive family, financial stability, genuine talent, a solid résumé, and a great team—this business is difficult. There are no guarantees that your child will succeed. Having these things helps, of course. And your child could succeed without some of them, but the road would be even more challenging. Pursuing a career as an actor—or helping your child to—is in many ways an exercise in faith.

Every audition is an exercise in faith. Faith that the time and energy spent preparing will not be wasted. Faith that this role is really yours (or your child's). Faith that if your kid is not cast, there is a reason for it that lines up with the greater good. Faith that everything happens for a reason.

Many people find faith in religious traditions, and some find it without organized support. But whatever direction you draw it from, I think you and your child must have some kind of faith and resilience to survive the constant uncertainty that is the daily experience of someone going after a career as an actor. Certainly these are good strengths for anyone to have.

I wish we had actually counted how many auditions Dove went out for before finally landing her first professional role—a recurring guest star on *Shameless*. But I do know that the audition just before that one—one day before, on a different series—was for "Mud-Covered Girl." That's right—a girl covered in actual mud, unrecognizable, who had one line. And she didn't get it. That night when we got off the phone with Dove's agent, who'd delivered the bad news (was it really bad news?) that she didn't get the role, Dove moaned, "This is ridiculous! I can't even get Mud-Covered Girl!" It was definitely a low point, and rather sobering. Really. If you can't get Mud-Covered Girl, what can you get?

It turns out that you can get the attention of a different casting director literally the next day—one who thinks you are perfect for what *they* need—and finally land on IMDb with a role on a critically acclaimed show and suddenly be vaulted into a whole different league of auditions, for much bigger roles. And it bears noticing that if Dove *had* been cast as Mud-Covered Girl, the guest star role would not have happened because she would not have been available.

This was encouraging, but it would be another eight long months before she was cast again—in the pilot that eventually became *Liv and Maddie*. There were many near misses along the way, and at that point, around a hundred auditions, mostly for leads and supporting leads, many for roles Dove *really* wanted. Some were for roles she didn't want as much, but her agent wanted her to get in front of the casting director just to begin a relationship.

If we had given up at twenty or fifty or even ninety-eight auditions, she might be attending Santa Monica Community College or FIDM right now instead of starring in her own show, promoting her fourth film, and collaborating with songwriters and music producers at the age of nineteen. There is nothing wrong with that other path—in fact, there is much that is right about it—but that wasn't the dream. Giving up means giving up the dream. But it also creates the space for a new dream to emerge.

It takes great inner strength and belief in yourself to get up and memorize new sides and then walk into a room in front of a casting director and camera over and over again when there is no definite evidence that you will succeed. The kids who do this are amazing to me, and so are their parents. Learning to take rejection without having it be personal is critical for this business and an important life skill. So is developing the emotional resilience to get out of bed and chase your dream despite the odds. Rejection is a part of life, but there are few paths that have so much of it baked in.

Remembering to not take things personally is one of the most important lessons that Hollywood offers.

Ultimately, I feel that there are enough valuable life experiences to be gained from the pursuit of this dream that even if it doesn't take you and your child where you hope to go, it is likely to be worth it. My personal mantra has become "May the right thing happen." I have given up believing that I always know what the right thing is. Too many times in my life, what looked like a gift was not, and what looked like disaster was actually a gift. At this point in my own journey—which, at this writing, has included five years as a Hollywood parent—I am firmly in the camp of "everything happens for a reason." This is my way, and the way of many other people I meet in this business, of trusting that the universe is guiding things in the right direction, and it supports my sense of faith when the inevitable curveballs come.

As I make the final edits to this manuscript and look at how our lives have been transformed by the leap of faith we made in coming to Hollywood—Los Angeles, really—I am in awe of all the wonderful people we have met and the incredible experiences we have had. I am proud to be friends with some of the most talented, generous artists and creators on the planet. I am incredibly grateful for our good fortune and excited to see what the future brings. And I wish all the very best of luck to you and your talented kid (or kids). May the right thing happen for you.

CHAPTER 38

Stories: Advice for Parents Considering This Journey

Words of Wisdom from Hollywood Parents

Victor Boyce

I would say—for sure—if your kid thinks they want to do it, you should definitely try. Because if you don't try, that's worse because you'll have that regret of never knowing what could have happened. I think what happens is, a lot of people, they'll try it, and then it won't be for them. And they'll say, "OK, we tried it, and it didn't work." But if you don't try it, you'll have regrets. Especially if your kid is serious and they really, really want to do it and try it. They might be resentful of it, even. So you don't want that. So if there's any possibility, if you have the time to go on some auditions, and your kid really thinks they want to do it, absolutely try it. Because you never know what can happen.

I had no clue. If you told me six years ago Cameron would be on five movies and thirty commercials and three music videos...and a guest star on this...and cameos...And he's got a million followers on Twitter. I'm like, "What? There's no way in hell." He's got a million followers on Twitter. I remember when he got forty thousand, and I thought that was amazing. I was blown away.

Right? So I would say absolutely give it a try. Because you don't want those regrets of not going for it. But, honestly, the odds are slim. But there is a chance, and so don't have any regrets—go for it, and have fun with it.

Pam McCartan

I think the one thing is to be really grounded in your understanding of the look. The look. Because I know—Ryan knows, he has a lot of confidence—that he's talented enough to be here and that it's always going to go down to what they're looking for. Sometimes, we were taught...sometimes you can change their mind.

I think we, as parents, we all have that thing, that Mama Bear, Papa Bear thing. You know. Where whether that's in sports or whether that's in education...whether that's in theater—whatever it is, we have that, "But they should have gotten an A. I can't believe they didn't get an A. They didn't get an A in Choir? What do you mean? They have the most beautiful voice." There's just nothing you can do about that.

You just have to be resilient, and you have to be able to move on. Because otherwise the business is not for you.

I think my big thing is do it for the right reasons. Just do it for the right reasons. Do it because your child really wants to do it and they really have, in my opinion, what it takes to do it. And that is the courage, the confidence. The talent is obvious, you know. Most of us have talented kids in one aspect or another. I mean, all of our kids are talented at something.

So given the fact that they might be talented in the arts, they've also got to have that courage and determination—that work ethic. There are a lot of sacrifices, a lot of sacrifices for everybody. You have to be—and your child has to be—willing to make those sacrifices and not say, "No, I want to stay back and play with my friends today. I don't want to go to that audition."

Because if they're going kicking and screaming, you are doing it for the wrong reasons. So it's got to be a really strong desire on everybody's part, and everybody has to be willing to make the sacrifices, because there are a lot of them. I mean, there are resource sacrifices... there's everything. Living arrangements, money, and friendships—all those things. It's a huge family commitment. Huge.

Clark Trainor

You've got a lot of parents out there who want it, but do their kids want it? That's the first, number one.

Number two, if you are in it for the fame, well, good luck with that. Because once you get the fame, first off, the fame ain't all that. The other thing I tell Tenzing: "All these things you see on Twitter are really sweet, really great, wonderful. But six months after the show has gone off the air and the next show comes, that *kid is the next big thing."*

It is not real; it is not lasting. If you are doing this for the fame, the minute you get into your thirties and roles start drying up, then your forties and then they really start drying up, and then your fifties, what is going to sustain you?

The only thing that can sustain you is the work—if they are passionate about the work and make sure that they are focusing on the work. It's entirely about the work at the end of the day. In thirty years—in fifty years—you are not going to look back and say, "Oh, remember when I was twenty and all those people...I had all those followers on Twitter."

You are going to look back, and you are going to look at your scenes, and you are going to say, "I remember the feeling I had in that scene" or "Look how I connected with the other actor in that scene." With the people.

[Another point] is just how small this big town is. Everybody knows everybody. And while on the outside you hear really bad things,

everyone I've met is fantastic. Really sweet, and they want you to do a good job because it makes them look good, and it makes their job easier. Everybody from the set decorator to the props to the lighting to sound—everybody wants you to succeed. When you walk into the room, you might feel like it's an adversarial process, but it's not at all. They want you to succeed.

Amy Anderson

Obviously, we know that stereotype of that crazy stage parent who is pushing their kid, trying to live vicariously or brainwashing their kid into, like, "Don't you want to be a star?" and stuff. I'm not even speaking to those people, because there's nothing we can do to convince those people to knock it off.

For those people who have young kids, and the kids have expressed their interest, it's just natural. Like we were saying before, even when your kid books huge things and seems happy, you still question whether you did the right thing. But I think the main thing is your kid will just tell you if it's what they like or not. A kid at that age can't understand the scope of what it means to be on TV and for someone all around the world to see you. Or even a commercial—everyone in the country is going to see you on this McDonald's commercial or whatever. They don't really understand that, but they will tell you in their own way what they love. That's really the best barometer you have, the best guidance, because even though Aubrey had never said, "I want to be an actor. I want to be on TV," until that moment when we specifically talked about it, she's a natural performer because I'm a performer. It's in her DNA. And she had always loved to sing, and she loves to dance. Her friends come over, and they put on the show.

It was in her personality, and even though it was shocking that she booked it, it wasn't shocking to me that she was good at it and that she had fun doing it. When she did her first audition and then her callback—especially I remember the callback—she came out of the room…I let her go in the room without me. The first one, I went with her. The second one, she went in alone because the producers wanted to know that she could, without me there. It was funny. I'll never forget it. My heart was pounding. I was like, "Oh my God. I'm just so worried that she's in there without me." I knew I could trust these people, but for a second I put my ear in the door. "Oh my God. If they open this door..." And I was like the one stooge, falling. I thought, "I will be so mortified." I literally said to myself, "Amy, press your back against the wall, and don't take it off until this door opens. Because you will never forgive yourself if that door opens and you're standing there." That would have been the worst.

I'll just never forget. The door opened, and she came skipping out. She was all smiles, and I said, "How did it go?"

She went, "It was good. I did my scene two times."

I just remember Steve Levitan looking around the door and going, "She did a really good job, Mom."

And I thought, "OK, great." Then they called her and wanted her to screen test. I told her, "OK, you're going to do this scene one more time, but it's going to be different. There's going to be a lot of people there. They're going to have a camera. They might put a microphone on you."

She kept saying, "Let's practice my scene again. Let's practice my scene," and she would ask me to tape it. She goes, "You make the video. Let's do my scene," and she memorized both. It was a scene between her and Jesse. She had the whole dialogue memorized, and she was, "Now you pretend to be the little girl, and I'm going to be the daddy." It was like a game to her.

Of course, she can't understand, "Yeah, I want to be on a hit show and be famous and have strangers come up to me in Target." That's not what I mean. It wasn't like she was driven to be famous; she enjoyed the game of it. It was fun to her. So I felt OK about letting her go ahead and do it. She told me through her actions. Her emotions and feelings. She never felt like she was being pushed to do it.

Yeah, your kid will let you know in their own way.

Pat Fisher

First of all, as we've already talked about, please make sure it's your kid's passion. The kid really has to really, really want to be on stage and really, really want to entertain people and really, really get a lot of joy out of doing that. And then, second of all, make sure you have some kind of family balance. Because I did spend months apart from my husband several times, and we have a very strong marriage. We did then, and we do now, and we did the whole time in between. But not everybody makes it. You know? Family balance is very, very important. And also one mistake I see parents make often is, once the kid starts making money, the parents quit parenting. It's like, "My kid's making more money than I am; now I can't tell them what to do anymore." You have to be Mom first or Dad first. I know dads that come out, too.

It's not just the mom and the kid. It's a dad and the kid, too—whatever works for your family. But don't quit parenting your child. You know, Jordan is twenty, and I'm still parenting him just as any loving, normal mom would do. He's independent, he's grounded, he knows who he is, where he's going, where he wants to be. But I'm still his mom, and I'm always going to be his mom. But it never got to the point that I quit parenting when he made money. So just because your kid makes money doesn't mean they don't need a mom and dad.

Kim Holt

I wish I would have known the timing that's in it because it was really complicated for our family to learn how to navigate through the time. We used to spend a lot of time together as a family, and now it's super challenging. I think it's challenging for all families today because families are generally busy, whether their kids are in sports or doing whatever.

I think we have the same challenges as people that have kids in competitive baseball that travel all over, or whatever they're doing. I think we have the same kind of challenges. As far as that goes, that has to be probably the most surprising thing to me…is that I just didn't realize how time-consuming it was. I didn't think anything could be more time-consuming than gymnastics.

Definitely make sure it's something that they really want to do. It's not something that you take lightly, especially if you don't live out here. You're picking up your family, and you're moving everything out here. I think you should definitely let your kids follow their dreams if you can do it—if it's manageable for your family—but I don't think… They always have when they turn eighteen, if it doesn't work for your family. I think that it has to work. Otherwise you could be spending a lot of your money, a lot of your retirement money. I don't think it's what people think it's going to be.

There is nothing good about fame, except that you can help with charity or things that are positive like that. I think that's the only good thing that comes from having a face that's famous. Other than that… I know in our situation, Olivia doesn't even think about that kind of stuff. She just wants to be a normal kid, and she does what she does because she loves it. I know other people don't understand that because I've been on the other side, too. You're like, "Why do you do that?" When you're twelve years old, you're not sitting in your bedroom, going, "I want to be famous."

From our standpoint, that wasn't her thing. She did it because she loved it. Like I said, she didn't even know…she didn't even want to know how much money she made until maybe a year or two ago. When we first started, she was asking, "How much do we have to pay them so I can do that again?"

I think the most important thing is to make sure it's something that's your kid's dream and it's nothing that you hope for your kid, even if they act like they have a little bit of interest in it. Make sure it's their wholehearted dream, not something that they may get sick of in six months, because it's a lot to give up to...It's a huge sacrifice, and they're sacrificing their childhood.

I know Olivia doesn't see that she sacrificed her childhood because she loves what she is doing. If you're not loving it, then you're sacrificing it.

We left at a perfect time in middle school—when middle-school girls are not very friendly—and then she started on it. She was always hanging out with her gymnastics friends and her cheerleading friends. She was a girlie girl. Then we came on a show, and she was the only girl, and she had no idea she was going to be the only girl. She was like, "Wait. Where are the girls?"

She grew up with these boys that became her brothers, and they were amazing. The good thing about it is that she knows how to be a friend to guys and knows that you don't have to just be a boyfriend or whatever. She likes that. No drama. There is not drama with boys. And if there is, they say what they have to say, and it's done. So it was a great way for her to grow up. I wouldn't trade it for anything in the world.

Allison Zuehlsdorff

I wish I would have known that it was going to be harder than I thought as a parent to navigate between being too hands-on and being invisible.

I think that we run the gamut, and those that are working with our kids can sometimes want us to be invisible. Sometimes they are expecting us to be overbearing when we're not planning on being any such thing, you know?

And sometimes we don't realize if we're being too hands-on. And I feel like our actors—especially our little actors—are going to end up being their best professional selves by them learning, through doing well, how much preparation it took to do what they really wanted to do. They have to start owning all that for themselves at some point, and so us parents need to have a healthiness about us, learning to let go at the right rate.

What I always say is, "Don't do it because you want to be famous." It's because you want to act, not because you want to get attention—not because you're looking to fill a longing in your soul.

There are enough hard things in this business that if you're not doing it for the sake of the art...

And I think that if your child starts not wanting to do it, it's hard for a parent to accept that, especially when they've invested a lot of money in headshots, training, gas, et cetera. I think we parents have to check in with ourselves all along the way to make sure that we are not so invested ourselves that we could become oblivious to the fact that our child actor may be done with the whole thing at some point.

Kenda Benward

My advice for parents who have kids that are constantly bugging you with "I want to go to LA, I want to be on Disney Channel, I want to be an actor..." My advice to you is make sure that acting—taking acting class, voice class, dance class—that that doesn't become their identity.

I believe that their identity has to be grounded in something that's stable and that's real. And that may be your faith, or it may be your family. It may be your community. It looks different for everybody.

But just don't make this industry define who they are. Because it will chew you up and spit you out and not care. And if the family environment can be the place of support, the place where the child can come back to and know that it's safe...and whether they get the audition or whether they don't, it doesn't matter. Life is still great, and we're still going to go to the football game. And we're still going to go roller-skating on Saturday and hang out with friends tomorrow, and you're still going to go to school on Monday.

As long as their life stays intact and the audition doesn't basically control the way that they feel about themselves, I think that is really important. Because when you audition as an actor, it's such a personal experience because you're putting your own creativity out there on the line for someone else to judge.

But at the same time, it's not personal from their perspective. They're not looking at you as a creative being. They're looking at you as something that they can sell. That they can market.

And so it's not personal to them. To them, it's like, "Do they have brown hair? Are they tall enough? Do they fit with the image that we're trying to create?"

So if it's your identity, then you begin to take it personally as opposed to just going, "Look, this is who I am. This is what I offer. And if it works for you, great. And if it doesn't, I've got a great life over here, and I'm going to go live it."

RESOURCES AND REFERENCES

There are some excellent online resources available to help parents navigate this often-confusing world. This list is by no means exhaustive, but these are sites that have been helpful to our journey.

Agents

The ATA, or Association of Talent Agents
http://www.agentassociation.com/
Licensed talent agents who belong to this nonprofit industry association are accountable to an additional supervising body of peers. This website also provides links to relevant industry news.

SAG-AFTRA
http://www.sagaftra.org/content/agents-and-managers
This link takes you to the union's excellent basic information on agents and managers, as well as advice on finding a good one.

The two links below will take you to lists of SAG and AFTRA franchised agents. Don't even consider working with an agent who is not on one of these lists.
http://www.sagaftra.org/professional-representatives/aftra-franchised-agents
http://www.sagaftra.org/professional-representatives/sag-franchised-agents

CHSPE Test

California High School Proficiency Exam
http://www.chspe.net/
Here you can find test dates, preparation, registration, and general information.

Coogan/Blocked Trust Accounts

http://www.sagaftra.org/content/coogan-law
Again, SAG-AFTRA is a great source of solid information. The following is from their website:

"Below you will find a partial list of banks, credit unions and brokerage firms that offer Coogan/Trust Accounts. Screen Actors Guild provides this list for information purposes only and does not endorse any particular institution… Some require a first paycheck to open the account, some a minimum deposit and the interest rates vary."

- AFTRA/SAG Credit Union
- Actors Federal Credit Union
- Bank of America
- Bank of the West
- City National bank
- First Entertainment Credit Union
- Morgan Stanley/Smith Barney
- Union Bank of California
- Wells Fargo

Author's note: This list was accurate at the time of this writing. Check with the SAG-AFTRA website to get an updated list of good Coogan account institutions.

Emancipation Grid from BizParentz.org

http://www.bizparentz.org/thebizness/emancipation.html
This chart spells out the differences between a child who is underage but a legal eighteen versus one who is emancipated. It is very useful. Click the icon on the top right of the web page.

Karaoke Tracks for Auditions
http://www.karaoke-version.com

Minor Work Permits
These sites provide laws, performer regulations, and general information on obtaining a work permit for your young actor.

California
http://www.dir.ca.gov/dlse/DLSE-CL.htm

National
http://www.sagaftra.org/content/state-statutes

Monologue Sources for Children and Teens
Magnificent Monologues for Kids by Chambers Stevens
Magnificent Monologues for Kids 2 by Chambers Stevens
Magnificent Monologues for Teens by Chambers Stevens

Sheet Music Resources
Music Notes
http://www.musicnotes.com

Sheet Music Plus
http://www.sheetmusicplus.com/

Sample résumé format for actor with agent:

SUPER FINE TALENT AGENCY

8888 Sunset Blvd, suite 100, Los Angeles, CA 90069
(555)111-1234, talent@superfinetalent.com

CATE RUIZ

SAG-AFTRA

Hair: Dark Brown — Weight: 110
Height: 5′1″ — Eyes: Brown
Age: 11

TELEVISION

THE PERFECTIONIST	Guest Star	CBS
MAGIC COAST (PILOT)	Series Regular	Disney Channel
GUILTY AS CHARGED	Featured	Warner Bros.
LOST AGAIN	Costar	ABC

FILM

NOW OR NEVER	Lead	Disney Channel
ALMOST KILLERS	Supporting	SKY Pictures
GIVE ME A SIGN	Featured	Traverso-Raye Prod.

THEATER

ANNIE	Annie	Dir. Deirdre Cory
ONCE UPON A MATTRESS	Nightingale of Samarkand	Dir. Daniel Fox
THE WIZARD OF OZ	Dorothy	Dir. Theresa Smith
LES MISERABLES	Little Cozette	Dir. Steven McAfee

RECORDING

YOU AND ME	Prod. Sam Jones	Wildwood Records

COMMERCIALS — List available on request

TRAINING

VOICE	Mary Reynolds
ACTING—Scene Study	Arthur Sackler
ACTING—For the Camera	Samantha Scrivener

SPECIAL SKILLS

Singing, swimming, tennis, horseback riding, gymnastics, dance, basic guitar. Can wiggle ears and do "the wave" with eyebrows.

Sample résumé format for young actor with no agent, less experience:

CATE RUIZ

(555)111-1234, catesmom@ymail.com

Hair: Dark Brown	Weight: 95
Height: 4'10"	Eyes: Brown
Age: 11	

THEATER

ANNIE	Orphan#4	Dir. Deirdre Cory
THE WIZARD OF OZ	Munchkin	Dir. Theresa Smith

COMMERCIALS

Kingston Toyota	Principal	Sunrise Productions

TRAINING

ACTING—Improv Class	Arthur Sackler
LITTLE STARS SUMMER CAMP	Denise Smithson

SPECIAL SKILLS

Singing, swimming, tennis, horseback riding, gymnastics, dance, basic guitar. Can wiggle ears and do "the wave" with eyebrows.

COMMON TAX DEDUCTIONS FOR ACTORS

Below is a list of some common tax deductions for actors and performers. These can be deducted up to the acting income earned.

I am not an accountant, and this list is not complete or necessarily applicable to your situation, but it's intended to get you thinking about and tracking relevant expenses as you incur them instead of at the end of the year. Keep accurate records, and consult an accountant before you deduct these expenses from your child's tax return.

Part of treating your child's career like the business that it is, is helping them keep as much of their hard-earned money as possible.

<u>Education Expenses</u>
coaching and lessons
dance training
voice training
rehearsal hall rental
CDs and downloaded recordings for training

<u>Promotional Expenses</u>
audition tapes/DVDs
business cards
headshots—photography
headshots—printing costs
mailing supplies (postage, envelopes)
website development, hosting

<u>Communication Expenses</u>
percentage of cell phone use for business
Skype or other software, if used for business

<u>Special Expenses and Supplies</u>
commissions (agent, manager, etc.)
dues (union, professional)

meals (if for business)
trade publications
trade subscriptions (IMDb, etc.)
camera/video equipment

Travel Expenses
car travel (in miles) to auditions
car travel (in miles) to business meetings
parking fees
airfare to auditions
taxi, train, bus, or subway expenses to auditions

INTERVIEW SOURCES

Amy Anderson November 19, 2014 (in-person interview)
Mother of Aubrey Anderson-Emmons, best known for playing Lily on *Modern Family.*

Kenda Benward October 1, 2014 (in-person interview)
Mother of Luke Benward, best known for *Ravenswood, Cloud 9, Good Luck Charlie, Minutemen, Dear John, How to Eat Fried Worms,* and *Because of Winn-Dixie.*

Victor Boyce October 7, 2014 (in-person interview)
Father of Cameron Boyce, best known for *Jessie, Gamer's Guide to Pretty Much Everything, Disney Descendants, Grown Ups, Mirrors,* and *Jake and the Never Land Pirates.*

Pamela Fisher December 17, 2014 (in-person interview)
Vice President, Abrams Artists Agency—Head of Youth and Young Adult.

Pat Fisher November 24, 2014 (in-person interview)
Mother of Jordan Fisher, best known for *Teen Beach Movie and Teen Beach Movie 2, Liv and Maddie,* and *The Secret Life of the American Teenager.*

Kim Holt December 19, 2014 (in-person interview)
Mother of Olivia Holt, best known for *I Didn't Do It, Kickin' It, Same Kind of Different as Me,* and *Girl Vs. Monster.*

Pam McCartan October 18, 2014 (in-person interview)
Mother of Ryan McCartan, best known for *Liv and Maddie, Summer Forever, Royal Pains, Monsterville: The Cabinet of Souls,* and *Heathers the Musical.*

Clark Trainor November 17, 2014 (in-person interview)
Father of Tenzing Norgay Trainor, best known for playing Parker on *Liv and Maddie*.

Bonnie Zane March 30, 2015 (phone interview)
Casting Director, Principal at Zane Pillsbury Casting.

Allison Zuehlsdorff December 8, 2014 (in-person interview)
Mother of Cozi Zuehlsdorff, best known for *Dolphin Tale, Dolphin Tale 2, Sofia the First, Mighty Med,* and *Liv and Maddie.*

GLOSSARY

Action

The cue the director calls when the cameras are ready to roll.

AD (Assistant Director)

The individual who relays instructions from the director to the actors and is in charge of logistics on set. There are often tiers of ADs: 1st AD, 2nd AD, even second 2nd and 3rd ADs.

ADR (Additional Dialogue Recording/Automatic Dialogue Replacement)

A postproduction studio recording that matches the actor's voice to picture. Also known as *looping*.

AFTRA (American Federation of Television and Radio Artists)

National labor union representing performers, journalists, and other artists working in entertainment and news. Merged with SAG to become SAG-AFTRA in March 2012.

Agent

Someone who represents talent. Agents' chief function is to secure work for their clients. Theatrical agents represent talent primarily for film and TV projects; commercial agents represent talent primarily for print and ad work. An actor might have both kinds of agents. Agents must be licensed, and franchised by SAG or AFTRA.

Audition

A meeting between an actor and a casting director through which the actor can demonstrate talent and ability for a certain role and the casting director can determine whether that actor is the person they want in the role.

Avail (short for *available*)

A status that means an actor is strongly being considered for a booking and should keep the requested period of time (the avail) open in order to be able to work, if booked. A few other actors may be held on avail for the same role at the same time. This status is promising but offers no guarantees. Actor on avail must let casting know if anything comes up to remove them from availability for that set time. Used more in commercial work. See also: *Pinned.*

Background

Actors with no lines, used to help set the scene. Also called *extras.*

Base Camp

An area near or on the shooting location where trucks, trailers, dressing rooms, wardrobe, hair and makeup, craft services, catering, bathrooms, equipment, and the background holding area are located. Generally not needed on a studio lot.

Billing

The order of the names in credits or title sequences. Often hotly negotiated in contracts.

Bio (Biography)

A brief résumé in paragraph form. Used in press releases, websites, or programs.

Blocking

The basic physical movements of actors on a stage or set. Blocking positions are often marked on the floor with tape.

Booking

A commitment made to an actor for a job. Generally followed by a contract.

Breakdown

The detailed description of a project, including key players (director, producers, casting director) story line, and roles available for casting. Often includes estimated start date and location of production.

Callback

A request to return for another audition for an actor being considered for a role.

Call Sheet

The daily shooting schedule. Lists scenes, cast, and key production people. Incredibly useful for learning names of the people on set.

Call Time

The time an actor is due on set. For a movie, this may be the time transportation picks an actor up to go to set.

Casting Assistant

The casting director's assistant, whose primary job is scheduling auditions, answering phones, and wrangling actors coming in to audition.

Casting Director

Also known (incorrectly) as a casting agent. Person responsible for choosing which actors will play the lead and supporting roles in a film or TV show, under the supervision of the director and producers.

Casting Service

An online service that allows performers to post their headshots, résumés, and special skills for consideration by casting directors.

Cattle Call

An audition where a very large number of actors turn out. Also known as an *open call*.

Cheating

A slight adjustment in an actor's position for the sake of the camera or stage audience.

Chemistry Read/Chemistry Test

One of the final stages of casting, in which actors are paired in different combinations to see which ones have the best "chemistry" together. Also known as a *mix and match*.

CHSPE (California High School Proficiency Exam, or "Chispy")

A proctored exam available to minors at age sixteen or after completing their first semester of their sophomore year. Passing this exam yields a certificate that is the equivalent of a high school diploma. Allows the minor to work as a legal eighteen (i.e., be legally finished with high school, no longer require a work permit or set teacher, and work adult hours).

Cold Read

An unrehearsed reading of a scene or sides. Used mainly in auditions.

Commission

The percentage of performers' income paid to their agent, manager, or other team members for their services.

Coogan Account

A blocked minor trust account required by law for all performers in California under the age of eighteen, into which 15 percent of their gross pay is directly deposited by the production company. Named after Jackie Coogan, child actor.

Copy

The script for a voice-over or commercial. Similar to *sides*.

Costar

A small guest star role on a TV show. Generally has under five lines and one or two scenes.

Craft Services ("Crafty")

On-set catering.

Day Player

A performer contracted on a daily basis, as opposed to having a longer-term contract.

Director

Person responsible for the ultimate result of a film or TV episode. The major creative visionary behind the actors' performances and the aesthetic feel of the work.

DP

Director of photography.

Drive-On Pass

A pass to drive onto and park in the studio lot.

Electronic Press Kit (EPK)

Interviews with actors and creative teams, as well as behind the scenes footage. Used for publicity purposes.

Emancipation

Legal adult status given by a judge to a minor. Allow minors to sign legally binding contracts and access their Coogan account funds. Does not allow them to work adult hours, leave school, or work without a permit.

Episodic

Multiple-episode TV series.

Episodic Season

Time of year when many TV series episodes are filmed and therefore guest star roles are cast, typically late summer to mid-December. This is a less clearly defined season as time goes by and series are filmed throughout the year. Counterpart to *pilot season*.

Equity

Union representing stage actors and artists, with jurisdiction over live theater.

Executive Producer

A producer who supervises other producers. On a TV show, may also be a writer or the creator of the series.

EXT (Exterior)

A scene shot outdoors.

Extra

A background actor with no lines. Can help give a sense of reality to the scene.

Film Commission

A city, state, or national organization set up to draw filming projects and assist with filming activity.

First Team

Principal actors.

Fitting

An appointment during which actors try on their costumes so alterations can be made if necessary.

Forced Call

A call to work fewer than twelve hours after the end of work the previous day. Often comes with financial penalties for production, depending on the actor's contract.

FX (Effects)

Special effects.

General Equivalency Diploma (GED)

Not the same as the CHSPE, though both are considered the equivalent of a high school diploma. The GED cannot be taken until the age of eighteen, which is why it is useless as a means to legal eighteen status.

Green Light

The go-ahead for a film or TV project to be made.

Guest Star

A larger role than costar on TV, frequently one that drives that episode's plot. Guest stars may or may not be recurring.

Headshot

Photo of an actor, typically eight by ten and in color, used for securing auditions.

Hiatus

The time between active production periods on a TV series. May refer to the period between whole seasons or to a week or more during the shooting of a single season.

Hold

A contractual obligation for a performer to be available to work.

Hot Set

A set that is perfectly lit and dressed with cameras positioned for filming. In other words, "Do not touch!"

Industrial

Films made for non-broadcast use, often for educational or industry purposes.

INT (Interior)

A scene shot indoors.

Local Hire

An actor hired locally, which eliminates the cost of housing, per diem, and travel for a production. Typically found in film rather than TV.

Location

Any place outside of a sound stage or studio lot where filming occurs.

Looping

Another term for ADR, or automatic dialogue replacement. Postproduction dialogue recording.

Manager

Someone who represents talent. A manager's chief function is to guide and advise actors on their careers. Not licensed.

Monologue

A solo performance used in theater auditions or agent auditions. Not used for TV or film auditions, which use sides, or scenes from the script.

MOW

A made-for-TV movie (originally Movie of the Week).

Off Book

The term for when an actor is expected to have their lines memorized, and no longer needs to look at a script.

On Hold

When an actor in a production is not currently scheduled to work but must be available to quickly come to work if called.

Production Assistant (PA)

Entry-level position on a set or in a production office.

Per Diem

A daily stipend paid to actors working on location for meals and incidentals. The dollar amount is generally set by union standards.

Photo Double

A stand-in who resembles the actor. Used for long shots or over-the-shoulder shots.

Pilot

The initial episode of a potential series. Used for testing and often not aired if the series is not picked up for production.

Pilot Season

The time of year when most pilots are typically cast, traditionally January to March. This period has become less clearly defined over time, as more networks cast pilots year-round. Only applies to traditional TV, not to film or web series.

Pinned

Similar to Avail; used more in film and TV. Imagine head-shots of the final choices for a role pinned to the wall as the last-minute casting decisions are made. Being pinned means an actor is in the final running for a role. The actor may or may not be the first choice or ultimately get the role, but the producers want to make sure the actor is available while they make a final decision.

Post/Postproduction:
The period after filming a movie or TV show when editing happens and effects are added.

Public Relations (PR):
A publicist (PR person) generates and manages press and media coverage for actors and represents them with the media.

Preproduction
All the work that occurs before actual filming begins, including writing, location scouting, casting, set design, and the like.

Principal Photography:
The main shooting period of a film, after preproduction and before postproduction.

Producer
The person who is responsible for decisions on a production, from original concept to completion, and ultimately responsible for the success or failure of a TV show or film.

Props/Property Master
Props are objects directly handled by the actors (their "property") on a set. The property master and props department are responsible for creating, managing, and setting these objects.

Reel

A digital résumé used by actors to show samples of their work.

Rep (Representative)

Can refer to an agent, manager, or even public relations representative.

Residuals

Additional income that an actor may generate from repeat airings of their show on TV. Generally only available to principal actors, and often not an option even for stars under many cable contracts.

Screen Actors Guild (SAG)

National labor union representing film actors and artists. Merged with AFTRA in March 2012.

SAG-AFTRA

A national labor union representing actors, announcers, broadcasters, journalists, dancers, recording artists, singers, voice-over artists, and other media professionals.

Second Assistant Director (AD)

The individual in charge of the cast, making sure the actors are where they are supposed to be at all times. Also draws up the call sheet daily.

Scale

Minimum required payment for services under union contracts.

Scale Plus Ten

Scale plus an additional 10 percent to cover an agent's commission.

Screen Test

A final audition for studio and/or network executives. May be in a conference room or a full soundstage.

Script Supervisor

The member of the crew who records all progress and aspects of a shoot and is responsible for internal continuity.

Series Regular

An actor who is in the main cast of a TV series.

Set Dresser

The member of the crew responsible for the décor/objects on a set that are not props. (Props are objects handled by an actor.)

Sides

Scenes or pages from a script used in auditions.

Sight and Sound

The right and responsibility of parents to be within sight and earshot of their child performer at all times.

Slate

Verbal statement of a performer's name at the start of a taped audition ("slate your name"). Also the small clapper device used to identify takes for editing.

Soundstage

A building on a stage lot designed especially for shooting film or TV.

Stage Right or Stage Left

Perspective from the actor's point of view as they face the camera or the audience.

Stand-In

A person used to help block and light a scene before the actor steps onto set. Often similar physically to the actor, but not always.

Studio Teacher/Set Teacher

The person hired to educate young performers while they are on set. Also in charge of enforcing welfare of all minors on set and child-labor laws.

Submission

An agent's suggestion of an actor to a casting director for a particular role or an actor's suggestion of themselves to an agent for representation. Also a taped audition sent for consideration.

Table Read

When the cast reads the entire script out loud (typically around a table) so the writers, director, and producers can hear how it sounds and make changes if necessary.

Taft-Hartley

A federal statute allowing a nonunion actor to be hired for a SAG-AFTRA job. Allows thirty days after first employment before mandatory union membership. Easier for child actors to get than for adults.

Turnaround

The period between when production wraps at the end of one day and starts again at the beginning of the next day. Actors are required to have twelve hours turnaround, or production may owe penalties.

Walk-On

A very minor role.

Wardrobe

The clothing worn by performers on camera.

Work Permit

A required legal document allowing a minor child to work. Permits are issued by a state or local agency. In Los Angeles, the Division of Labor Standards Enforcement issues them.

Work Session

A chance for an actor to work with the casting director or director before a big audition or screen test.

Wrap

Completion of a production, or a particular actor's role in that production. "That's a wrap!"

Youth Agent

A theatrical agent who represents actors who either are under eighteen or can play under eighteen.

About the Author

Bonnie J. Wallace speaks, writes, and teaches workshops to help parents navigate Hollywood so they can effectively help their child become a professional actor. Mother of Dove Cameron, star of *Liv and Maddie, Disney Descendants, Barely Lethal,* and more, Bonnie is dedicated to inspiring others on this journey. A believer in leaps of faith, Bonnie is a Hollywood mom, a small-business owner, and a former nonprofit theater board member. She lives in Los Angeles.

For information on workshops Bonnie offers, visit:
http://hollywoodparentsguide.com/workshops/

For information on booking Bonnie to speak to your group, visit:
http://hollywoodparentsguide.com/speaking/

For bonus material and other cool stuff, visit:
http://hollywoodparentsguide.com/bonus/

For bulk inquiries (25 books or more) please contact: bonnie@hollywoodparentsguide.com

INDEX
HOLLYWOOD PARENTS GUIDE

CPSIA information can be obtained
at www.ICGtesting.com
Printed in the USA
FSHW010726220919
62264FS